Double Emperor

Double Emperor

The Life and Times of Francis of Austria

Chip Wagar

HAMILTON BOOKS
Lanham • Boulder • New York • London

An imprint of The Rowman & Littlefield Publishing Group, Inc.
4501 Forbes Boulevard, Suite 200, Lanham, Maryland 20706
Hamilton Books Acquisitions Department (301) 459-3366
www.rowman.com

6 Tinworth Street, London SE11 5AL

Copyright © 2018 by The Rowman & Littlefield Publishing Group, Inc.

All rights reserved. No part of this book may be reproduced in any form or by any electronic or mechanical means, including information storage and retrieval systems, without written permission from the publisher, except by a reviewer who may quote passages in a review.

British Library Cataloguing in Publication Information Available

Library of Congress Cataloging-in-Publication Data

Library of Congress Control Number: 2018959555
ISBN: 798-0-7618-7077-7 (pbk : alk paper)
ISBN: 978-0-7618-7078-4 (electronic)

∞™ The paper used in this publication meets the minimum requirements of American National Standard for Information Sciences—Permanence of Paper for Printed Library Materials, ANSI/NISO Z39.48-1992.

Printed in the United States of America

Contents

List of Figures   vii

Preface   xi

PART I

1   Birth and the Florentine Years   3
2   Coming of Age—Vienna and Joseph II   15
3   A Brief Transition—Leopold II   31
4   Accession to Power—1792   49

PART II

5   The Economics of War and Peace   57
6   The Habsburg Inheritance   69
7   The Second Coalition   83
8   Beethoven, The Third Coalition, and The Birth of the Austrian Empire   101
9   Conservative Reform in the Franciscan Era   115
10   Wagram   125

PART III

11   Metternich, Radetzky, and the Policy of Collaboration   141
12   Resurrection   153

13	Triumph and Redemption	167
14	Finis Napoleon	177
15	The Congress of Vienna	187

PART IV

16	After the Congress—Biedermeier Austria	199
17	Family	217
18	Francis and the Post War Era	225
19	Luxury and Austrian Biedermeier Culture	235
20	Revolution and Reaction	239
21	Franciscan Twilight	245

Epilogue	255
Bibliography	261
Index	265
About the Author	273

List of Figures

Figure 0.1	Francis I, Emperor of Austria by Anton Einsle, 1841; The Wellington Collection, Apsley House, London. This painting was posthumous and given to the Duke of Wellington by the Emperor's son, Ferdinand	xiv
Figure 1.1	Francis as a young child of seven years, in Florence, circa 1775. By Johann Zoffany. Kunsthistoriches Museum, Vienna	5
Figure 1.2	The Archduke Leopold's family as Grand Duke of Tuscany in the Pitti Palace, Florence, circa 1776. By Johann Zoffany. Bundesmobilienverwaltung Collection, Vienna	6
Figure 1.3	Maria Theresa circa 1772, by Anton von Maron; Ptuj Ormoz Regional Museum, Ptuj, Slovenia	10
Figure 2.1	Joseph II by Georg Weikert; Heeresgeschichtliches Museum, Vienna	16
Figure 2.2	Leopold (left) and Joseph II, circa 1769 by Pompeo Batoni; Kunsthistoriches Museum, Vienna	19
Figure 2.3	Elizabeth Wilhelmine von Württemberg, circa 1784. By Giovanni Battista Lampi; Kunsthistoriches Museum, Vienna.	23
Figure 2.4	State Chancellor Wenzel Anton Kaunitz, circa 1762; By Jean-Étienne Liotard	28
Figure 3.1	Leopold II (1747–1792) by Heinrich Füger, Circa 1790; National Gallery, Prague	33
Figure 3.2	Maria Therese of Naples. Second wife and "double cousin" of Francis II. By Marie Louise Elisabeth Vigée-Lebrun, circa 1790. Musée Condé, Paris	36

List of Figures

Figure 3.3	Francis II, in coronation regalia of a Holy Roman Emperor by Ludwig Streitenfeld. The Hofburg, Vienna.	45
Figure 4.1	The young Metternich by François Gérard, circa 1807	51
Figure 5.1	Archduke Charles, Duke of Teschen. Circa 1819, by Thomas Lawrence. The Royal Collection. Windsor Castle.	65
Figure 6.1	Napoleon, First Counsel, circa 1804. By Charles Meynier. Musée de la Ville de Bruxelles, Hotel de Ville.	79
Figure 7.1	Tsar Paul of Russia (1754–1801), son of Catherine the Great and the second of four Russian tsars during Francis' reign. By Vladimir Borovikovsky; State Russian Museum. St. Petersburg.	84
Figure 7.2	George III, King of Great Britain and of Hannover, about 1799. Portrait by Sir William Beechey. National Portrait Gallery, London.	85
Figure 7.3	Francis the Emperor and his family, circa 1806.	90
Figure 7.4	Frederick William III, king of Prussia 1797–1840. Wilhelm Herbig. The Wellington Collection, Apsley House.	97
Figure 8.1	Beethoven, circa 1792 by Joseph Mähler. Archiv fur Kunst und Geschichte, Berlin	102
Figure 8.2	December 5, 1805—Napoleon and Francis After the Battle of Austerlitz. Jean-Antoine Gros. Chateau de Versailles	108
Figure 8.3	Field Marshal Karl Phillip, Prince of Schwarzenberg. Artist Unknown.	110
Figure 9.1	Maria Ludovica, Empress of Austria 1808–1816.	122
Figure 10.1	Johann Phillip von Stadion by Johann Ender	128
Figure 10.2	The Tyrolean Rebellion of 1809 by Franz Defregger. Alte Nationalgalerie, Berlin	131
Figure 10.3	Victory over Napoleon at Aspern by Johann Krafft.	133
Figure 11.1	Klemens von Metternich, Foreign Minister, circa 1815. Sir Thomas Lawrence. Kunsthistoriches Museum, Vienna.	142
Figure 11.2	Marie Louise, Empress of the French 1810–1814. Francois Gerard. The Louvre Museum, Paris	147
Figure 11.3	Joseph, Graf Radetzky von Radetz. Carl Gutsch circa 1840.	149

List of Figures ix

Figure 12.1	Napoleon, Russia—1812. Adolph Northen.	155
Figure 12.2	Tsar Alexander of Russia by Franz Kruger, circa 1837. The Hermitage Museum, St. Petersburg	159
Figure 12.3	Metternich and Napoleon, Marcolini Palace, Dresden. Woldemar Friedrich.	163
Figure 13.1	The Battle of Leipzig—October 18, 1813	169
Figure 13.2	Baron vom Stein, Prussian Minister, circa 1804 by Johann Rincklake. The Westphalian State Museum of Art and Cultural History	170
Figure 13.3	Victory at Leipzig by Johann Krafft, circa 1839. The Deutsches Historiches Museum, Berlin. Tsar Alexander I, Emperor Francis I and King Frederick Wilhelm III at center right receive the news of Napoleon's defeat from Field Marshal Karl Phillip von Schwarzenberg, center left.	171
Figure 13.4	Gebhard Leberecht von Blücher, Prussian Field Marshal. Sir Thomas Lawrence. Waterloo Gallery, Windsor Castle	174
Figure 14.1	Francis I on campaign by Johann Krafft, circa 1832. The Hermitage Museum, St. Petersburg.	179
Figure 15.1	Triumphal Entry of Emperor Francis. Johann Krafft, circa 1828. The Belvedere, Vienna.	188
Figure 15.2	The Congress of Vienna by Jean Isabey, circa 1819	191
Figure 16.1	Wilhelm Joseph Heine's Inmates at the Prison Church, 1837. Deutsches Historiches Museum, Berlin.	202
Figure 17.1	Ferdinand, Archduke of Austria by Caspar Jele, circa 1834. Monastery of Stift Wilten, Innsbruck	220
Figure 18.1	Joseph Kreutzinger's portrait of Francis at 52 years of age. Heeresgeschichtliches Museum, Vienna.	226
Figure 18.2	Francis rowing a man on the pond at Laxenburg by Johann Krafft. The Belvedere, Vienna. The castle he built—Franzensburg—can be seen in the background. A typical Biedermeier scene that Francis seemed content for his subjects to see.	227
Figure 18.3	Sir Thomas Lawrence's portrait, circa 1818. Waterloo Chamber, Windsor Castle.	229
Figure 20.1	Louis Philippe d'Orleans—the wily king of the French. Artist Unknown. Musée Condé, Chantilly, France.	240
Figure 20.2	Lord Palmerston—British Foreign Secretary. Francis Cruikshank circa 1855.	243

List of Figures

Figure 21.1	Francis in formal regalia by Friedrich von Amerling, 1832. The Hofburg Schatzkammer, Vienna.	246
Figure 21.2	Close up of Amerling's portrait.	247
Figure 21.3	Napoleon François, grandson of Francis and Duke of Reichstadt. Leopold Bucher, 1832.	248
Figure 21.4	Napoleon Franz in family portrait, third from left, by Leopold Fertbauer, 1828.	248
Figure 21.5	Count Franz von Kolowrat by Johann Ender	251
Figure E.1	Sarcophagus of Francis, last Holy Roman Emperor and First Austrian Emperor, Imperial Crypt, Vienna.	256
Figure E.2	Bust of Francis I of Austria by Camillo Pacetti, Kunsthistoriches Museum, Vienna	258

Preface

The study and history of the Habsburg dynasty is the study and history of Europe. Although the dynasty disappeared as a political entity a century ago in the ashes of the First World War, its six-hundred-year existence rivals and to some extent exceeds the footprint of the ancient Roman Empire.

In space, its territorial reach extended as far as California and the Philippines, the Netherlands, Spain, Poland, Germany, Hungary and Italy to name only some of its possessions. It was Habsburg power that defeated and ruled the Aztec and Incan empires in the Americas. It was Habsburg power that defeated the Turkish Empire on land at the gates of Vienna in 1529 and at sea at Lepanto in 1571. There was a Habsburg Emperor of Mexico and a Habsburg king of England. Its patrimony grew so large that famously, by 1556, it was divided in two.

In the last century of its existence, the dynasty ruled over one of the largest empires of continental Europe. It touched or interacted with every other major political and social power during this time. It was the Habsburgs who contended time and again with the Sun King, Frederick the Great and Napoleon and, in each case, eventually led a coalition that defeated them all. As the great historian A.J.P. Taylor once wrote "the Habsburgs were the greatest dynasty of modern history, and the history of central Europe revolves round them, not they round it."[1]

For this reason, the study of the rise and fall of this great dynasty and the empire it created and lost in 1918 has been the subject of many scholars and books. This even though, like the Romanovs, the Hohenzollerns, the Manchus and, for the most part, the Bourbons—all comparative *parvenus*–the Habsburgs have vanished into the twilight of history. The world would be a very different place had this dynasty not existed. This is what gives the subject of the Habsburgs such enduring interest.

The other fascinating aspect of the Habsburgs and their empire is the multi-lingual, multi-ethnic and multi-cultural nature of their imperium. Alone among the European powers, the Habsburgs ruled over an empire with no single dominant ethnic/linguistic group. This diversity, usually fatal to the longevity of even the greatest empires, and the balancing act required to hold it intact, astonishes and confounds historians and political scientists to this day. The explanation for the staying power of a nearly unbroken succession of rulers from Rudolf in 1278 to Franz Joseph and 1918 consumes volumes and thousands of pages to explain how, for example, Hungarian, Croatian, Slovenian and Austrian military units were still occupying Italian, Romanian, Ukrainian, Serbian, Albanian and Polish soil, fighting under the Habsburg flag, when the guns fell silent in November 1918.

This book is a biography of the life and times of the nineteenth and last Habsburg Holy Roman Emperor and the first of four Austrian Emperors. I decided to write this book partly due to my own fascination with the history of Central Europe and the Balkans and partly when I discovered, as the incomparable Frederick Kagan remarked ". . . Amazingly, there has been no biography of Francis in English." This is not exactly true.

There exists a remarkably well researched and well written biography of his early life and formative years by Dr. Walter Consuelo Langsam, former president of Wagner College, entitled *Francis the Good* and published by Macmillan in 1949. This biography, however, only takes us roughly to 1792 when Francis became king and emperor at 24 years of age. Even more surprisingly, there are few biographies written in German either; one a two-volume set by Colestin Wolfsgruber, *Franz I, Kaiser von Österreich*, published in Vienna in 1899 and another by Hermann Meynert, *Kaiser Franz I, Zur Geschichte seiner Regierung und seiner Zeit*, again published in Vienna in 1872. There exists no modern biography of Francis in the German language either.

Francis Joseph Charles von Habsburg-Lothringen, the oldest son of the Habsburg Archduke Leopold of Tuscany and his wife the Archduchess Marie Louise of Spain was born on February 12, 1768 in Florence. He died on March 2, 1835 in Vienna at the age of 67. Forty-three of his sixty-seven years he ruled the vast Habsburg domains in Europe first as the elected Holy Roman Emperor, later as hereditary Emperor of Austria, and always as king of Hungary, Bohemia, Croatia, Slavonia, Galicia and Lodomeria, Grand Duke of Cracow, Grand Prince of Transylvania, Margrave of Moravia, Duke or Count of innumerable other provinces and cities and the only "Double Emperor" in history. He was the father of Marie Louise, second wife of his great rival, Napoleon Bonaparte, and thus his father-in-law, and the grandfather of Napoleon's only legitimate male heir, Napoleon II, the Duke of Reichstadt.

This book, due to my own shortcomings in time, talent and poor command of the German language (and, hence, realistic access to whatever original source material exists in Austrian or German archives), is an attempt to address a vacuum in biographical history. I have sought to amalgamate material from various, disparate sources on other subject matter in which the personality or actions of this man fleetingly appear. For this reason, the bar is set very low and I can only hope that readers will judge it as a very basic *opus* that will inspire others with greater talent, time and resources to finish a complete work comparable to the many excellent biographies of my subject's grandson, Kaiser Franz Joseph (1830–1916) which abound.

Indeed, the reason for the paucity of biographical information about Francis is one of the issues I explore in this book. It is intriguing to consider that this man had a 43-year reign that witnessed the coming and going of three British kings, four French kings and one emperor, three Russian tsars, three Prussian kings, and seven American presidents. How curious that his presence astride the continent of Europe has not warranted further inquiry.

The first word that usually comes to mind regarding Francis is the word "reactionary." It is not usually meant in a complimentary way, either. He is invariably portrayed as a dour, humorless man who wanted to "turn back the clock" of human progress and the impulse toward freedom and democracy. Francis is often presented as the iron fisted champion of absolutism and the old order within the velvet glove of his famous chancellor, Klemens von Metternich. As a perceived reactionary by historians living in an age of rampant and triumphant democracy, where the virtues of liberal or parliamentary government are unquestioned, Francis has tended to be viewed negatively through this lens.

For those who have read a bit more deeply, he has been often compared invidiously to his contemporaries and even his own family. His younger brother, the Archduke Charles, is, for example, often considered his superior in intellect and talent; certainly, where military matters were concerned. Francis has been often considered a mediocre intellect, a poor strategist, misguided, out-maneuvered and out-fought, often defeated and humiliated during his reign by his great opponent, Napoleon. His chancellors, Kaunitz and Metternich, also overshadow their master. Napoleon and even Tsar Alexander of Russia eclipse him in fame, if not in fortune. With all this, this book attempts to tackle the mystery of how such a supposed mediocrity managed not merely to survive, but to transform his inheritance and the continent of Europe.

In the last decade of the reign of the Austrian Emperor, Francis I, the Austrian Empire sat on the continent of Europe as a colossus, its most powerful and influential state, and the undeniable fulcrum of the European and, hence, world balance of power. His dynasty reached the apex of its influence, territorial size and cultural predominance in the long annals of the Austrian branch of the family. This, then, is the attempt to tell the story of how this unassuming and mysterious man did it, despite all his personal shortcomings, mistakes and the unwieldy, almost un-governable empire he inherited and transformed.

Francis I, Emperor of Austria by Anton Einsle, 1841; The Wellington Collection, Apsley House, London. This painting was posthumous and given to the Duke of Wellington by the Emperor's son, Ferdinand.

NOTE

1. Taylor, A.J.P. *The Habsburg Monarchy 1809–1918*, (Chicago: University of Chicago Press, 1948, reprint 1976).

Part I

Chapter One

Birth and the Florentine Years

It was the height of Carnival Season in Florence, a time of masked balls, revelry and celebration in the streets of the City of Lilies before Ash Wednesday and the beginning of the penitent season of Lent on the Christian calendar. On the evening of February 11, 1768, the reigning Grand Duke Leopold and his very pregnant wife, Maria Luisa, had been enjoying Carnival in the streets and piazzas of the capital city of Tuscany with their subjects. Suddenly, the Grand Duchess felt the pangs and symptoms that signaled her time had come. She knew the signs. This was her second child. A baby girl, Maria Theresa, had been born just a little more than a year earlier.

Quickly her husband ordered their carriage to return them to the Pitti Palace, the ducal residence. Several hours later, in the early hours of February 12, after a relatively easy delivery, the mother, a Spanish princess of the reigning Bourbon family, gave birth to a future emperor. He was named Franz Joseph Karl by his parents in honor of his late paternal grandfather, his uncle and his maternal grandfather. He would be the second of sixteen children born of the marriage of his father, the Grand Duke Peter Leopold Joseph Anton of the House of Habsburg-Lorraine and the daughter of King Charles III of Spain.

The entry of this baby into the world, even at the time, was thought to be significant, although his eventual impact on the world could not have been imagined. Upon his entry into the world, the boy was the presumptive male heir of the very popular Grand Duke of Tuscany who was, in turn, the presumptive heir to his childless brother, the Holy Roman Emperor in Vienna. The birth of a male heir called for hearty celebrations. Three days of fireworks, illuminations and revelry were held and all public offices were closed for six days in Florence. The child was baptized later in the evening on the day of his birth by no less than the bishops of Florence, Fiesole and

Montalcino while news of the child's birth was dispatched to Vienna on horseback.[1]

The news arrived at the medieval palace of the Hofburg in Vienna on the evening of February 19 when a courier breathlessly informed the baby's grandmother, the Dowager Empress Maria Theresa. She was alone in her apartments when the news came, while other members of her family had gone to the Burgtheater to be entertained on the last day of Carnival. Still dressed in black mourning for her late husband, who had died three years earlier, she realized right away that her grandson had been born on the same day as her marriage to Francis, Duke of Lorraine, 32 years earlier.

The Empress was so excited that she quickly made her way to the Burgtheater, entered the darkened imperial loge and delivered the news herself to her startled but delighted family: "My Poldy's got a boy!"[2] The entourage included her oldest son, Joseph Benedikt August, the child's uncle and godfather; a figure who would become immensely important in the development of this special child in the years to come.

Other contemporaries who would loom large in the life and times of Franz Joseph Karl von Habsburg-Lorraine were or would soon be entering the world as well. Arthur Wellsley, to become the Duke of Wellington, would be born in Dublin, Ireland in another year. Napoleon Bonaparte would be born in Ajaccio on the island of Corsica the following year, in August 1769. Napoleon's older brother Joseph was born the same year as Francis. The future King Louis XVI of France, who would marry his aunt, was twelve. Ludwig van Beethoven was born two years later.

George Washington, by contrast, was already 36 years old. King George III of Great Britain was also in his thirties when the young prince was born. Wolfgang Mozart was 12. Haydn, like Washington, was 36. Jean Jacques Rousseau was 56, Voltaire 74, Edmund Burke 39, and Klemens von Metternich would not be born in Koblenz for another seven years.

The child was the grandson of the Bourbon King of Spain, Charles III, on his mother's side and of the Habsburg Empress-Queen Maria Theresa on his father's. He was the nephew of the Holy Roman Emperor, Joseph II. His father, would eventually become Emperor Leopold II, but at the time of Francis' birth was Grand Duke of Tuscany. Francis would also have eleven brothers and sisters, some of whom figured more prominently than others during his reign. He was also the nephew of the Archduchess Marie Antoinette and future Queen of France.

The eventual Emperor Francis would spend his young, formative years in Tuscany at the court of his father, in Florence most of the time. Florentine culture of the mid-18th century constituted the milieu in which the young Francis accumulated his first impressions of the planet he would inhabit. The

Figure 1.1. Francis as a young child of seven years, in Florence, circa 1775. By Johann Zoffany. Kunsthistoriches Museum, Vienna

Figure 1.2. The Archduke Leopold's family as Grand Duke of Tuscany in the Pitti Palace, Florence, circa 1776. By Johann Zoffany. Bundesmobilienverwaltung Collection, Vienna

nature of his parents and his family are important clues to his personality and his method of perception and thought. And for a prince of the blood, whose early life occurred in the dead center of the Age of Enlightenment, the prevailing socio-cultural environment in which Francis was educated, lived and breathed cannot be overlooked.

The immediate family into which this child was born and raised, at least in his early years, is generally described as one dominated by a liberal, somewhat indulgent and loving home family life, perhaps to a fault. When compared, for example, to the critical, demanding and strict regime imposed on Frederick the Great, for example, or on King Edward VII by his parents, Victoria and Albert, this future ruler had it much easier, at least at first.

Correspondence by the child's father, Leopold, make clear his deep affection for his oldest son to the day he died. For just one example, upon receiving the news in Florence of the sudden death of his brother and his own accession to the imperial throne in 1790, Leopold wrote Francis in Vienna:

> . . . Omit from your letters to me all titles of majesty and all compliments. We are and should try to remain two friends who love each other cordially, have nothing to hide from each other, and contribute together to the well-being of the

public and the state. You will accomplish through your strength and youth those things which I can no longer do . . ."[3]

This is but one evidence of a father's deep love for his son who was then 22 years old. His keen interest in his son's education and resentment at his brother's—the Emperor's—interference in his son's upbringing is another. More about this later. Little direct evidence or correspondence from his mother, Maria Luisa, exists to footnote her love and affection for Francis, but there is no evidence to doubt it. In fact, the indulgent personalities of most of the other children of Leopold and Maria Luisa for the rest of their lives tends to bolster the impression that family life in the Palazzo Pitti and the Tuscan capital was likely to have been quite relaxed, informal and even fun.

To anyone who has not been to Florence, the ducal palace on the southern bank of the River Arno that winds through the city is one of its signature landmarks. Built in the late 15th century by a banker named Pitti, it became the main residence of the fabulously wealthy and powerful di Medici family by the mid-16th century. The palace, located near the equally famous Ponte Vecchio bridge crossing the Arno, remained the property of the House of Habsburg-Lorraine until 1860 and the Second War of Italian Independence.

The children of the Grand Duke Leopold would have been able to play in the extensive gardens and grounds of the palace itself, walk the Ponte Vecchio with its stalls of vendors clinging to the sides of the bridge, and explore the architecture and culture of Florence, the "cradle of the Renaissance," as millions of tourists do to this day. The Medici's Uffizi Gallery and fabulous art collection was all there. Michelangelo's David. The shops and taverns that populated the narrow, medieval streets and piazzas of the center of the city, at most a thirty-minute walk from the palace grounds, the magnificent domed cathedral by Brunelleschi would all have been known to the young Francis, his brothers and sisters. The ambience of Florence was and still is quite distinct from that of cities of northern Europe with its relatively warm climate, surrounded by the beauty of the Tuscan countryside and not far from other architectural and cultural gems such as Siena and Pisa, to name only a few. Not surprisingly, the mature Emperor Francis would have a deep love and take great pleasure in art and culture and became quite a collector of it, as we shall see.

And so, the early life of this man from the standpoint of family and the ambience of location could hardly seem to have been better. Few people in 18th century Europe could imagine a more idyllic and perfect way to begin life and it is difficult to conceive of one that could have more pleasant. This would change as Francis reached his teens; gradually at first and then suddenly in 1784 when, at the age of 16, he was summoned to Vienna by his uncle, the Emperor.

The impact this sudden and dramatic change in circumstances on the young Francis cannot be fully understood without some digression into the lives and personalities of the boy's extended family—his relatives–in Vienna. At this point in our narrative, however, we look at the Habsburgs not as the imperial, dynastic power brokers that they were and had been for some four centuries, but as a family with personalities, prejudices, opinions and viewpoints that interacted with and influenced other family members, as our own have done in our own lives.

One of the first points to realize was that Francis was not immediately assumed to be the heir to one of the largest family fortunes and inheritances in 18th century Europe. On the day Francis was born, his paternal grandfather, the Emperor Francis Stephen of Lorraine, had been dead for two and a half years. His widowed grandmother, the Queen and Dowager Empress Maria Theresa, had quickly arranged the election of her oldest son, Joseph, as Holy Roman Emperor in August 1765. That monarchy was an elected one. Joseph II would succeed his mother only on her death as her heir to the hereditary Habsburg family possessions including, most importantly, as king of Hungary, Bohemia and innumerable other kingdoms, principalities, duchies and counties as the eldest male son. In turn, his son would have succeeded him, if he had any sons, but he never did.

It was an unusual arrangement. The Empress Queen, Maria Theresa, whose reign is generally thought of as the Golden Age of the "Austrian" (as opposed to the Spanish) Habsburg dynasty, had been the actual ruler of the sprawling Habsburg possessions in Europe since 1740. With the death of her husband in 1765, she went into deep mourning like Queen Victoria of England after the death of her husband, Prince Albert, a century later. She lived another fifteen years, dressed always in black, until 1780. With the imperial throne vacant once again the dowager Empress, had little choice but to put forward her son Joseph as the next emperor and, at least in title, co-regent of the Empire, since by law no female could hold the imperial title.

For the next fifteen years, she endured an increasingly fractious and uneasy relationship with her son. In this power-sharing, the Empress retained the ultimate loyalty of her ministers, most importantly Wenzel Anton, Prince of Kaunitz-Reitberg, her state chancellor and one of the most gifted, wily servants of the dynasty in its history. She retained the final authority to veto her sometimes impetuous son's edicts and policies, but this arrangement left both parties frustrated. Often angry with his mother, Joseph II repeatedly threatened to resign the co-regency and spent inordinate amounts of time away from the capital and his mother's court. For her part, the Empress dreaded the rows with her son and likewise, often threatened to abdicate or simply gave in for a time to Joseph's latest policy.

Yet neither one of them ever resigned or abdicated. Despite their clashing viewpoints–she the conservative, religious, cautious improviser and he the bold, "enlightened," iconoclastic reformer—the result was a period of remarkable stability and achievement, despite occasional missteps. Joseph's expansionist tendencies that led up to the War of the Bavarian Succession was perhaps their most serious breakdown, driving the Empress to near panic when her old enemy, Frederick II, entered the lists. She quickly intervened to end the war at the first opportunity but already Joseph II had antagonized Bavaria and caused other south German dynasties to wonder how safe their sinecures were with this new, aggressive ruler on the throne in Vienna.

Despite the frequent and increasingly desperate pleas of Maria Theresa, Joseph refused to marry for a third time after the death of his second wife of just two years, Princess Maria Josepha of Bavaria in 1767, the year before Francis was born. Joseph's only child, a daughter also named Maria Theresa, died in January 1770. The Archduchess Maria Theresa was the daughter of his first wife, Isabella. The tragedy of these deaths left Joseph II emotionally desolated. He had attended his daughter personally, at her bedside, after she fell ill with a fatal respiratory infection, and was inconsolable when she died at the Schönbrunn palace at only seven years of age.

Infants were, of course, vulnerable to often deadly infectious diseases that became easily treated in the latter 20th and early 21st centuries. Antibiotics such as penicillin were unknown and would not be discovered until the early 20th century. Public sanitation and preventative public health measures were only dimly understood after repeated scourges of plague in the preceding centuries. Lister would not unravel the mystery of microbes, infection and disinfectant until the latter half of the 19th century.

Thus, quite many Habsburgs, like everyone else, were carried off to their early graves by smallpox, cholera, tuberculosis, influenza, and pneumonia, to name a few, rather than diseases like cancer, heart attack and Alzheimer's that post-modern medical advances and longer lives have made the common, mortal threat. The Emperor Joseph's two daughters had died of smallpox and respiratory disease. Maria Theresa lost a daughter to smallpox she was convinced she had contracted from prayer at the tomb of another child who died of the same disease. In fact, in late 18th century Europe, smallpox alone was responsible for some 400,000 deaths a year on the continent.[4]

Apparently, Joseph's refusal to remarry again was, at first, not taken as final and definitive by his mother and the imperial family in Vienna, but as the years passed, Joseph's decision had to be reluctantly accepted. There had been no legal impediment to Joseph's daughter inheriting the possessions of the dynasty upon his death. After all, his own mother had done so upon the death of her father who had no male heir. Whatever might have happened to

Figure 1.3. Maria Theresa circa 1772, by Anton von Maron; Ptuj Ormoz Regional Museum, Ptuj, Slovenia

the history of Europe and the House of Habsburg-Lorraine had Joseph II's daughter lived, with her passing the succession after 1770 became definitive and the importance of Francis and the children of the Grand Duke Leopold paramount. Nonetheless, Francis was only two years old at that point and Joseph had only been Emperor and co-regent of the Habsburg dynastic possessions (with his mother) for five years.

The family in Vienna, given the state of the roads between the seat of Habsburg power and Florence, along with the threat of highwaymen in the independent Venetian Republic, required armed bodyguards for travel. This made the headquarters of the family business quite distant to the Florentine branch in the early life Francis led. Further, distancing himself and his family from the Viennese court as much as he could, Leopold had secured from his mother and brother a free hand in the governance of the Tuscan duchy in 1770.

As her grandson would do, Maria Theresa had faced down an existential threat to the dynasty in the War of the Austrian Succession and the even more wrenching Seven Years War early in her reign. Interestingly, she too faced the greatest military mind of her age in these wars, Frederick the Great of Prussia. Having survived the crucible of war, she became an inspiration to her countrymen and presided over a period of unprecedented reform and consolidation that enabled a bankrupt and shaky inheritance to assume a place among the foremost powers of Europe by the time of her death.

Maria Theresa appreciated the power of charm and charisma and had used it when at times, she had little else. She is also credited with a sort of pragmatic realism that in turn allowed her to listen to often wise and careful ministers whose intellect or experience in some things were greater than her own. She was served by some of the greatest political advisors in Austrian history: Friedrich Wilhelm von Haugwitz, Gerard van Swieten and, above all, Wenzel Anton, Prince of Kaunitz and future father in law of Metternich. Her son, Joseph II, lacked these qualities but had others she did not.

Joseph II is one of the most controversial sovereigns of the Habsburg dynasty in its six-hundred-year run. He is controversial for many socio-political reasons as a king-emperor that we will touch on briefly later, but here we concern ourselves with his personality as a man, since that is what most impacted his young nephew.

While he too came from a very large family and loved his mother, Joseph was quite different from her. Her intolerant, Catholic faith was a major influence in her life to the point of aggressive anti-Semitism and anti-Protestantism. Joseph II was largely ambivalent toward religion and saw his mother's intense Catholicism as "superstitious" and "ridiculous" as well as harmful to an empire made up of significant Protestant and Jewish populations.[5]

The boy's grandmother, the Empress Maria Theresa and his uncle, the Emperor Joseph II were intimately involved in the education of the young boy even from the distance of Vienna. As Francis would likely be the dynastic successor to his uncle or his father, no chance could be taken with his upbringing. The Emperor visited Florence on more than one occasion to see for himself the growing boy and ensure his proper education.

One of the first surprising things to learn about the man who would be credited after his death as the very symbol of monarchical absolutism and reaction in Europe was that he was not raised or educated that way. In fact, the young Francis was rigorously taught precisely the opposite and his two predecessors as emperor, his uncle Joseph II and his father Leopold II, were both unquestionably disciples of the theory of "enlightened" monarchy and the social contract. For example, consider the written instructions given by his father, the then Grand Duke Leopold, to one of his son's tutors, Count von Colloredo-Waldsee:

> ... The princes must, above all, be convinced of the equality of man ... They should be made to realize that their inclinations and pleasures, their entire existence must ever be subordinate to their duties ... that they are human beings; that they hold their position only through the sanction of other human beings . . . Every prince who loves war or avidly seeks the glory or fame which is ac-

quired thereby is a tyrant over his people; one should seek only the glory which attaches to justice, humanity and the fulfillment of one's duties.

And further:

> No pains must be spared to acquaint the princes with their country and make them respect the proprieties. Establish in them an aversion to taxation and make clear to them that their sole passion should be humanitarianism, compassion, the desire to advance the happiness of their people. Stir their sensibilities on behalf of the poor and make plain that the rich must never be favored over the poor. Explain that the greatest misfortune for a prince lies in his not having seen things with his own eyes and not being informed on the true state of his country's affairs . . .[6]

Eventually, Joseph and the Empress suggested other tutors, including the Marquis Frederick Ferdinand di Manfredini and Count Sigismund von Hohenwart, both of whom Leopold agreed should assist Colloredo. The significance of these appointments is only that both men also advocated a thoroughly "modern" and enlightened curriculum. Francis was introduced to the thoughts and philosophies of John Locke and Jean Jacques Rousseau by Manfredini. Hohenwart, who arrived in Florence in 1777, has been regarded as perhaps the most influential teacher in Francis' life.[7] He introduced the young prince to the thoughts of Montesquieu, Rousseau and even Frederick the Great of Prussia, the great enemy of the Habsburgs. In a small handbook prepared for Francis in 1784 before his departure to the imperial court in Vienna, Hohenwart's own thoughts regarding the duty and role of a monarch were clearly displayed:

> . . . The monarch will lie awake nights so that his citizens may enjoy carefree sleep; he will work so that they may enjoy leisure . . . Life, property, a reasonable liberty, these most tangible evidences of human happiness will be protected and firmly secured by him . . . the shepherd exists for the flock, not the flock for the shepherd . . . From the time that he ascends his post he belongs to the state, not to himself. He may no longer follow his own inclinations; he may have no desires other than to serve and make happy his people . . . Every mistake of his state servants falls back on him, for he selects them . . . Since his people regard him as a kind of visible deity, it expects him to be well-nigh infallible . . . He is the guardian spirit of security, property and liberty . . .[8]

The truth of his upbringing and education belies the assessment of no less an authority than Robert Kann, whose 1974 classic, *The History of the Habsburg Empire*, seems to have entirely ignored the detailed facts regarding this time so painstakingly researched and documented a quarter century earlier in Langsam's book. Kann, for example, described Francis' education this way:

Francis had been raised in Tuscany in the atmosphere of the enlightened government of the then grand duke Leopold. He spent the latter part of Joseph's reign either at the seat of the emperor's government or as observer in the eastern theater of war. His hard taskmaster thoroughly indoctrinated him with the principles and practice of Josephin reformism . . .[9]

Dismissing the Enlightenment tutoring of several teachers for years in a sentence, Kann concludes Francis was "too small in intellectual attainment" and "mediocre in ability but not stupid . . . suspicious of new ideas . . . incapable to [sic] grasp complex ideas . . . Brilliance of any kind, even of a highly conservative character was suspect to him, since it might turn into unpredictable directions . . ."[10]

This kind of indictment, while not always as comprehensively negative as Kann's, seems to uncritically recur without much thought or citation to any authority in the historiography of other authors, and yet conflicts with known facts of his life. Anecdotes about him are often taken out of context to arrive at this characterization. The truth seems more complex and nuanced. It ignores the metamorphosis of a maturing mind over time, based upon this man's experience in the crucible of the Europe of his era. The reader must judge this for himself but with an awareness that the conventional wisdom regarding the character and intellectual rigor of Francis may lack much support in evidence.

Francis was deemed a handsome youth even from early childhood, although somewhat slight of build and thin. This seemingly frail appearance became an issue with his uncle after the boy was summoned to Vienna at 16 years old to complete his education and upbringing under the direct and, unfortunately, baleful eye of his uncle, the Emperor. Although Joseph had directly been involved in the selection of the boys' tutors while he was growing up in Florence, and even issued instructions and required detailed, frequent reports from the tutors and his brother, Francis' arrival in Vienna in 1784 began a difficult and painful period for the young archduke.

At about the same time, in Paris, on October 19, 1784, the Ecole Militaire in Paris admitted a fifteen-year-old gentleman cadet from Corsica, Napoleone de Buonaparte. His artillery examiner, Louis Monge, described this unusual student this way:

Reserved and studious, he prefers studying to any kind of amusement. He enjoys reading good authors and applies himself very well to the abstract sciences only, with a solid knowledge of mathematics and geography. He is quiet and solitary, capricious, haughty, and frightfully egotistical. He replies energetically to questions in class and is swift and sharp in his repartee at other times. He is most proud, ambitious, aspiring to everything. This young man merits our consideration and help.[11]

In February 1785, Cadet Buonaparte's father died, plunging his family at home in Corsica into financial distress. At sixteen, on September 28, 1785, he received his commission in the army artillery, since the naval exam for gunners he had intended to pursue was not given that year. By November 6, he arrived at his first posting with the La Fère artillery regiment at Valence, about 90 miles south of Lyons. There he continued to contemplate how he might liberate his native Corsica from France.

NOTES

1. Langsam, Walter, *Francis the Good* (New York: The Macmillan Company, 1949) 1,2.

2. Vovk, Justin, *In Destiny's Hands, Five Tragic Rulers, Children of Maria Theresa* (New York: iUniverse, Inc., 2010) 61.

3. Letter of February 6, 1790: Arneth, Alfred, *Marie Antoinette; Joseph II, und Leopold II* (Vienna: Wilhelm Braumüller, 1866) 177.

4. Perlin, David and Cohen, Ann. *The Complete Idiot's Guide to Dangerous Diseases and Epidemics* (Royersford: Alpha, 2002)

5. Mahan, Alexander, *Maria Theresa of Austria* (Whitefish: Kessinger Publishing, LLC, 2010).

6. Austrian State Archive. "Points d'education pour les enfants." *Haus-, Hof- und Staatsarchiv, Faszikel 56, Erziehungsplane betr. Die Erziehung der Kinder Leopolds II.* 1775–1784, Konvolut 7, folios 1–4.

7. Langsam 22

8. Wolfsgruber, Cölestin, *Franz I. Kaiser von Österreich, und Sein Zeitalter* (Vienna: Wilhelm Braumüller, 1899) *289–297*

9. Kann, Robert, *History of the Habsburg Empire* (Berkley: University of California Press, 1974) 209

10. Kann 210

11. Madelin, Louis, *La Jeunesse de Bonaparte* (Paris: Hachette, 1937) 12–13.

Chapter Two

Coming of Age–Vienna and Joseph II

Once his nephew arrived in Vienna, the Emperor Joseph II quickly decided that his development to date was seriously deficient and lacking. Wholesale changes to the young man's curriculum and daily activities were demanded of his teachers and critiqued by the Emperor. Francis himself was required to keep a journal of his daily activities which he was required to give to the Emperor who personally reviewed and commented on his progress, usually in critical and sometimes harsh terms.

Francis lost weight and was often reduced to misery and tears by the insistent and seemingly unrelenting criticism of his uncle which was then repeated and amplified by his tutors who were duly frightened by the indignant comments directed to them by the Emperor. Nothing seemed to be sufficient to please the Emperor. In a letter to Francis on August 18, 1784, one can appreciate the flavor of the stinging criticisms that regularly rained down on Francis, of which this was only the beginning:

> When one looks upon him as a youth of seventeen and compares him with others of the same age and recalls one's own status in those years, one is convinced forthwith that his physical development has hitherto been wholly neglected. He is retarded in size and strength and backward in physical skills and bearing. He represents, in short, a mollycoddle who regards as tremendously important and momentous everything which he does or that affects his person, and counts as naught those things which others do for themselves or suffer . . . In view of the present status of the Archduke's character, a character partly native and partly molded by circumstances and bad example, it would be a great error, and one involving the loss of much care and work, to continue in the disadvantageous and sleepy manner hitherto pursued. Count Colloredo and the two adjutants-general must therefore carefully and painstakingly try, on all occasions, to encourage the

Figure 2.1. Joseph II by Georg Weikert; Heeresgeschichtliches Museum, Vienna

Archduke to act according to the principles here outlined. . . . From all this it follows that, the more the Archduke shows conceit over his imaginary perfection, the more he is to be confronted with and convinced of the truth. . . .[1]

The references to the young Archduke in the third person add a particularly debasing texture to a diatribe that went on for several pages. Another similar written critique was delivered on February 4, 1785. On November 4, 1785, there was a terrible scene and another memorable dressing down by the Emperor, this time verbally and in front of the Archduke's tutors in which Joseph described his nephew as a "soulless machine," accused him of laziness and seeking the easiest way out of things.[2] On another occasion when Francis appeared awkward on horseback, the Emperor shouted at the startled adolescent in public. He derided Francis as "dim-witted" "timid" "awkward" and "lethargic" at various times, apparently in the belief that such harsh criticism would cure his nephew of these undesirable traits and that coming from him, Francis could not avoid or ignore addressing these deficits.[3]

Indeed, Joseph II developed a system of "fear and unpleasantness" including the strict admonition that Francis was not to "eat, sleep or enjoy himself until he had completed his daily duties."[4] There was to be no mingling or interaction with friends, acquaintances or even servants, at times, to ensure that Francis alone carried out his instructions because otherwise, he "failed to lead himself, to do his own thinking."[5]

By January 1786, the Emperor's sister, Marie Christine, reproved the Emperor to his face regarding his all too frequent criticisms of the Archduke and it appears to have finally caused Joseph to relent and reconsider his methods. By May 25, 1786, Joseph wrote his brother Leopold concerning his son, stating that Francis was "for the first time since he came into the world . . . acquitting himself fairly well on all points."[6] Yet, paradoxically, a bond of sorts developed between uncle and nephew.

It is difficult to obtain a true picture of the young Archduke's personality during these critical years because of the biased or narrow viewpoints of those individuals around Francis whose descriptions of him then survive to the present day. His father, Leopold, seems to have been the most realistic and indulgent and was, at times, apparently exasperated with his brother's fault-finding and pedantic letters. The Emperor's views must be regarded with some suspicion given his own rather exacting, perfectionist and sometimes impulsive personality. The observations of the tutors, particularly Colloredo, are suspect because they often sought to deflect criticism away from themselves by emphatically agreeing with the monarch about Francis' deficiencies and blaming the youth himself for lack of effort or defects in his personality rather than any deficiency in their methods.

In truth, it seems the young Archduke's personality was not terribly different than most young, adolescent men and, indeed, he seems to have conscientiously applied himself to his education and physical training with a determination that would be far beyond the expectations of modern education. He seems by most accounts to have had an early gift for memory, especially for names and places. He had a keen intelligence that enabled him to "grasp things" quickly, even in the opinion of the Emperor.[7]

Other personality traits gradually come into focus. Francis seems to have been plagued in adolescence by shyness or "timidity." Once in Vienna, Francis was rarely allowed to spend much time with young people his own age, particularly outside the family. References to his narcissism are too frequent to ignore in these years and suggest at the very least an awareness by Francis of his eventual fate and at least some feelings of entitlement. These "defects" in personality, as we have seen, were ruthlessly exposed by his uncle and relentlessly confronted until the young man was "convinced of the truth" of his "imaginary perfection."

What other characteristics emerge about him? He loved to read. By the time he was eighteen, he had already a significant collection of volumes in both quality and size located in his apartments in the Hofburg. He retained the library throughout his life, assiduously adding to its collection and receiving with special pleasure rare or significant books as gifts from his fellow monarchs, diplomats, family and friends. He designated the collection a family heirloom to be handed down from eldest son to eldest son in the imperial line after his death.[8]

He also loved art, especially portraits. In its day, the Emperor Francis' portrait collection was considered one of the world's greatest. Francis especially collected portraits of contemporaneous, famous individuals such as fellow royalty, military commanders and statesmen. Often, when he was a young prince, Francis composed short essays and commentaries to explain the portraits he collected.[9]

Perhaps the greatest qualities remarked on by virtually all who recorded their impressions of the young Francis was his phenomenal memory, his quick grasp of the essence of an issue or thing and his eye for details. A tour of a town, a fortress, cathedral or prison, a factory, a theatre or people he met along the way would and could be appraised quickly and in detail and recalled perfectly years later. He was keenly interested in commerce and trade to a far greater degree than other young men his age. Even as an elderly man, Francis would keep some of his own accounts in his own hand.

From his days in Florence, at an early age, Francis learned Italian. He was also taught French, German and Latin by his tutors. He is known to have been quite proficient in translating between French and German in his teen-

Figure 2.2. Leopold (left) and Joseph II, circa 1769 by Pompeo Batoni; Kunsthistoriches Museum, Vienna

age years. Gradually and by late adolescence, Francis came to prefer holding conversations in German and was known to complain at times when certain figures at court persisted speaking to him in French, notwithstanding his abilities in that tongue. Nonetheless, like most Habsburg monarchs before and since, Francis spoke several languages fluently.

He developed a taste for hunting deer and waterfowl and was a decent shot. He would enjoy hunting in the Austrian style in the woods and mountains all his life when the opportunity presented itself. Although initially clumsy at horse riding, as observed with annoyance by his uncle, Francis applied himself and in time became an accomplished horseman.

VIENNA IN THE JOSEPHIN ERA

The Vienna of the late 18th century that Francis discovered was, as it has remained to this day, a city of high culture. This was especially true in comparison to all but a few of the other European capitals and major cities of that time. The Burgtheater had been constructed in 1741 and was the most important German language theater in the world when Francis arrived in Vienna. Three Mozart operas would premiere there as would Beethoven's First Symphony in 1800.

Francis' grandfather, Emperor Francis I sponsored in 1752, the building of the zoo on the grounds of the imperial palace at Schönbrunn. By 1779, his son, Joseph II, opened the zoo and the grounds to the public. The *Tiergarten Schönbrunn* remains today the oldest continuously operating zoo in the world.

Joseph's barely concealed contempt for the nobility and its exclusive privileges found expression in many similar actions. Another was the opening of the ballrooms of the Hofburg to the public for dancing in 1773. One of the unintended consequences of the Emperor throwing open the doors was the appearance of a dance that had been popular with peasants and common folk in Austria and Bavaria for the past century: the waltz. By Francis' time in Vienna, the waltz had been introduced to the higher ranks of society before anywhere else in Europe. It quickly caught on as a popular dance for celebrating Carnival in Vienna.

Yet another Josephin gesture to the common folk in Vienna was the opening to the public in 1766 of the hunting grounds outside the city walls known as the *Prater* that had been purchased by Emperor Maximillian in 1560. Joseph II also allowed merchants to open coffeehouses in the park for public consumption and convenience.

In 1786, Wolfgang Amadeus Mozart's opera *The Marriage of Figaro* premiered in Vienna before the Emperor and the imperial court, to rapturous receptions, as described in this contemporaneous account:

> Crowded houses proved that nothing ever on the stage produced a more powerful effect; the audience were convulsed with laughter, in which Mozart himself joined. The Emperor repeatedly cried out Bravo! And the piece was loudly applauded and encored. . . . Never was anything more complete than the triumph of Mozart and his '*Nozze di Figaro*' to which numerous overflowing audiences bore witness.[10]

Although there is apparently no record of Francis attending the premiere or meeting Mozart on this occasion, there can be little doubt that he would have. This would not have been his first time. Mozart and his father had visited Francis' family and performed for the Grand Duke Leopold in the Pitti Palace in 1770 when Francis would have been only two years old and Mozart 14. On a second Italian tour in 1773, Mozart's father had applied for a position for his son at the court of the Grand Duke, but was turned down.

By 1786, nonetheless, Mozart had been living in Vienna for five years and was already famous as a pianist and composer. He had a very strong and growing fan base who attended his concerts that often took place in ballrooms of expensive restaurants or even in apartment buildings in Vienna. Mozart produced many of his own concerts in which he was often but not always a solo performer. In addition, he was composing and presenting on average three or four new piano concertos every year. *Figaro* was followed in 1787 by *Don Giovanni* and, in December of that year, Mozart was appointed Chamber Composer by Joseph II.

Mozart was known for his extravagant lifestyle in these days when he reached the peak of his fame and fortune. The British tenor Michael Kelley became close friends with him and described him in his autobiographical Reminisces:

> He was a remarkably small man, very thin and pale, with a profusion of fine hair, of which he was rather vain . . . He always received me with kindness and hospitality [at his house]. . . . He was remarkably fond of punch, of which beverage I have seen him take copious draughts. He was also fond of billiards, and had an excellent billiard table in his house. Many and many a game have I played with him, but always came off second best. . . . He was kind-hearted and always ready to oblige; but so very particular, when he played, that if the slightest noise were made, he instantly left off. . . .[11]

In 1787, a little-known pianist from Bonn—Ludwig van Beethoven—arrived in Vienna for a brief stay. Although there is apparently no contemporaneous documentation, it is believed that Beethoven and Mozart may have met and that Beethoven even played for the Viennese superstar in his apartment. Unfortunately, Beethoven's mother fell ill that year of tuberculosis, forcing his return to Bonn. He would return in 1792 but by then, Mozart was dead.

A late 18th century Englishman, William Hunter, gave his countrymen and, today, gives us a glimpse into the architecture and ambience of Vienna in 1792:

> ... Within the walls, which are not quite three miles in circumference, it is very confined. The houses, which are chiefly plastered and white washed, are well built, and the streets, though narrow, are regular and well paved. At night they are lighted and watched, and the passengers may walk out at all hours with the greatest security. Three of the squares are decorated with handsome monuments, which have been raised, on different occasions, at great expense, to be erected. This regulation was enacted on account of the fortifications, which are considered as of the utmost importance, and which, indeed, have enabled the inhabitants to sustain several vigorous sieges. Vienna has a gay and busy appearance. The streets are crowded with people, who flock in from the suburbs; and such is the concourse of strangers, that you frequently have an opportunity of seeing the habits and manners of almost every nation in Europe congregated on the same spot. Provisions are plentiful and cheap, but lodgings are expensive. The houses, in fact, are not sufficient for the inhabitants, and a different family occupies every floor. Including the suburbs, the population of Vienna is computed to amount to two hundred and ten thousand souls ...

Vienna was still a walled city at that time and would remain so until after the 1848 revolutions and the reign of Francis' grandson, the Emperor Franz Joseph. Nonetheless, the great walls had fallen into disrepair and, in some places, were in ruins.

THE TURKISH WAR

In 1786, the Emperor deemed it time for his young ward and future successor to learn the arts of war. In typical Josephin fashion, no favors were to be afforded to the heir. Francis was introduced to the duties and responsibilities of a second lieutenant and was expected to learn the function and responsibilities of each officer's rank and grade up to division commander.[12] Francis was popular with the officers of the army and the camaraderie with men more his own age was a relief from the isolated life he had been allowed most of the time at court. He was stationed in Hungary for over a year, out from under the watchful eye of the Emperor, until a few months before his marriage on January 6, 1788 in Vienna to Elisabeth Wilhelmina, a young duchess of Württemberg.

Like many members of the Habsburg dynasty, it was accepted as a matter of fact and due course that the marriage of the heir would be arranged for

Figure 2.3. Elizabeth Wilhelmine von Württemberg, circa 1784. By Giovanni Battista Lampi; Kunsthistoriches Museum, Vienna.

reasons of state. His father had informed him of this marriage years earlier, in 1782, when Francis was only fourteen years old.

The motivation for consummating the marriage at that time was the interest Joseph II had in further cementing the Habsburg relationship with the Russian Romanov dynasty, with whom he had signed an alliance in 1781. The 58-year-old Empress Catherine (the Great) was nearing the end of her long reign that had seen her dynasty become one of the most powerful European monarchies. Her son, the future Tsar Paul, had already married Marie from the Duchy of Wurttemberg. It was deemed advantageous by Joseph that his nephew should marry Marie's sister, Elisabeth, who had already become the future Tsar's sister-in-law.

It was an arranged marriage, without question, but the famous dynasty with a long and illustrious history of fabulously advantageous marriages was often lucky in love as well. Even though Elisabeth was not considered particularly attractive, Francis liked her immediately, as well as her parents. Francis accepted his own marriage without question and dutifully returned to Vienna when the time came. The Emperor Joseph, normally frugal and unostentatious, lavished the couple with an elaborate wedding including a formal court ball with buffet supper for forty-six hundred invited guests.[13]

Francis had little time to spend with his new bride because in February 1788, just a month after the marriage, Joseph II formally joined the Russo-Turkish War that had begun in August 1787, when the Ottoman Turkish Empire had declared war on Russia. The terms of the 1781 alliance between the two dynasties required Joseph II to assist the Russians in such a war and furthermore, having been blocked twice from territorial expansion in Germany, Joseph II, ever the expansionist, saw the possibility of acquiring territory in the Balkans from the ancient enemy of his House in conjunction with a rising and powerful ally.

The Austro-Turkish War of 1788-91 is an often overlooked and obscure war fought in a far corner of Europe. From a military point of view, its obscurity may be deserved and can be summarized in a few paragraphs. The implications of the war on the Habsburg monarchy and its precarious position in Europe, however, deserve more scrutiny. We will begin with the military aspects, since this part of the story can be summarized quickly.

Francis and his uncle joined the army being assembled in Hungary after his wedding. It was the largest imperial army ever assembled and at enormous cost. An estimated 300,000 troops with more than 1000 field guns were eventually marshalled by the Emperor and placed at the command of the eminent Field Marshal Franz Moritz von Lacy. Although this war is often described as a military failure and blamed on the Emperor personally, the record contradicts this common misconception. In fact, the opposite occurred.

The slow mobilization and positioning of the massive Habsburg army allowed the Turks, who had already been mobilized and fighting with Russia for a year, to take the initiative. Shortly after hostilities were underway there was a Turkish invasion of southern Hungary (the Banat) from Turkish Serbia, which was initially successful in breaking through thin Imperial defenses. Tens of thousands of Serbian refugees poured into Hungary, many of whom flocked to the Habsburg standard to fight the dreaded Turks.[14] Ironically, based upon what was to come a century later, the Serbians looked for annexation by the Monarchy and to save themselves from the heavy hand of the "infidel" Muslim Turks in favor of the Christian Habsburgs. They fought hard under the Emperor's standard.

This advance was checked in the summer of 1788 as the Emperor and his young aide-de-camp remained with the army and calmly brought more resources to bear in this theatre of the war. The war then degenerated into a stalemate during the disease riddled autumn and winter of 1788-89.

Francis witnessed an immense imperial army wracked by dysentery, typhus and all manner of infectious diseases assisting his uncle in southern Hungary. At one point, contagious diseases sickened between 300-400 Habsburg soldiers every day. By the Fall of 1789, it has been estimated that some 172,000 soldiers were sick or wounded and of those, 33,000 died.[15]

Joseph II was unimpressed by and impatient with the lackluster martial command of the aging von Lacy and for a time, took personal command of the army. Eventually, he appointed the equally elderly but much more aggressive Field Marshal Ernst von Laudon. By September 1789, von Laudon besieged and captured the Turkish stronghold of Belgrade in a brilliant campaign of three weeks. Bosnia and Serbia thereafter fell. Another Habsburg army in cooperation with the exceptionally talented Russian general Suvarov captured Bucharest and Wallachia (Romania), which was then occupied.

Unfortunately, disease was not confined to the rank and file. While campaigning in Romania, Joseph II was infected with tuberculosis and became increasingly ill and weak. The Emperor returned to Vienna with his nephew in the latter part of 1789, essentially, a slowly dying man. Nonetheless, having failed to aggrandize the Habsburg dynastic holdings in central Europe, a vast Balkan empire was now coming under the control of Joseph II.

Unlike Napoleon, his brothers or even his grandson, the future emperor Franz Joseph, Francis would never take actual command of any of his armies during his lifetime. There is little evidence regarding exactly how much Francis learned from his uncle or the imperial commanders in the field about military logistics, strategy or tactics between 1788-90. He was tutored by one of the best Habsburg generals at that time, Jozsef Alvinczi, later Baron von Borberek, whose career Francis would advance after becoming emperor and one of the few generals in history to have defeated Napoleon himself in the field. Nonetheless, for four of the six years leading up to his own accession to the crown, Francis observed much of war that may have influenced his thinking and, hence, his actions later in life.

While the war had been militarily a success, it was a failure in every other respect. In fact, the Austro-Turkish War would have disastrous consequences in both the short term and the long term on Habsburg power in Europe.

Internally, within the Habsburg lands, the war was immensely unpopular. Conscription of the aristocracy and common people was rigorously enforced in typical Josephin fashion and created enormous resentment, especially in Vienna. The immense cost of the war dramatically increased the indebtedness of the Monarchy to such a point that it threatened its survival when it was thereafter faced with a series of ever more serious and expensive existential wars with France during Francis' reign. This will be discussed in more detail later.

On the international front, the Turkish War created a power vacuum within the Holy Roman Empire for Prussian mischief. When the Austrian Netherlands (Belgium) flamed into open revolt in 1787 followed by the Turkish War, the opportunistic King Frederick Wilhelm II contemplated the possibility of renewing Prussia's bid for equality or even supremacy within Germany and found the temptation irresistible.

Frederick William bided his time, awaiting developments. As von Laudon and Suvarov routed the Turks, the prospect of a far more powerful Habsburg dynastic power that sprawled from the Adriatic and Black Seas to the heart of central Europe prompted the King and his ministers to make a move to restore the balance of power. In 1790, he concluded an alliance with the Sultan of Turkey. Its terms included the promise of a Prussian invasion of Bohemia to take pressure off the Turks. Prussia also sponsored an influx of spies and *agents provocateurs* to arouse both the Belgians and the Hungarians:

> Confident of Prussian help, many Magyar nobles began calling for a diet to dethrone the Habsburgs; Frederick William even suggested replacing them with the pro-Prussian duke of Saxe-Weimar. At the same time, the Belgian exiles in Liège re-entered the Austrian Netherlands at the head of a small army. By the end of 1789 they had expelled all Austrian forces from the western half of the country. Although Luxemburg remained under Habsburg control, the other estates now declared their independence as the États belgiques unis.[16]

The Prussian king's agents found fertile ground for incitement in both Hungary and Belgium. Other Josephin reforms, such as ending serfdom in 1785, confiscation of all church property, dismantling the power of the nobility by ignoring or abolishing local diets and estates and, above all, subjecting the nobility to the hated land tax had produced simmering resentment to his reforms throughout the empire, but especially in Belgium and Hungary. The war, with its taxation and conscription, was a burden too far and simultaneously placed Habsburg military power that would be needed to put down such mutinies far away in the Balkans, fully engaged against the Turks.

Francis witnessed the slow collapse of his uncle under the weight of the failure and swelling resistance to his well-intentioned but increasingly toxic errors of judgment and timing. Rather than contenting himself with seeing through a program of domestic reform, which would alone have met stiff resistance and engaged the most extraordinary ruler, Joseph's expansionist foreign and military policy conducted at the same time had brought him and his empire to ruin. By 1790, he and his Monarchy were besieged from within and without by enemies and the Emperor was dying of tuberculosis.

Joseph despaired, and his increasing ill health sapped him of energy and hope. He found himself a lonely and largely despised figure in Vienna. His empire, wracked with dissent and its treasury exhausted by the Turkish war, Joseph II had to face the dreadful fact that unless something dramatic was done, his empire might just fall apart.

His state chancellor, Kaunitz, like the late Empress he had served for four decades, had been dead-set against expansionism and, therefore, Joseph's wars. A few weeks before Kaunitz' death in 1794, he gave the same advice to Francis that he had given to his uncle and his grandmother, years earlier:

> "It is a matter of common knowledge that I have long been of the opinion that the Austrian Monarchy is in a position to procure such power and strength through wise domestic reforms as to make the most spectacular [foreign] conquests superfluous."[17]

Kaunitz had steadfastly rejected Joseph's vast expenditures on the army and war, arguing that no matter how numerous the army was, it could never outnumber the combination of all potential adversaries.[18] Appalled at the results of his master's policies, he refused to even visit the Emperor as he became increasingly sick and depressed and was largely confined to his bedchamber. His advice having been repeatedly spurned by Joseph II, Kaunitz watched with tart dismay the bitter harvest his master had sown by 1790.

Joseph wrote his brother, Leopold, in Florence:

> I confess to you that, humiliated by what has happened to me, seeing that I am unfortunate in everything I undertake, the appalling ingratitude with which my good arrangements are received and I am treated—for there is now no conceivable insolence or curse that people do not allow themselves to utter about me publicly—all this makes me doubt myself; I no longer dare to have an opinion and put it into effect, I allow myself to be ruled by the advice of the ministers even when I don't think it is the best, since I dare not hold out for my view and indeed I haven't the strength to impose it and argue for it.[19]

Leopold remained in Florence, nonetheless, despite pleas from his brother to come quickly to Vienna and form a co-regency, for fear that the unpopularity of his brother would then smother him and the Monarchy.

Figure 2.4. State Chancellor Wenzel Anton Kaunitz, circa 1762; By Jean-Étienne Liotard

Only Francis continued to serve the Emperor whom he had come to love and revere as a second father. A despondent and desperate Joseph II finally signed a decree on January 30, 1790, rescinding many of his reforms; an act that seems to have inspired him to direct that the epitaph to be inscribed on his simple copper coffin at the foot of his mother's tomb would be: "Here lies Joseph II who failed in all he undertook."[20] He died on February 20, 1790 with only his nephew attending him. He was 48 years old.

On a day that might have been one of joy to Francis and only two days before the death of the Emperor, on February 18, 1790, his wife Elisabeth died in childbirth. Their daughter, the Archduchess Ludovika Elisabeth, turned out to be mentally ill and died herself sixteen months later. It is a melancholy fact that infant mortality and female death in childbirth was still, at the end of the 18th century, not uncommon. It struck high and low alike. Childbirth was a difficult, rigorous and extremely painful process even when things went well, especially for first-born children. The agonies of his wife's painful death as the hours of labor ticked by and her struggles were increasingly recognized as hopeless was as difficult and wrenching for a privileged archduke as it was for a common peasant.

Francis found himself alone in the Hofburg palace on February 21, 1790; a widower at the age of twenty-two with an infant child. As he returned to his rooms in the Hofburg, he might have remembered that the exquisite décor and furnishings had been specifically chosen and meticulously placed with care by the late Emperor himself shortly before Francis arrived in Vienna six years earlier. Francis would live in these same rooms when he was at the Hofburg for the rest of his life. On his command, not one stick of furniture, not one portrait or sculpture was ever allowed to be moved or changed from the way his uncle had arranged it for him. When he became Emperor, Francis commissioned a massive bronze equestrian statue of his uncle, with his arm outstretched to protect his people, in what became the *Josephsplatz* within the Hofburg palace complex. It remains there to this day.

Joseph's meteoric reign had flashed wide and deep past his observant nephew who knew that someday, sooner or later, if he lived long enough, the immense power and responsibility he watched his uncle wield with rapt attention would be his. What might the young Francis have already observed that would stay with him from the reign of his uncle? A distaste for and distrust of war that he had seen arouse resentment from his subjects at its taxes and blood? A tempering of the enthusiasm he had been taught for enlightened "reforms" that had engendered "appalling ingratitude," rebellion and even treason from those for whom they had been enacted,?

These predilections have often been attributed to Francis as having arisen out of the French Revolution, and there can be little doubt that the cataclysm of war and revolution in France that was yet to come would have a major impact on his thinking. Yet the education of this young man in more conservative and cautious governance might well have had their origins in this, a much earlier time.

The double death of his wife and his uncle were undoubtedly the first heavy blows that life had imposed on this young man. Many, many more were to follow that would likewise, undoubtedly temper the personality of the man who had just ten years earlier wandered the gardens and piazzas in the sun of Florence with his brothers and sisters. But now he was in a darkened palace, in a cold city while he waited for his father to arrive.

NOTES

1. Feil, Joseph *"Kaiser Joseph II. Als Erzieher"* in *Sylvester-Spenden eines Kreises von Freunden vaterländischer Geschichtsforschung* (Vienna: 1852) 2–5.

2. Langsam 67–68: *Tagebuch Colloredos*, October 22, 1785.
3. Blanning, T.C.W, *Joseph II.* (London: Routledge, 2013) 201.
4. Blanning 60.
5. Wheatcroft, Andrew, *The Habsburgs: Embodying Empire* (London: Penguin Books, 1997) 201.
6. Arneth 34.
7. Langsam 47.
8. Langsam 48.
9. Langsam 67.
10. Kelly, Michael, *Reminiscences of Michael Kelly, of the King's Theatre, and Theatre Royal Drury Lane* (London: H. Colburn, 1826).
11. Ibid.
12. Langsam 69, 70.
13. Vovk 214, 215.
14. Aksan, Virginia, *Ottoman Wars 1700-1870: An Empire Besieged* (London: Longman/Pearson, 2007) 163-166.
15. Ibid.
16. Ingrao, Charles, *The Habsburg Monarchy, 1618–1815* (New York: Cambridge University Press, 2nd edition, 2000) 208.
17. Szabo, Franz A. J. *Kaunitz and Enlightened Absolutism, 1753–1780* (Cambridge: Cambridge University Press, 1994) 2.
18. Szabo 286.
19. Emperor Joseph II to Grand Duke Leopold, 21 January 1790. Beales, Derek, *Joseph II, In the Shadow of Maria Theresa*, (New York: Cambridge University Press, 2008) 5.
20. Davies, Norman, *Europe: A History,* (New York: Harper Perennial, 1998).

Chapter Three

A Brief Transition–Leopold II

News of the unexpected death of the Holy Roman Emperor and head of the House of Habsburg-Lorraine rippled outward from Vienna across the continent of Europe, catching governments, family and ordinary people by surprise. Alone in Vienna, the *de facto* Habsburg ruler of an empire teetering on the brink of disaster and revolution, Francis temporized with the elderly State Chancellor, Kaunitz, until his father could arrive.

Francis' father was not surprised when the news reached him in Florence, although he had come to dread the premature death of his brother as a personal calamity. Over the years, he had joined the ranks of those who had come to resent what they perceived to be the overbearing, hectoring and sometimes impulsive rule of his brother. Joseph's meddling in his family's affairs, including the education of Francis, were ultimately obeyed with increasing distaste and even anger by Leopold and his wife.

Leopold's loving, brotherly feelings toward Joseph had been shattered years earlier in 1781 when Joseph had first become co-regent and Emperor. It involved a dispute regarding a large endowment of some two million florins their father had left deposited in a Tuscan bank for public works and the general benefit of the people of Tuscany. Joseph had demanded it be returned to the imperial treasury in Vienna.[1] Leopold initially refused, and a series of increasingly angry and bitter letters flew back and forth between them to the point that their mother had to intercede.[2] Most, but not all the money was eventually released to the Emperor. Joseph in time forgave and forgot the matter and assumed Leopold had done the same. Such was not the case. Leopold's love for his brother died in this affair and never returned. By the end of Joseph's life, Leopold's feelings were those of contempt and almost hatred.[3]

Far more cautious and pessimistic than Joseph, Leopold's attitude toward reform could best be described as somewhere between his mother and his brother, albeit for different reasons. Where Maria Theresa's caution for reform welled up from her strong religious convictions and natural conservatism, Leopold's skepticism arose from more practical worries about the reaction they might provoke in the aristocracy and the people. While intellectually steeped in the Enlightenment in his youth, with his brother Joseph, he was more patient, practical and far more devious.

Leopold's reforms in Tuscany tended to be popular but incremental and geared toward creating infrastructure and public works that made life easier and more pleasant than, for example, rescinding press censorship or abolishing feudal obligations, as his brother had done. Leopold was no longer the idealistic man of the Enlightenment who had authored the powerful, liberal missives to his son's tutors. He had by 1790 developed a sometimes sullen and paranoid personality as Grand Duke that probably arose from his discovery that he was always being spied upon either by his mother or his brother.[4] Spying and informing became an accepted part of life for the Grand Duke and soon Leopold had developed an elaborate network of informers and spies of his own in Tuscany. His altruistic impulse to work for the good of his people remained, but his enthusiasm for the *avant-garde* reforms of the type his brother favored, if he ever shared them, had waned.

For the past decade, Leopold watched as Joseph alienated one group after another, one class after another, one national community after another, capped off by expensive wars, as he saw it. Leopold, unlike his brother but like Kaunitz, had little interest in military affairs or territorial aggrandizement. He had abolished the military in Tuscany shortly after his arrival, avoiding the expense of maintaining a military establishment that freed him to expend money on public works.

The Potato War with The Netherlands, the War of the Bavarian Succession with Prussia and then the Turkish war, Leopold watched from afar with the same dismay and alarm his mother had felt while she was alive. Yet these wars were not his wars and until his brother's health began to fail, there was little he could do. Nor did he fully appreciate the dangerous position in which the latest, on-going war had placed the Monarchy. It became all too apparent to Leopold when he arrived in Vienna from Florence, as revealed by a letter to his sister on March 15, 1790:

> My health is fair . . . It is not the trip which has made me suffer so; it is the sad state and situation of the monarchy and the confusion which reigns everywhere throughout the realm.[5]

Figure 3.1. Leopold II (1747-1792) by Heinrich Füger, Circa 1790; National Gallery, Prague

BEETHOEVEN IN VIENNA

Maximilian Franz was the youngest child of the Empress Maria Theresa and youngest brother of Emperor Joseph. Since 1784 he had been Archbishop of Cologne and, therefore, one of the Electors of the Holy Roman Empire. His court was held in Bonn and as the Pope's anointed deputy, would place the crown on the head of his brother, Leopold II and then his nephew, Francis.

Maximilian was a keen patron of the arts, especially music, and had as his court *Kapellmeister* Ludwig van Beethoven, grandfather of the famous Beethoven of the same name. Shortly after Maximilian's installation in Bonn, his court organist, Christian Neefe, introduced him to his young pupil, the grandson of his Kapellmeister. Maximilian was surprised and delighted at the amazing talent of the young Ludwig van Beethoven and appointed him assistant court organist under Neefe's supervision. By 1787, the Elector and Neefe believed that Beethoven might be the "next Mozart" and that he should go to

Vienna to develop his talents there with the musical giants such as Mozart, Haydn and Antonio Salieri. Maximilian and several other local nobles financed Beethoven's trip to Vienna in that year but, unfortunately, as we have seen, his stay in Vienna was cut short with the illness and death of his mother which forced his return to Bonn. He would not return to Vienna until 1792.

Beethoven's connection to the Habsburgs would not end with the patronage of the Elector and while the composer would have a lifelong and hypocritically hostile relationship with the nobility and aristocracy, there is no evidence that this extended so far as the monarchy itself. In fact, at least early in his life, he seems to have been an admirer of the Emperor Joseph, possibly due to the influence of Maximilian Franz. The Elector was an enthusiastic reformer and imported into his territory of the Empire many of the Enlightenment policies of his brother. While the late Emperor's policies had been anathema to the conservative nobility, his reforms were received with enthusiasm in the intellectual circles the young Beethoven frequented where the reforming Emperor was regarded as a hero.

In 1790, Beethoven composed the "Cantata on the Death of Joseph II" at the behest of the Elector which, it was hoped, would be played at a memorial mass in Bonn. For reasons which are obscure today, it was never played and Beethoven himself never promoted it to the public. In 1813, the composer Johann Nepomuk Hummel is said to have purchased the score at an auction and then it languished in obscurity. It was discovered again at another auction in 1884. Upon its reappearance, it was immediately performed in Vienna that same year. Beethoven also composed a companion piece, "Cantata on the Accession of Emperor Leopold II." It seems certain that Beethoven showed the Joseph Cantata to Haydn when he visited Bonn in 1792 on his way back to Vienna from London. Haydn was sufficiently impressed with this piece to encourage Beethoven to return to Vienna to study with him. Beethoven did so and became Haydn's most famous protégé, introducing the sensational pianist to the salons and concert halls of Vienna's wealthiest music patrons.

Francis, while alarmed at the mounting issues facing the Monarchy, could console himself with the fact that he was not inheriting the throne and had no expectation of doing so for a long time. His father was only 43. One of his father's first priorities, after his arrival, was finding Francis a second wife. Leopold was not particularly concerned with influencing international ties with another great power, as Joseph had been. Leopold was interested in dynastic consolidation and settled on princess Maria Therese, the 18-year-old, eldest daughter of his sister, Maria Carolina, the Queen of Naples. Incredibly, Leopold also arranged the marriage of his second son, Ferdinand, to another daughter, Luisa, and gave his daughter Clementine to the Queen's son, Prince Francesco.

The tendency of the Habsburg dynasty to intermarriage with close relatives had already had disastrous consequences to the family and Europe. The danger of genetic inbreeding was, of course, unknown in the 18th century. The founder of the study of genetics, Gregor Mendel, would not publish his first paper on the theory of heredity until 1866 and the concept would not be widely understood until after 1925. Accordingly, the disastrous genetic consequences of intermarriage continued to wreak havoc in the family that, if anything, considered the benefit of intermarriage to be self-evident; much like breeding of fine horses.

The Spanish Habsburg line had become extinct with the death of King Charles II in 1700, after nearly two hundred years of marriages of uncles to nieces, first cousins and other similar close family. Charles II was described as:

> . . . sadly, degenerated with an enormous misshapen head. His . . . jaw stood so much out that his two rows of teeth could not meet; he was unable to chew. His tongue was so large that he was barely able to speak. . . . His brief life consisted chiefly of a passage from prolonged infancy to premature senility. . . . He had been fed by wet nurses until the age of 5 or 6 and was not allowed to walk until almost fully grown. . . . His body remained that of an invalid child. . . . The nature of his upbringing . . . helped to create a mentally retarded and hypersensitive monarch. . . . [6]

Epilepsy was a common, inherited trait of the Habsburgs and would plague numerous members of the family including Francis' eldest son and heir, Ferdinand, who was born in 1793. Nonetheless, unaware of these genetic perils, Francis wed his second wife, a "double cousin," in a triple wedding ceremony in Vienna on September 15, 1790 with his brother and sister. The spectacular wedding was followed by weeks of fireworks, operas and gala parties that reinvigorated Viennese society after years of the frugal and dull court of Joseph II.[7]

IMPERIAL RETREAT AND RETRENCHMENT

On September 30, Leopold was informed of his election as Holy Roman Emperor. His coronation in Frankfurt followed on October 9, 1790; a magnificent ceremony of imperial pomp with thousands of people watching the procession and coronation.[8] On November 15, Leopold was crowned king of Hungary in the Cathedral of St. Martin at Bratislava in another suitably opulent ceremony meant to impress his fractious Hungarian subjects, no doubt, with the dynasty's wealth and power.

Figure 3.2. Maria Therese of Naples. Second wife and "double cousin" of Francis II. By Marie Louise Elisabeth Vigée-Lebrun, circa 1790. Musée Condé, Paris

Leopold, despite the dire financial straits weighing on the Empire, about which we will discuss more shortly, was not as personally frugal as were other members of his family, including his son. And the personal wealth of the Habsburg family should not and cannot be confused with the imperial treasury.

Some decades earlier, his father, Francis I, had established the Habsburg "mutual support" fund that would last until 1918 and, perhaps, even later than that for the financial support and comfort of the imperial family.[9] This fund comprised a stupendous source of wealth, not merely in cash and investments, but in precious objects of art, paintings, real estate, palaces and other corporeal assets. The fund was always under the personal control of the head of the House of Habsburg-Lorraine, including the granting of allowances and living expenses. This gave the Emperor considerable bargaining power and authority over sometimes unruly uncles, nephews, cousins, sons and daughters dependent upon the generosity of the Emperor to support them in a style becoming of their status and to which they naturally became accustomed.

As for Francis, Maria Therese, unlike his first wife, was considered quite attractive, vivacious and spoke German fluently. She would bear him twelve children. There is no doubt that Francis loved her during her life, calling her his "heart and soul." Sixteen years later, upon her death, his brother the Archduke Charles had to physically remove a heart-broken Francis from her deathbed.[10]

Upon his accession, Leopold wasted little time in becoming the imperial brake-man, grasping the lever of his late brother's runaway reforms and wars with both hands and pulling it back with all his might. The internal, financial reforms, taxes and increased revenues that had inured to the treasury over the years by the careful management of Francis I and Maria Theresa had been exhausted and significant debt incurred. Continuing the war in the Balkans against Turkey, let alone dealing with the revolution that had broken out in Belgium and seemed about to erupt in Hungary, and now Bohemia and Transylvania as well, was an oppressive burden the state simply could not bear and had to be addressed. Leopold's empire was further threatened on virtually every front by external enemies; in the south by an active war with Turkey, in the north by an impending invasion by Prussia and to the west, France was in the throes of revolution.

The drain on the state treasury had also burned the economy and had been widely felt by Viennese society during the Turkish War, including by artists and musicians such as Wolfgang Amadeus Mozart. Conscription, taxes and a constricting economy in Vienna had resulted in a dramatic reduction in subscriptions for music by the aristocracy and wealthy patrons. Likewise, concerts and performances became sparsely attended and infrequent during the period of the Turkish War for lack of money.

Mozart, as an example, increasingly borrowed money from friends and acquaintances to keep up his lavish lifestyle, but by 1788 he and his wife Constanza had been forced to move to the suburban district of Alsergrund at Währinger Strasse 26, to economize. This was outside the walls of the city, in what is now the Ninth District, not far from the Votivkirche, the Josephinum (just completed in 1785) and the present-day Sigmund Freud Museum. The actual apartment building in which he lived was pulled down in 1891 and replaced by the present building that stands there today. It was here that Mozart wrote his opera *Cosi Fan Tutti* and three symphonies, among other pieces, in ever-increasing poverty. He died in 1791, three months after the opening of his opera, *The Magic Flute* and during the first year of Leopold's reign at the age of 35.

Had Joseph II lived, with his experience in ruling the Empire, chastened as he might have been, different solutions might have been worked out in time, but Leopold was thrust into the imperial chair without many resources or much time. He acted decisively, reversing his late brother's policies to save the Monarchy, as he saw it.

First was peace with the Turks. In an astonishing climb-down, in the Treaty of Sistova, signed on August 17, 1791, Leopold ceded virtually all his brother's military gains, retaining only a sliver of territory and abandoning the Serbs to their fate at the hands of the returning Turkish overlords. The Habsburgs last bid for a Balkan empire, held at the point of a sword, evaporated with the stroke of a pen.

The Turkish War would mark the last, best chance for the Monarchy to establish a vast Balkan empire. The Habsburg and later Austrian Empire would never again annex Turkish territory until 1908 when it briefly absorbed Turkish Bosnia before the collapse of the Monarchy altogether in 1918. The incorporation of Serbia and Bosnia into the Empire at the end of the 18th century, together with Wallachia, would have transformed the Habsburg *Erblande* into a largely Slavic power with a window on the Black Sea.[11] Instead, the Treaty of Sistova confirmed that the Imperial army that had suffered significant losses to disease and battle at immense cost had done so essentially for nothing. The financial drain, however, had left Leopold in no position for a military confrontation with Prussia.

As for the simmering treason of the nobility of Bohemia, Leopold would go further than his brother in his dying days, rescinding the emancipation of the serfs and thereby pacifying the people who mattered most to the regime. Concessions were made to the aristocracy in the Austrian Netherlands, Transylvania and Hungary as well. These included, most importantly, restoration of the Estates in various provinces that re-established the rights and privileges of the nobility that had been so disdained by his brother. Again, like his mother, Leopold was far more willing to compromise than Joseph II and accommodate himself to limitations on his own powers against which Joseph had rebelled.

Leopold's thorough system of surveillance, spies and informers established in Tuscany was imported to Vienna and replicated throughout the Empire. There would be no conspiracies or unforeseen rebellions now. Letters were opened. Reports were demanded.

The young heir Francis, formerly his uncle's most trusted aide-de-camp and personal assistant, worked hand-in-glove with his father and was privy to his thoughts and solutions. Under these circumstances, it would be an unusual student of politics indeed, in 1790, not to have connected the reforms his uncle had unleashed since the death of Maria Theresa with the welling up of revolution, with which his father had been forced to contend. The gauzy optimism and idealism of Francis' youth in the 1770s, with which he and his brothers had been indoctrinated, was evolving into a more cautious if not yet cynical understanding of what was required for the *Imperium* to survive.

The results of Leopold's counter-reformation were dramatic. The Austrian Netherlands, Bohemia, Hungary and Transylvania were largely, if not completely pacified. The loyalty of the aristocracy was generally restored. The ruinous wars, heavy taxation and economic decline that had pushed France over the brink in 1789 could just as easily have done the same in the Habsburg possessions, but Leopold had rescued the situation for his dynasty without a moment to lose. His son watched and learned a lesson that was to be reinforced quickly and repeatedly throughout his early reign.

After quelling the domestic sources of discontent, Leopold could take stock of the world around him and his inheritance. It was not a favorable moment in history for his monarchy. The façade of the European world of 1790 was irrevocably cracking down to its foundations. The American Revolution had resulted in a significant defeat for Great Britain in 1781, and in American independence in 1783. George Washington, the first American president, had just taken office in 1789 pursuant to a constitution that had been ratified by the Thirteen Colonies who now formed the United States of America.

In the meantime, a humbled Great Britain had embarked on a sustained period of financial reform and restraint under the administration of King George III's *wunderkind* First Minister, William Pitt. Unlike the Habsburgs, Britain had managed to avoid war for the better part of a decade since the debacle of Yorktown in 1781, husbanding its resources. Britain was also experiencing the onset of the industrial revolution that would make her the richest and most powerful country in Europe over the next two and a half decades.

The victory of the Franco-American alliance over Britain was a Pyrrhic one for France. Plunged into near bankruptcy that was not relieved by any sane financial policy, her dire straits were made worse by subsequent disastrous harvests that produced conditions of near famine. While Francis and his uncle were in the Balkans fighting the Turks, Louis XVI, the king of France, had been forced to ask for more taxes from the aristocracy and bourgeoisie to deal with these crises.

France had been an ancient foe of the Habsburgs for the better part of two centuries until, because of the need for allies against the menace of Frederick the Great and Prussia, Maria Theresa's great chancellor, Kaunitz, had reversed the alliance system of Europe over time. France and the Empire, along with Russia, had become allies against Prussia and Britain. In furtherance of this rapprochement between the Bourbons and the Habsburgs, the youngest daughter of Maria Theresa was betrothed to the Dauphin of France. Several other, older daughters of the Empress were also married off to various Bourbon kings and dukes in Italy; children of the Spanish Bourbon king, Carlos III. The relationship between the Habsburg and Bourbon dynasties had reached a zenith of mutual understanding by the time of the death of the Empress and had continued under Joseph II. All that was about to end.

The response of the long-repressed aristocracy of France, once the Estates General convened in Paris, was no less truculent and even more belligerent than that of the aristocracy of the Habsburg Empire had been. Without an autocrat to face down the Estates that was as quick and canny as Leopold II, the French aristocracy had demanded reforms; essentially an end to the absolute monarchy. Leopold encouraged the French monarchy through his sister, Queen Marie Antoinette, to grant concessions, including a constitution. Nonetheless, as Leopold was energetically patching and repairing his own house, that of his brother-in-law caught fire.

The French Revolution, it can be credibly argued, was the most significant event of the late 18th century; certainly, in the Western world. Although he could not have imagined it at the time, it would be one of the most significant events in Francis' life until he died more than four decades later. As the months went by in 1790 and 1791, the enlightened French aristocracy also lost power to increasingly radical Jacobins supported and goaded on by a hungry, poor and angry urban population in Paris. What had begun as a showdown between the king, on one side, and the aristocracy and wealthy bourgeoisie, on the other, metamorphosed into something else entirely. Yet this was not the only danger in Europe facing the Emperor. There was Prussia.

With the decline and fall of the French monarchy, what is often overlooked is the fact that the Habsburgs were losing their best continental ally against their mortal enemy in Berlin. Prussia and the Hohenzollern dynasty under Frederick the Great had begun a century long struggle with the Habsburg Monarchy that would continue until the defeat of the Austrian army at Königgratz in 1866. Frederick II had openly defied the Monarchy in two long, bitter and expensive wars earlier in the century as we have seen. He had also blocked the ambitions of Joseph II, twice, to absorb Bavaria into the Habsburg hereditary possessions, including in the brief War of the Bavarian Succession. "Old Fritz," as his soldiers called him affectionately, had died at last in 1786 and was succeeded by his licentious nephew Frederick William II.

Aware of impending war with Prussia upon his accession to the throne, Leopold reached out to Frederick William, assuring him in a personal letter that the Prussian king had nothing to fear from him; that he wanted no more than friendly relations:

> I solemnly protest, no views of aggrandizement will ever enter into my political system. . . . To your majesty in particular, I will act as you act towards me, and will spare no efforts to preserve perfect harmony.[12]

The humble and sincere tone of the letter met with an equally conciliatory one from Prussia and a preliminary meeting at Reichenbach between the two monarchs. An understanding was reached there that included a disclaimer by Leopold of any intention of keeping the territorial conquests made in the

Balkans by his brother that had un-nerved the Prussian court. When Leopold proved as good as his word in the Treaty of Sistova with Selim III and the Turkish Empire in August 1791, a thaw in relations began and war was averted.

THE FRENCH REVOLUTION AND APPROACH OF WAR

The termination of the war, the Treaty of Sistova and the Treaty of Reichenbach allowed Leopold II to complete his pacification of Hungary, Transylvania and the Austrian Netherlands while observing the deteriorating situation in France. After numerous frightening riots and intrusions into the royal apartments at the Tuileries in Paris that had terrorized the royal family, an escape was attempted on June 21, 1791 and failed. The abortive escape deeply discredited the King among moderates in the government who were preparing a constitution. Among the radicals and much of the urban population of Paris, Louis XVI was thereafter regarded with deep suspicion as a possible traitor and colluder with foreign enemies. The presence of the Habsburg Queen was further confirmation of the popular suspicion that the royal family was biding its time before French émigrés with military support from the Habsburgs and Prussia would arrive to crush them.

In fact, the King's brother, Charles, the Count d'Artois, had fled France and was actively seeking military support from Leopold II to intervene and save the French monarchy, but not receiving it. In July 1791, Leopold reluctantly agreed to meet with the Count d'Artois after many months of avoiding doing so. The meeting between the brother of the Queen and the brother of the King was reportedly quite emotional and contentious, but Leopold would not be moved to invade France and advised the Count "from making a move which [could] compromise the life and safety of the king and the queen for no reason. . . ."[13]

The rapprochement between Prussia and Austria continued to strengthen due to continuing and ominous threats to the very lives and safety of the royal family in Paris. This concern for the royal family cannot be overstated as a major cause for the rapid deterioration of relations between France and the other courts of Europe. There was a second meeting at Pillnitz Castle, the summer residence of King Frederick Augustus of Saxony, near Dresden, on August 27, 1791. The Count d'Artois and the King of Saxony also attended the consultations. Eventually, the Declaration of Pillnitz stated that the two monarchs:

> . . . [v]iew the situation in which the king of France currently finds himself as a subject of common interest for all of Europe's sovereigns . . . [and] they will

use the most efficient means in relation to their strengths to place the king of France in a position to be totally free to consolidate the bases of a monarchical government that shall be as amenable to the rights of sovereigns as it is to the well-being of the French nation . . . are resolved to act quickly, in mutual agreement, and with the forces necessary . . . [and] shall issue their troops the necessary orders to prepare them for action."

Although it was the intention of the Emperor at that time that no military intervention would occur unless all the other great powers joined him, the Declaration itself did not say that and it was not received that way by the government in Paris. Many radicals there viewed it as tantamount to a declaration of war, but still nothing happened while Leopold II was alive. Nonetheless, Leopold's diplomatic outreach to Prussia paid immediate dividends when only months earlier, Prussia had been inciting his Hungarian subjects to riot and contemplating war.

In Russia, the affable former German princess, Catherine the Great, still sat on the throne of Russia and would continue to do so until 1796. The relationship between the Romanovs and the Habsburgs, as we have seen, was a close and mutually supportive one; the only point of the compass that had not posed an imminent external threat in 1790. The ever-acquisitive Empress and her ministers continued to pursue expansion and, in the case of most concern to the Habsburgs, were looking to absorb more of the kingdom of Poland that lay directly on the northeastern borderlands of the Reich. This posed a dangerous problem for the Monarchy.

Catholic Poland had long been a friendly borderland to the Habsburg core of Austria, Hungary and Bohemia/Moravia. Maria Theresa had been alarmed during her reign at the ambition of Russia and Prussia that culminated in the First Partition of Poland in 1772. Upon realizing that Prussia and Russia were going to annex territory regardless of her objections and averse to war with a weak Polish kingdom as her only ally, the Empress had reluctantly accepted compensation in Polish Galicia and adjoining areas. Now internal strife roiled the kingdom that would provide a pretext for a Russian invasion in 1792 and a second partition by Prussia and Russia. A long-time ally and buffer between the Habsburg Empire, Prussia and Russia was ominously disappearing from the map.

In June 1791, Francis suffered the death of his sixteen-month-old daughter, Ludovica, from influenza. She had been frail and mentally challenged since birth. Francis would ultimately suffer the death of six of his children during his lifetime. Ludovica was the only living tie that had remained to him with his first wife Elisabeth. On December 12, 1791, however, Francis and Theresa had their first child, Marie Louise, at the Hofburg Palace. She would live to adulthood and become an international celebrity in her own right.

By February 1792, the French National Assembly issued an ultimatum to Leopold II demanding that unless he "renounce all intentions and acts against the sovereignty and independence of the French nation," France would declare war on the Empire. He did not respond to the threat directly, but advised his ministers to prepare for war. Yet, it was apparent that, for reasons that are unclear, the Emperor's health began to rapidly decline.

It has been suspected that Leopold may have had a stroke but the relatively primitive diagnostic resources of the time make it difficult to know for certain. Indeed, it has been said that Leopold "worked himself to death"[14] in the brief two years of his reign. His memory suddenly became an issue. At the end of February, Leopold was diagnosed with rheumatic fever, a contagious, inflammatory disease emanating from an infection by the streptococcus bacteria. In serious cases, it can spread to the heart, as it must have done in his case. He was bled by court physicians on February 28 and died suddenly in the arms of his wife the next day, on March 1, 1792.[15] He was just 44 years of age. Francis was just 24.

The failure of the late Emperor to respond to the French ultimatum after Pillnitz is seldom remarked in European history, but had momentous consequences. One cannot help but consider the counter-factual, what-might-have-been had Leopold not died at this precise moment when the chance to avoid war was hanging in the air. It is perhaps not too fanciful to compare the situation in February 1792 to the moment, just two years earlier, when Leopold had reached out to the Prussian king and avoided war over the spoils of the collapse of the Turkish Empire.

The situation was analogous in many respects. Leopold was facing unrest within his own Empire and a destitute imperial treasury. The French revolutionary government, like the Prussian king, was fearful of Habsburg (and Prussian) power and felt it must confront it before it grew too great. The French government, amid a dynamic, domestic constitutional crisis did not want war, nor did Kaunitz nor the Emperor. Had Leopold II reached out to negotiate the fate of the royal family of France at this point and in return, responded affirmatively to the French ultimatum, it seems likely that war would have been avoided and, perhaps, so much more. Yet at precisely the moment when all hung in the balance, the Emperor succumbed and his successor was too young, too inexperienced and too influenced by events to seize the moment to preserve the peace and conserve his Empire. The consequences of this missed opportunity comprise the history of the Revolutionary and Napoleonic wars. The possibilities of what might have been the history of Europe had it been otherwise boggles the mind.

Francis conveyed his grief and despair to his brother Charles in a letter:

> ... The greatest misfortune which might befall our family now forces me to write to you. Our father died of a stroke at four o'clock today, without receiving the last sacrament, but in the arms of my mother. I am too frightened in my monstrous calamity to write any more. Preserve for me your gentle love and friendship, which I need now more than ever. . . . [16]

THE FIRST COALITION—WAR WITH FRANCE

At the age of 24, Archduke Francis became King of Bohemia, Hungary, and Croatia. All the hereditary Habsburg realms automatically became his upon the death of his father. Thanks to the prodigious labors of his father, Francis did not inherit an empire wracked by internal breakdown and revolution, as his grandson Franz Joseph would do in 1848. On the other hand, the increasingly dire international situation was probably equal to what his grandmother, the Empress, had confronted in 1740 at the age of 23.

On April 20, 1792, the French National Assembly, having received no definitive reply to its ultimatum to the late emperor, declared war on the Empire because of its toleration of the formation of an alleged "émigré army" led by the Count d'Artois on its soil in the Austrian Netherlands. This force, while very small, had been seen by some in the French government as a threat to its national security in the context of the Pillnitz Declaration and the silence from Vienna in response to the French ultimatum. True to his word, the King of Prussia declared his solidarity with the new Emperor and joined the war in May. Russia, contemplating the new situation, saw the opportunity to invade and occupy more of Poland without the possibility of any active resistance from Prussia or the Empire and prudently remained neutral in the conflict with France, as did Britain for the time being.

The imperial coronation at Frankfurt of Francis II, the last Holy Roman Emperor, occurred only months after the French declaration on July 14, 1792 and during a mobilization of forces for the invasion of France by the First Coalition consisting of Prussia and the Holy Roman Empire. Prussian land forces were under the command of the Duke of Brunswick and there was an air of optimism among the assembled royal and noble families who came to witness the coronation spectacle and enjoy the festivities that followed.

French émigrés who had fled their estates in Alsace congregated at Frankfurt with the *glitterati* of the Imperial court. The young Metternich described the feelings of the aristocrats:

> Great hopes were placed on the result and certain victory was generally expected. The French emigrants thought the undertaking sure of success and the

Figure 3.3. Francis II, in coronation regalia of a Holy Roman Emperor by Ludwig Streitenfeld. The Hofburg, Vienna.

only complaint they were heard to utter related to unavoidable delays in the assembling of the army. According to their idea, the dispatch of a few battalions only was needed in order that the white flag should immediately appear on all the towers of France. No doubt these lofty delusions brought about the defeat which the Prussian army soon afterwards sustained. . . . [17]

On August 10, a Parisian mob attacked the King's Swiss guards at the Tuileries and massacred them. The royal family was then imprisoned in the Temple Tower; essentially a medieval fortress prison originally constructed in the 13th century by the Knights Templar and scene of past grisly tortures and executions. On August 30, the monarchy was abolished and France was declared a republic.

The facts surrounding the outbreak of war in 1792 between France and the Austro-Prussian coalition, which would soon be joined by Britain, draws into question the common belief that France's rightful desire for republican democracy and the liberties of man was opposed by reactionary monarchies anxious to snuff it out before the "infection" spread to their country. This is particularly so regarding the young emperor Francis II. Therefore, it bears some careful consideration.

In the first place, the France that declared war had already passed the point of reasonable and responsible transformation into a constitutional democracy with the rule of law. It was already lurching toward the Terror with more in common with the later Russian revolution of 1917 than the American one of 1776.

More to the point, however, neither Francis, his late father nor their advisors had sought to interfere in the evolving French revolution and had even encouraged the King to agree to a constitution, which Louis XVI had done in 1791. Until the last moment, when the lives of the royal family were threatened by the radicals in Paris, both Prussia and the Empire rejected the émigrés, the Count d'Artois in particular, denying them military support and cautioning them against the precipitous use of violence.

The Imperial crown had not been placed on Francis' head before France declared war on him and his Empire, and not the other way around. The French also made the first military move, attacking the nearest, contiguous Habsburg possessions—in Belgium—while the Imperial army was being mobilized on the Rhine with Prussia.

The only complicity the Habsburg monarchy had in the initiation of military hostilities with the French appears to have been its toleration of the increasingly panicky and dispossessed French émigrés led by the king's brother, Charles. For him, the cause was primarily personal; he was frantic to save his brother and the royal family from the clutches of the Temple and the mortal threat to their lives he saw coming from the Radicals in the French government. History shows his fears were not exaggerated or misplaced.

The abolition of the monarchy had been accompanied by the forfeiture and confiscation of many aristocratic estates throughout France, as well as church lands, monasteries, abbeys and so forth, all of which had been exempt from taxation before 1789. Naturally, this created a very hostile and belligerent class of clergy and nobility who fled across the borders of France to the Austrian Netherlands or the Rhineland states that were part of the Empire.

While the presence of these émigrés were a source of irritation and anxiety to the French government, their power to rescue the royal family or invade the country was vastly overrated. No less a personage than the Queen of France understood it when she had written to Leopold II on May 22, 1791:

"The times are extremely pressing, and it is wished that you would make a decision promptly. The princes, the comte d'Artois and all those that follow them, absolutely want to act; they do not have their own means to do so and will lose us without your agreeing to help. . . ."[18]

As inept as the Revolutionary army would turn out to be in the opening phase of the war, it would have been more than adequate to vanquish even a thousand aristocrats on horseback. It does not follow that meeting with or tolerating the presence of the Count or the exiled French aristocracy should have provoked a declaration of war from Paris.

Rather than the conventional explanation of twentieth century historians, influenced no doubt by the "inevitability" of the triumph of freedom and democracy, the French declaration of war was motivated more by a dose of paranoia and the impulse of an unstable, Jacobin government to unify its people by resistance to a claimed foreign threat.

To underscore the reluctance of the Habsburgs to use force or invade France, it has been remarked that the 81-year old Imperial *Staatskanzler* Wentzel Anton von Kaunitz advised both Leopold II and Francis II against war with France. He believed that France would stay weak and divided if it were left alone and that Prussia was the more dangerous enemy. It was reputedly due to the reversal of his policy of alliance with France and isolation of Prussia that he had brought about in the middle of the century that led to Kaunitz's resignation at the outset of the reign of Francis II on August 19, 1792.[19] Nonetheless, at the time of the French declaration of war, Kauntiz was still State Chancellor. Thus, neither the monarchy nor its ministers favored or sought war with France.

Francis was not alone in his reluctance to confront the revolutionary government in Paris. Prussia had also declined to initiate hostilities, let alone declare war. Nor did Britain or Russia. Horrified as the monarchy of George III was at the execution of the King of France, it was France who declared war on Britain on February 1, 1793; not the other way around. Russia, perhaps the most autocratic monarchy in Europe, never joined what became known in history as the War of the First Coalition.

Francis had war thrust upon him barely a month after the unforeseen and shocking death of his father with little choice in the matter. The false narrative that the reactionary monarchies of Europe sought war with France is apparently another one of the reasons Francis has been written off as a reactionary from the beginning. His personality was more complex than that and the sources of his later conservatism more varied than is often credited. For now, it was up to Francis II to conduct a war with France that was thrust upon him; the first of five that he would fight over the next 23 years.

NOTES

1. Cochrane, Eric, *Florence in the Forgotten Centuries 1527–1800,* (Chicago: University of Chicago Press, 2013) 423.
2. Vovk 55, 56.
3. Vovk 56.
4. Coxe, William, *History of the House of Austria,* (London: Bell & Dalby, 1873) 435.
5. Vovk 236.
6. Kahn, Razib. *Inbreeding and the Fall of the Spanish Habsburgs.* Discover Magazine, April 14, 2009.
7. Vovk 238.
8. Ibid.
9. The Holy Roman Emperor Francis I, as noted previously, was the husband of Empress Maria Theresa, father of Joseph II and Leopold II and grandfather of Francis II whom he predeceased two years prior to his birth. It was Francis I who put the "Lorraine" in Habsburg-Lorraine. As for the creation of this family fund, it remained in existence until the downfall of the monarchy in 1918. See: Anonymous. *The Czechoslovak Review, Volume II,* (New York, Bohemian Review Company, 1918).
10. Vovk 90.
11. The "Erblande" is a German term used to describe and differentiate the "inherited" lands of the Habsburg dynasty over which they exercised direct rule from the "elected" lands of the independent princes of the Holy Roman Empire over which they exercised indirect and limited control.
12. Abbott, J.S.C., *The Monarchies of Continental Europe,* (New York: Mason Brothers, 1861) 500; Vovk 244.
13. Vovk 243.
14. Langsam 88.
15. Vovk 249.
16. Wolfsgruber 227.
17. Metternich, Clemens, *Metternich, The Autobiography, 1773–1815,* (Welwyn Garden City: Ravenhall Books, 2004) 13.
18. Vovk 243; Letter XCIV, Arneth 166.
19. Seward, Desmond, *Metternich, The First European,* (London: Viking Penguin, 1991) 16.

Chapter Four

Accession to Power

The Habsburg Empire inherited by Francis II, so unique and unusual in the history of Europe and the world, has been dismissively described as a collection of nationalities that ran against the tide of rising "nation-states" in Europe, particularly in the later 19th century. Multi-national empires were not thought particularly unusual or remarkable in the late 18th century, but even by the standards of that day, the Habsburg collection was unsurpassed in variety and complexity. Metternich himself described it thusly:

> The kingdom, which only since 1806 has taken the name of the Austrian Empire, is like no other either in its origin or its maturity. To the Ostmark of the Empire many other districts have been added under the House of Habsburg, which were formerly separated from each other by history or nationality. These have brought to this dynasty in the course of generations a great possession, not, with few exceptions, by way of conquest, but by hereditary succession, contracts of marriage, and voluntary submission with reservation of individual rights. That these rights and reservations were generally maintained by the rulers, when they were not forfeited by single portions of the Empire, is a truth which the party spirit and political strife of foreigners may attack but can never destroy. . . . From the singular formation of the whole kingdom, united under a succession of rulers unbroken for centuries, arose the extraordinary want of a name for this whole—a want which is shown by its appellation of the "House of Habsburg," or the "House of Austria." This case is unique in the history of states, for in no other country has the name of the ruling family been used instead of the name of the country in ordinary, and still less in diplomatic usage.[1]

The Habsburg monarchs had been constrained and sometimes hamstrung by the conditions imposed upon them by the aristocracy and bourgeoisie of the various kingdoms, duchies, principalities, cities, counties and provinces their family had acquired over the centuries. As feudal overlords, of course, they had the right and privilege to summon great armies, dispense grants of titles and lands, resolve disputes, and dispense justice, as did the kings of France or Spain or the Tsars of Russia. Yet they were far more bound by the rule of law and "reservation of individual rights" to their authority than almost any other ruling house in Europe. After all, their Imperial crown was an elected one and could be withheld, as it was recently after the death of Maria Theresa's father in 1740 when the Bavarian Wittlesbach heir was elected instead.

Francis had witnessed, in the last few years before his inheritance, the perils of straying too far in the direction of authoritarian rule. His uncle, with the best of intentions, had nearly ruined the monarchy with liberal reforms and by taxing and commanding far more than his mother or, for that matter, most of his predecessors had ever dared to do. Joseph's goal of a unitary state, like that of Louis XV, unencumbered by the nobility, Diets or Estates of the various sub-parts of his realm, had led him to ride roughshod over the financial and political power elites of the Empire, such as they were, until they rebelled. The "enlightened despotism" of Joseph II had unraveled before Francis' very eyes and was not a model he could emulate when his own time arrived.

Francis' father had rescued the situation, tacking back to the right and the aristocracy but that had not helped Louis XVI against a rebellious French aristocracy that was playing out before his eyes in the autumn of 1792. Concession after concession by the French King seemed only to encourage more demands and violence. There was a limit on how far one could placate the aristocracy and the people before the same thing might happen in Vienna.

Francis would have to walk a fine line indeed between the "enlightened despotism" of his uncle and the more relaxed, cautious consensus-seeking style of his father. He had to consider a recently antagonized aristocracy, on the one hand, and an awakened rural peasantry to whom rights had been granted and then rescinded, on the other.

Francis and his ministers needed no pretext or precedent for surveillance and detention of known or suspected radicals. As will be seen in chapters to come, Francis would indeed preside over an extensive, intrusive system of secret police, spies and informers but this system had long been in place when his father died. Furthermore, Francis would have an abiding respect for the law and the existing judicial system even in the face of known revolutionary activity within his own lands.

Early in his reign came the discovery of a conspiracy against the crown in Budapest. Historians have often treated the impact of this conspiracy contemptuously where Francis is concerned. It is usually condemned as a paranoid over-reaction to a virtually harmless and small group of hapless

Figure 4.1. The young Metternich by François Gérard, circa 1807

revolutionaries or a pretext for instituting a repressive police-state. In part, this may be because the conspiracies were headed by the mentally unstable Ignac Martinovic, but there really were secret Jacobin societies; at least two run by Martinovic. One was among the aristocracy fomenting Hungarian independence, the other among the common people for depriving the nobility of their legal and tax privileges.[2]

The paranoid overreaction theme ignores the reality that as many as 200-300 people were involved in these conspiracies alone. Historical figures must be judged in context, and not from the comfort of an age of predominant, liberal democracy. Even in the context of the 21st century, however, with the enactment of the Patriot Act in 2001, widespread surveillance of e mails and cell phone communications, martial law, espionage, extraordinary rendition and similar measures, the actions of this Emperor and his ministers cannot be piously condemned.

But few responsible governments of that day would or did let such subversive activity pass. The infant American government would itself enact the

Alien and Sedition Act in 1798 that criminalized "false statements" critical of the federal government. In Prussia, the Edict on Religion of August 9, 1788 was followed by a censorship edict in December. Russian censorship since 1700 and the time of Peter the Great had never experienced any relaxation during the Enlightenment period and, if anything, became more efficient and pervasive under Catherine and her son Paul in the late 18th century.

In the event, the discovery of the Budapest conspiracy confirmed in the young emperor's mind the advice he was receiving from his ministers—that unseen conspiracies of Jacobin radicals were a serious threat that must be quickly discovered and suppressed before they spread and erupted, as had happened in France. A hyper-vigilant system of police spies, agents provocateurs and censorship within the Empire was deemed a necessity.[3]

In the years to come, it must be conceded that the existence of this police state, albeit a mild one by 20th century standards, probably had much to do with the absence of any serious revolutionary activity within the Empire during Francis' 43-year reign. While this had the unfortunate consequence of delaying the advent of constitutional monarchy in the Habsburg domains until 1850, long after the emperor's death, it also consequentially ensconced the Austrian Empire in the quiet and peaceful Biedermeier period that we will discuss later. This is not to justify but merely to contextualize the regime of a man whom history has judged as a harsh reactionary from the first moment of his rule.

Another unsavory blot on the legacy of Francis is the way he dealt with the plight of his paternal aunt, Queen Marie Antoinette. On January 21, 1793, after a brief trial, Louis Capet, formerly Louis XVI, King of France, was executed. Stunned, King George III expelled the French ambassador and France replied by declaring war on Britain on February 1, adding the British Empire to the membership of the First Coalition. Once again, the conduct of Francis with respect to his aunt is often condemned as indifferent, cold-blooded and consistent with the imagined personality of "the old stick" that has been contrived over two centuries.

The eventual fate of Marie Antoinette was not known to Francis when Danton and the French Jacobins in Paris reached out to bargain with him for her life. While a living king represented a threat to the legitimacy and continuity of the revolutionary government of France, much as the Tsar would be to the Bolsheviks in 1918, the foreign-born widow of the late King was not. To credit Francis with foreknowledge that Robespierre's Terror would necessarily execute the Queen out of blind hatred is unfair.

Nonetheless, the Emperor refused to be blackmailed, on the theory, no doubt, that to bargain with terrorists or revolutionaries in return for the life of one person must necessarily invite more of the same. The Emperor understood this then as well as modern presidents and prime ministers understand it today. Although the terms Danton was prepared to discuss with the Emperor are apparently unknown, it is immaterial because Francis was unwilling to make any concessions for the release of a member of his own family and to the detriment of the Empire.[4]

Finally, while he had never met his aunt, the youngest daughter of the Empress Maria Theresa, who was sent to France before Francis ever set foot in Vienna, there is no evidence to suggest that Francis had any animosity or ill-feelings for her. Indeed, he would have witnessed his uncle's and his father's unmistakable affection for their sister while at the court of both.

Few people outside of France did not sympathize with the dire circumstances of the Queen and her children then, particularly after the execution of Louis XVI, let alone her nephew in Vienna. The horror of the people of Europe, outside France, to the pitiful and seemingly pointless execution of the Queen rocked the continent then and ever since. Although his personal reaction upon receipt of the news has never been recorded, it can only be imagined that Francis would been as grieved and outraged as anyone; more than most.

Marie Antoinette, a Habsburg, a daughter of Empress Maria Theresa, sister to Joseph II and Leopold II and aunt to Francis II was brought to the Place de la Concorde in an open cart on October 16, 1793, past jeering mobs pelting her with mud. Her head was severed by the blade of the guillotine at 12:15 PM that afternoon. Francis' cousin, Louis Charles the Dauphin of France, was never seen in public after that and died of tuberculosis ten months later in the Temple Tower at the age of ten.

NOTES

1. Metternich 262–63.

2. Palmer, Robert, *The World of the French Revolution,* (London: Routledge, 1971).

3. Silagi, Denis, *Jakobiner in der Habsburger-Monarchie,* (Vienna: Verlag Herold, 1962) 128–131.

4. Frasier, Antonia, *Marie Antoinette: The Journey,* (London: Phoenix, 2002) 492.

Part II

Chapter Five

The Economics of War and Peace

Cicero once said, "the sinews of war are infinite money." The war of the First Coalition (1792–97) that began for Francis on April 20, 1792, like it or not, would be expensive, like any war before or since. The enormous expenses incurred by Joseph II in the Turkish War that had just been terminated a year earlier, and his two smaller but still expensive wars with Prussia and the Netherlands would significantly impair the Empire's ability to wage this one. Indeed, the state of the Imperial treasury that Francis inherited was nothing short of frightening.

Francis confronted the war with France with a meagre treasury to finance it. The Habsburg Monarchy had been spending more than it raised in taxes for years and was heavily in debt. It was a dangerous situation but, ironically, not too different from that of France which was already in revolution that had toppled its monarchy and would plunge it and Europe into confusion and war for the next quarter century.

In 1792, the basic currency in use in Germany and the Habsburg Empire was the gulden. The gulden or *Rhinegulden* in other parts of Germany was equivalent to and sometimes called a florin. The florin was a similar coin in size, weight and gold and called this in many other parts of Europe. Both coins derived from the Florentine florin, a gold coin struck there in 1252 and used in much of Europe in the centuries since. The two will be used at times interchangeably in this narrative.

Extrapolating the worth of this unit of currency into today's money is a difficult and inexact science, as pointed out in an essay by Francis Turner entitled *Money and Exchange Rates in 1632*. For our purposes, we will assume that the worth of one gulden or florin is the equivalent of US$ 36.00 in 21st century money.

In 1792, the year Francis became Emperor, revenue of the Habsburg Empire was $2.952 billion with expenditures of $3.312 billion and state debt of $14.976 billion. In the same year, interest payments on the state debt were $612 million with payments on debt redemption of $342 million; absorbing nearly a third of state income. Military expenditures from 1790, when the Turkish War was at its peak, had been a staggering $1.512 billion on top of an "ordinary" military expenditure of some $954 million per year.

By 1792, after Leopold II had abruptly ended the Turkish War, "extraordinary" military expenses had been slashed by nearly two-thirds to $597 million per year.[1] By 1793, after France declared war on Britain on February 1, the government in Vienna was forced to ask for and received some $300 million in subsidies from Britain to fund and victual the Habsburg military forces in the Netherlands alone against France. Thus began a pattern of dependence upon Britain, as well as other sources of private credit, for the funds necessary to carry on the war that would continue in the decades to come.

Nonetheless, contemplating war with France in 1792, the ministers advising Francis could not have been very sanguine. Not that the Habsburg Empire was alone in financial distress. In France, the annual government deficit increased from 10% of gross national product in 1789 to 64% in 1793. By 1795, after the bad harvest of 1794 and the removal of price controls, inflation had reached a level of 3500%.[2]

Thanks to Pitt's reforms and restrained expenditures over a decade since the end of the American War of Independence, Britain could negotiate sovereign debt at interest rates lower than the other great powers. In addition, its rising industrial manufacturing production produced further state revenues and taxes. Yet Britain's national debt was still 123% of its GDP by 1792; down from 156% after the American War.[3] Nonetheless, over time, Britain was able not only to raise money for its own war effort, but to subsidize the other Great Powers: Russia, Prussia and the Empire.

As Cicero had observed, the ability to wage and sustain war in the time of Francis II was circumscribed more by money than by population or territory. The armies of the French Revolutionary and later Napoleonic Wars would number in the hundreds of thousands, not millions. Whether a so-called "Great" power was really great depended more upon its ability to fund a war of major significance, not whether it could conscript enough men.

The population of Europe in 1800 ranged from a high of approximately 35.5 million for Russia down to about 2.9 million for Portugal. The fact was that even tiny Portugal, if it could afford it, could come up with an relatively potent-sized army of 150,000 or more, based solely upon population.

The key questions in 1793, as the First Coalition and the new French Republic girded for war, were how the conflict would or could be funded by each side and the quality of the armed forces and officers who would lead it. Both sides struggled mightily on both accounts. The French struggled more at first.

The French general and foreign minister, Charles Francois Dumouriez, immediately organized an invasion of the adjoining Austrian Netherlands which failed miserably. French soldiers deserted in prodigious numbers and even murdered one of their generals. The invasion collapsed.[4] This left France open to invasion with the remnants of a disorganized and demoralized army which led, no doubt, to the optimism of the émigrés in Frankfurt described by Metternich.

Imperial forces congregated meanwhile along the Rhine/Moselle were under the command of Field Marshal Frederick William Hohenlohe and consisted of approximately 50,000 men. Another army formed further north around Koblenz consisting of approximately 34,000 Prussians and French émigrés was led by the Duke of Condé and Field Marshal Charles William Ferdinand, the Duke of Brunswick.

Francis initially camped with his army for a short time after his coronation in Frankfurt but soon returned to Vienna as the campaign unfolded. The experienced Hohenlohe was a very good choice as a military leader and the emperor's younger brother, the Archduke Charles, was left with the aging Marshal. Charles would learn much from Marshal Hohenlohe and go on to a very distinguished military career of his own very soon.

Imperial forces initially fared well, taking Thionville and Verdun but the Duke of Brunswick's defeat at Valmy on September 20 marked a psychological turning point in the initial campaign far out of proportion to the scale of a loss in which the Duke's army sustained 184 casualties to some 300 for the French. For reasons that remain controversial to this day, the Prussians retreated rapidly to the east and across the Rhine, leaving the Imperial army on its own.

Doumouriez returned to the attack, driving north into Belgium again while the victor of Valmy, Francois Kellerman, turned east and captured the fortress city of Metz. By November, after defeat at Jemappes by an overwhelmingly larger French army, the Austrian Netherlands was evacuated and temporarily occupied by France.

French successes astonished even themselves. Much blame has been attributed to a declaration by the Duke of Brunswick when he began his invasion in July. In these heady days, the Duke threatened huge reprisals on the population if harm came to the royal family. The result was the opposite of what was intended. Far from intimidating the Jacobins and the mob in Paris, the King was executed as a traitor. Worse, the now radicalized government resorted to unprecedented measures to defend the country.

The male population of France was conscripted into several large "citizen" armies motivated by compulsion but also by a deep sense of patriotism for the new French Republic that they felt was their own. This was the so-called *"levée en masse."* The National Convention, now the ruling authority in Paris, decreed on August 23, 1793 that:

> From this moment until such time as its enemies shall have been driven from the soil of the Republic, all Frenchmen are in permanent requisition for the services of the armies. The young men shall fight; the married men shall forge arms and transport provisions; the women shall make tents and clothes and shall serve in the hospitals; the children shall turn old lint into linen; the old men shall betake themselves to the public squares in order to arouse the courage of the warriors and preach hatred of kings and the unity of the Republic. . . .[5]

Young men between the ages of 18 and 25 were conscripted, raising the estimated size of the French army to a staggering 1.5 million men under arms by late 1794; an unprecedented number of soldiers equivalent to about five times the size of the professional Imperial army. Nor was that all:

> The Committee of Public Safety is charged for taking all measures necessary for establishing, without delay, a special manufacture of arms of all kinds, in harmony with the élan and the energy of the French people. Accordingly, it is authorized to constitute all establishments, manufactories, workshops, and factories deemed necessary for the execution of such works, as well as the requisition for such purpose, throughout the entire extent of the Republic, the artists and workmen who may contribute to their success. . . . The central establishment of said special manufacture shall be established at Paris.[6]

The government mobilized every available resource to support these ill-equipped and poorly trained but large armies, with uniforms, boots, horses, provisions and all necessary articles of war upon which the government could lay hands pressed into service. Finally, many career officers in the former Royal army, among the best in Europe, were willing to lead these armies. Many even shared the "republican" sentiments of their soldiers and dread of the invading foreign armies.

This was the equivalent of Goebbels' "total war" and "strength through fear" conception in the Third Reich when dread of invasion and occupation by Bolshevik Russia motivated a frightened population to resistance. Nor were those now commanding the French government less demanding than the Nazi regime would be in preserving their revolution. By April of 1783, the French government had evolved to the point of a virtual dictatorship by the infamous Committee of Public Safety. This group of nine legislators included

Georges Danton and, in July, Maximillian Robespierre. Terror became policy by the time of the invasion:

> It is time that equality bore its scythe above all heads. It is time to horrify all the conspirators. So legislators, place Terror on the order of the day! Let us be in revolution, because everywhere counter-revolution is being woven by our enemies. The blade of the law should hover over all the guilty.[7]

In thirteen months in 1794–95, it is estimated that some 1300 "enemies" of the people were guillotined as the Terror spread and deepened.

It is difficult to conceive of the truly revolutionary nature of the French government in the history of the European continent up to that time. Europe had never seen anything like this. The Habsburg dynasty had never contended with something like this. Francis and his ministers were facing a revolutionary power motivated by passionate hatred not merely of foreign invasion, but now the ancient regimes of its enemies, of which Francis and his Empire was the leading one.

Far from buckling under the weight of both internal strife and foreign invasion, those in power in France became ever more determined and radical. If the Revolution had freed the masses from autocracy and feudalism, the masses now had the obligation to defend what they had won, their government demanded. There would be no compromise; no going back. It was now an existential war not just for those who had overthrown the *ancien regime* and executed the royal family; it was an existential war for all and all would contribute to the collective defense.

This motivational factor made up for poor discipline and tactics in the early battles with the drilled, professional armies of Prussia and the Empire but also tended to produce high casualties. Yet many of the French officers of the royal army who were willing to serve the Republic, such as Kellerman, could command them well enough to prevail in many, but not all encounters. Another initially overlooked factor was the superiority of French artillery which proved to be the most modern and deadly in Europe, regardless whether used by royalists or republicans in the field.

One such artillery officer in the formerly Royal army, a Lieutenant Napoleon Bonaparte, was promoted to the rank of captain in the summer of 1793. After authoring a pro-Jacobin pamphlet, *Le Souper de Beaucaire*, that established him as a politically "safe" officer, he was promoted again to major in the 2nd Regiment of Artillery on September 7 and assigned to the siege of Toulon which was then under occupation protected by the British Royal Navy. There, he conceived of a simple but effective plan to seize a fort on the hills to the west of the harbor. Showing great personal bravery, he was wounded when an English gunner stabbed his left thigh with a pike while taking the fort. On December 17, the fort was taken and on December 22, Napoleon Bonaparte was promoted to brigadier-general; the youngest man ever to achieve this rank in the French army to this day.

DECLINE AND COLLAPSE OF THE FIRST COALITION

The unity of purpose between Prussia and the Habsburg Empire that had been forged at Pillnitz just a year earlier unraveled very quickly when war came. The retreat of the Prussian army far into Germany after the miniscule setback at Valmy was inexplicable unless one considers the situation in the East where Russia appeared ready to absorb virtually all of Poland. Polish land and population was worth far more to the Prussian kingdom than an ideologically based war with France and besides, leaving the Habsburgs in the lurch to confront France alone served the purpose of weakening both.

Indeed, Prussia was sufficiently concerned at the prospect of Russian annexation in Poland that only a token rump of its army remained in the French theatre of war, essentially inactive, while the bulk of it was moved east after Valmy in a show of force toward Russia that had its intended effect. On January 23, 1793, after months of secret negotiations between them, Prussia and Russia agreed to mutual annexations of Polish territory while Francis and his army were attempting to hold the line against France in the West. This was the "Second Partition" of Poland that Russian and Prussian agents bribed or bullied the Polish Parliament into ratifying thereafter.

While Prussia technically remained in the war in 1794, negotiations began in secret with the French that year and culminated in the Peace of Basle on April 5, 1795. At that point, Prussia formally dropped out of the First Coalition in which it had been fighting since Valmy only in name. In addition, Prussia secretly conceded the German lands west of the Rhine to France. Almost simultaneously, France agreed to peace treaties with Spain and Hesse-Kassel that removed them from the war as well. Only Britain remained steadfast but other than financial support, contributed negligible land forces to fight the French on the continent.

The so-called ideological war of the monarchies against Revolution was proved, in the event, to be paper thin or even mythological. Indeed, the rather unpretentious Frederick William II would add more territory to the Prussian kingdom in the Second and Third Partitions of Poland than any other Prussian king before or since, and it all occurred during this time.

By 1794, the Habsburg Empire was effectively the only major power confronting the French on the continent. Francis would continue the war for three more long and lonely years, essentially alone. It would not be the last time that Prussia and Russia would prove to be less than reliable allies. Yet this begs the question why the Habsburg Empire remained at war on the continent as the only great power facing France when Russia, Prussia, Spain and, one by one, the other German states left Francis to fend for himself? The answer seems to have been: necessity.

Unlike the other powers, Francis lost territory to the French and wanted to get it back. Furthermore, resurgent French power encroached on Imperial and Habsburg interests in both Germany and Italy. Prussia was still, in this era, a truly "eastern" monarchy who valued contiguous territory in Poland far more than its meagre western holdings, such as Cleves:

> Faced with the prospect of a French victory, the other European monarchs offered Austria no aid. Frederick William II and his son, who succeeded him in 1797, and Paul I of Russia, who took power in 1796, continued to revile the Revolution and its leaders but did not join the struggle. The British, who had made common cause with Austria in 1793 following the French invasion of Belgium, continued the belligerent status but offered Francis no material assistance.... Prussia's betrayal of Austria in 1795 convinced Francis that he faced perfidious allies and predators throughout Europe....[8]

One of the recurrent themes of the French Revolutionary period and the Napoleonic one that followed is how France alone could defy the combined might of at least five other Great Powers? The answer is only in part through her military prowess. Far greater was the greed and mutual suspicion the other Great Powers had regarding one another, even in the face of repeated and menacing French aggression. Russia and Prussia, as we have seen, were far more interested in Poland and territorial expansion than they were about a revolution, however distasteful, on the other side of the continent. Britain's age old struggle with France was not to be settled on the continent but at sea and overseas, in her colonial possessions. And Spain, geographically isolated as she was on the wrong side of France from the other powers, eventually threw in with the French calculating more safety and gain with Paris than against it. In this *sauve qui peut* landscape, Francis and his cabinet would soon attempt their own self-serving deal with France.

In the meantime, Francis fought on, increasingly alone and without terrible results for several years, especially in Germany. His younger brother, Charles, began his brief but distinguished military career during this time becoming the most able Habsburg family commander in the history of the monarchy, before or since. On August 24, 1796, defending against a French invasion of southern Germany by Jean-Baptiste Jourdan, the Archduke won a sharp victory at Amberg, forcing Jourdan to retreat. Another victory over Jourdan followed at Würzburg on September 3 after which Charles rounded on General

Moreau, inflicting yet another significant defeat on his 32,000-strong force at Emmendingden, and essentially forcing all French armies back to the Rhine.

Charles, Duke of Teschen, had also grown up at the Pitti Palace in Florence and was six years younger than Francis. He suffered from the Habsburg genetic curse of epilepsy and was likely bi-polar; certainly suffering often from black moods of what was then called melancholia but would now be diagnosed as deep depression. As the third son, fifth child of Leopold II, Charles was not a likely heir to the imperial throne. At a young age, his father allowed him to be adopted by his childless aunt, the Archduchess Maria Christine to be raised and educated in Vienna. When his aunt and uncle, Prince Albert of Saxony, were appointed governors of the Austrian Netherlands, Charles finished his education there.

Charles had embarked early on a military career that sprang not merely from his lofty station but from merit as well. He learned his craft assiduously and came into his own at a time of maximum peril to his family and his country. He commanded a brigade at the Battle of Jemappes at the age of 21. In due course, after beating most of Napoleon's generals most of the time, he would face the master himself at Aspern and Wagram in 1809, as we shall see.

A fair bit has been written about a growing bitterness between Francis and his younger brother by several historians after Francis became Emperor. Some of these writers have speculated that Francis envied his brother's military success and allowed jealousy to poison their filial relationship. There is, not surprisingly, no direct evidence of this. Another speculation is that Francis resented the suggestion by Napoleon, much later, that he abdicate in favor of Charles who refused to consider it. Again, there is no evidence of this as a cause either. Instead, what coolness there was between them, eventually, seems to have arisen from Charles' outspoken opinions against the Monarchy going to war with France either in 1805 or 1809 capped by his defeat by Napoleon at Wagram.

Surprisingly for a young Emperor who had spent several years in the army and had enjoyed a front-row seat at the highest levels of command with his uncle, Francis took an inexplicably negligible interest in military command. Since his monarchy would be rocked by the vicissitudes of war for more than two decades, it seems little short of astonishing that Francis left the command of his armies to others with not even an attempt to learn the craft more deeply. His disinterest would cost him dearly.

Until the winter of 1796, the Habsburg armies held their own, especially in Germany, but suddenly in the early Spring of 1796 the French under Napoleon Bonaparte defeated the kingdom of Piedmont and then won a major victory at Lodi on May 10. Napoleon's campaign continued in northern Italy for the remainder of the year, culminating with his victory at the Battle of Rivoli on January 14, 1797. Thereafter, the capture of the bastion fortress of Mantua a few weeks later saw the disintegration of the Imperial field army in Lombardy and the opening of a southern approach from Italy into Upper and Lower Austria itself.

The disastrous campaign in Italy, in which so much was lost, so decisively and in so short a time, compelled Francis to direct Maximilian, Count von Merveldt to request an armistice at Loeben, which was granted on April 18, 1797. Successes in Germany the previous year and the resistance to French penetration of the Empire again in 1797 could not make up for the defeats in Italy which, with the fall of Venice, brought the French under Napoleon nearer and nearer to Vienna itself.

Figure 5.1. Archduke Charles, Duke of Teschen. Circa 1819, by Thomas Lawrence. The Royal Collection. Windsor Castle.

The armistice was followed by a formal treaty of peace signed at Campo Formio on October 18, 1797 ringing down the curtain on the War of the First Coalition, with Britain the only remaining belligerent from the original alliance.

The peace treaty of Campo Formio was negotiated by Johann Philipp von Cobenzl who had been formerly Francis' first appointed *Staatskanzler*, or State Chancellor—the highest official and advisor to the Emperor. He had succeeded the great Kaunitz but served the shortest time of any State Chancellor appointed by Francis; a brief seven months from August 1792 to March 1793. By 1797, Cobenzl had returned to the diplomatic service and was given the unenviable task of negotiating with Napoleon.

A career diplomat since the 1770s, Cobenzl was a long-time protégé of Kaunitz who had secured his appointment as "vice chancellor" in 1779 to relieve himself of the daily burden of administration. This amiable diplomat had also been a favorite of Joseph II, having grown up in a prominent noble family. Cobenzl had accompanied the late emperor in 1777 on his visit to Paris to visit his sister, Marie Antoinette, when Joseph had traveled incognito as Count Falkenstein.

Cobenzl seems to have receded into the shadows of the Habsburg bureaucracy for a decade or so after his appointment as Vice Chancellor, quietly serving his patron and friend as well as Emperor Joseph II. Kaunitz is reported to have described him as having "a perceptive mind, a ready practicality and a conciliatory nature."[9]

Creative solutions to the Habsburg diplomatic and political dilemma of 1792 would probably have eluded the most talented of civil servants, but Cobenzl fell far short of that. In fairness, he was faced in quick succession with the Prussian desertion after Valmy and exclusion from the Second Partition of Poland. Now, with the collapse of imperial resistance in Italy that had compelled Francis to seek peace with France he would be the chief negotiator for the Habsburg Empire with little leverage. Campo Formio, however, would prove disastrous not because of the cession of territory to France in the Netherlands, but due to perfidy toward Vienna's allies in Germany.

Francis was compelled to cede the Austrian Netherlands (Belgium) to France and, in return, Francis acquired the adjoining Venetian Republic, or what was left of it, after French occupation earlier in the year. Further negotiations between the Holy Roman Empire and France were to be conducted later, at a Congress in Rastatt, to reach a final peace. But that was not all.

Facing the seemingly irresistible military pressure of the French army and the temptation to salvage his dignity, Francis contributed to the demise of the thousand-year-old Holy Roman Empire by agreeing in secret with the French to pressure the lesser German states into surrender of the Empire's lands west of the Rhine, to France. In return, the Emperor was to receive French support in his annexation of the rich bishopric of Salzburg and Bavarian territory adjoining Austria to the Inn River. These annexations would be to the private benefit of the Habsburg dynasty; not to the Empire.

This secret agreement was a blunder of the first order for two reasons.

The first reason was that once the Congress of Rastatt had agreed to the cession of the Holy Roman Empire's ancient territories west of the Rhine to France, it set off a diplomatic free-for-all among the dispossessed for compensation at the expense of the smallest, weakest German states least able to defend themselves. As the very young Metternich, who attended the Congress with his father, remarked: "I do not wish to be quoted, but according to my way of seeing things, everything is gone to the devil and the time is come when everyone must save from the wreck what he can."

The very *raison d'etre* of the Empire, and the purpose of the Holy Roman Emperor was to prevent such predatory behavior outside the laws and customs of the Imperial Diet. Not only would Francis as king of Hungary, Elector of Bohemia and Archduke of Austria—the most powerful state within the Empire—not lift a finger to prevent the resulting feeding frenzy, but was accepting his 30 pieces of silver not to do so.

The result, as events played out and became known in time, was a moral degradation of the prestige of the Habsburg monarchy as imperial guarantor. While the formal dissolution of the Empire was still years away, its moral foundation was shattered by the secret arrangements made at Campo Formio that played out at Rastatt.

The second reason was that while the French simply occupied the west bank of the Rhine and even clamored for more, Francis never received Salzburg nor Bavarian territory since the Congress was eventually aborted with no final agreement that would, with dignity, allow the annexations. Thus, while Habsburg duplicity became exposed eventually, when the French made known the secret protocols after war was declared in 1799, it gained nothing but the enmity of most German rulers. Few of them trusted Vienna to guarantee their freedom and security, not least Bavaria who would gladly become a steadfast ally of the French, almost to the end.

In truth, Francis had inherited a difficult and dangerous international situation at his coronation that had deteriorated from there whether he elected war or peace. It rivaled the existential threat faced by his grandmother when she had taken the throne in 1740 and faced defeat and partition of her inheritance. The situation left Francis in an unenviable and precarious position in Europe. He had discovered that he had no reliable friends. France could exploit divisions and divergences of interest among the other European powers. The most exposed, time and again, was Francis. His increasingly impossible position was exacerbated by his Empire's financial poverty and military weakness.

NOTES

1. Langsam 129, 131.
2. Brezis, Elise and Crouzet, François, "Seven Centuries of European Economic Growth and Decline," *Journal of European Economic History* (London: 1995) Vol 24:1, 7–40.
3. Mitchell, B.R. *British Historical Statistics.* Cambridge: Cambridge University Press; Reissue edition, 2011.
4. Holland, Arthur William. "The French Revolution." *Encyclopedia Britannica, 11th ed.* Cambridge University Press. Cambridge: 1911.
5. Stewart, John Hall, *A Documentary Survey of the French Revolution*, (New York. Macmillan, 1951) 472–474.
6. Ibid.
7. Andress, David, *The Terror: The Merciless War for Freedom in Revolutionary France,* (New York. Farrar, Straus and Giroux, 2005) 178–179.
8. Kagan, Frederick W., *The End of the Old Order, Napoleon and Europe, 1801-1805,* (Boston: Da Capo Press, 2006) 8.
9. Szabo, Franz A. J., *Kaunitz and Enlightened Absolutism, 1753-1780,* (New York: Cambridge University Press, 1994) 71.

Chapter Six

The Habsburg Inheritance

The Habsburg inheritance of Francis II is one of the most complex things for an historian or political scientist to understand, let alone a lay person with just passing interest in the structure of the government that Francis and his predecessors ruled. To understand it completely would be beyond the purpose and capacity of a biography such as this, but some understanding of it is imperative to address another lingering myth of Francis as a man and as a ruler: that he was the supreme autocrat of a highly authoritarian empire. This myth is supplemented by his characterization as a reactionary; a subject we will deal with later in this book.

Autocracy is a concept incompatible with the true essence of the Habsburg dynasty before and after the reign of Francis. The closest the dynasty would ever come to absolute monarchy would occur briefly after the crushing of the revolution of 1848, a half century later, by a military junta in the name of the then-emperor, Franz Joseph. Even then, the 18-year-old Habsburg monarch enthroned to perpetuate the dynasty for another half century granted a constitution in 1850; just two years later.

Normal, in terms of the Habsburgs, was a chaotic myriad of competing and overlapping bureaucracies whose jurisdictions were poorly defined and ever changing. I will describe only a couple of the most important institutions to illustrate the point and provide just enough understanding to appreciate the dilemma constantly faced by each successive Habsburg ruler to the end of the dynasty, including Francis.

The chaotic organization of the government inherited by Francis in 1792 was superimposed on essentially two separate, co-dependent and yet often antagonistic political organizations. One was the Holy Roman Empire of which Francis and his predecessors were elected Emperors. The second was the *Erblande* or the "hereditary possessions" of the dynasty of which, confusingly, some parts were within the Empire and some were not. For example, the archduchy of Austria, the kingdom of Bohemia and the Austrian Netherlands were within the Empire. The kingdoms of Hungary and Croatia, Transylvania, Galicia and the Grand Duchy of Tuscany, among other possessions, were not. Each of these entities had their own constraints.

The Holy Roman Empire of 1792 was comprised of nearly 100 separate, autonomous or independent entities sprawling across the center of Europe including, mainly, German speaking territories and populations. Chief among these were Austria and Prussia who, as we have already seen, were often antagonistic rivals. There were middling states, powerful because they had an army or because their ruling dynasty was extremely wealthy or both. Saxony, Bavaria, Wurttemberg, Hessen-Kassel and Hanover fell into this category. And then there were the rest; city states, tiny duchies, bishoprics, principalities and so on.

The Emperor was elected by nine "electors" who, naturally, were among the most powerful states within the Empire. Oddly, Austria was not one of the "elector" states but Bohemia was and furnished the Habsburgs a single vote.[1] Upon the death or abdication of an Emperor, the new, incoming ruler was, over the centuries, forced essentially to "renegotiate" the terms of his power with the Electors and the Imperial Diet. As one might imagine, this led to progressive weakening of the powers of the Emperor.

The Imperial Diet was the elected legislature of the Empire, but the term "elected" really meant entitled or designated representatives of the religious, aristocratic or royal (in the case of Prussia) classes and not, as one might expect, of the common folk comprising 99% of the population. The complex mechanism of voting and representation of the Diet is, again, unimportant for our purposes but often proved slow, cumbersome and replete with devolutions of power to committees, deputations and so on that met to deliberate, investigate, advise and consent to the issues of the day. Laws, customs and treaties, some of which dated back nearly a millennium, further bound up the motive power of the Empire and the Emperor.

The power of the Emperor to raise money necessary to do anything rested, in the end, on the willingness and consent of the constituent parts and pieces of the Empire who were all too often reluctant and recalcitrant unless faced with an overwhelming foreign threat or emergency. The Emperor could not so much command the raising of an army as request, invite or persuade the "estates" comprising the Diet to consent to do so. As the power of the Emperor deteriorated, generally, over the centuries, his right to intervene within the various duchies, principalities, counties, and city-states became virtually non-existent.

By 1792, the principal role of the Emperor was to protect the Empire from foreign threats and its weaker component members from predatory behavior or annexation by the larger, more powerful members. Understanding this, one can appreciate the magnitude of the mistake Francis and his ministers made at Campo Formio. In effect, a conflict of interest had arisen between Francis as hereditary ruler of his dynasty's possessions and his duties as the elected Emperor. Before resuming our narrative in that regard, we need understand his position as Archduke of Austria, King of Bohemia, Hungary, Croatia, and Grand Duke of Cracow, among many other titles and possessions.

THE HEREDITARY LANDS OF THE HABSBURGS

Within the *Erblande*, the monarchical power was far greater but still more constrained and limited than that of nearly any other monarchy in Europe save the British one. In the all-important matter of money and revenue, by custom and by law, much of the treasury was filled by taxes and contributions granted by the so-called "Estates" of these innumerable duchies and kingdoms that had developed within the feudal societies of the Middle Ages. Most comprised set numbers of aristocrats, bishops, abbots, and an *haute bourgeoisie* of wealthy townspeople or burghers, guild meisters and so on. The hodge-podge of mini legislatures was often "inherited" by the Habsburgs from arrangements made long ago in the mists of time by extinct dynasties whose lands they inherited or acquired by marriage.

As with the component members of the Holy Roman Empire, tension was ever-present between the local estates and the central treasury in Vienna. Naturally, the Estates tended to favor keeping as much money as possible at home to spend locally or to maintain taxes at minimal levels. In times of war or foreign menace, the Estates tended to be much more willing to contribute or raise taxes; in times of peace and relative tranquility, not so much. Thus, depending on the situation, the "domestic" politics of the Habsburg hereditary possessions also tended to be characterized by a constant process of back-and-forth bargaining and cajoling between Vienna and the various provincial estates for money. Of course, strong-arm tactics using military force or the threat of it could be employed, but this had negative consequences too, as Joseph II had come to find out.

As if this were not enough, within the *Erblande* there was the special challenge of Hungary whose governance was separate, apart and unique from the rest of the hereditary possessions. Hungary presented a special problem to the Habsburgs, particularly after the reign of Maria Theresa, that arose from this kingdom's special status since its submission to the Habsburg Archduke Ferdinand I of Austria in 1526.

As happened so fortuitously and so often to the Habsburgs, the dynasty was in the right place at the right time to pick up the pieces of another ruling family's misfortune. In this case, it was the extinction of the Jagiellon dynasty of Hungary, whose last king was killed and died childless after the epic battle of Mohacs against the Turks. His sister, Anne, had married Ferdinand in 1515 and, as the kingdom was overrun, the Hungarian nobility "elected" Ferdinand king on the hope that he would save them from the Turkish "infidels." He was the first of an unbroken succession of Habsburgs who remained hereditary kings of Hungary in exchange for a solemn pact with its nobility, maintaining a separate Hungarian Diet and constitution which, again, limited the powers of the king.

Hungary was to the Habsburgs what a combination of Scotland and Ireland was to the British crown. Like Scotland, Hungarian nobles usually, voluntarily fell into collaboration with the "Austrian" part of the Habsburg lands, especially in times of external threat to dynasty. These nobles were often "Germanized," speaking the language, being appointed to imperial titles and office and achieving high rank at Court. So long as the dynasty upheld their ancient privileges, the Habsburgs could count on the loyalty of this powerful class. But like Ireland, there were periodic rebellions and risings in Hungary and Transylvania among the lower nobility or "gentry" that would continue until 1867 and an increasing resentment at never being treated as an equal partner.

Gaining money, men and arms from Hungary was at least as contentious as from any other part of the Habsburg possessions but more important than most for several reasons. Its high nobility—the magnates—were often stupendously wealthy with absolute, feudal power on estates as large as many of the German principalities within the Holy Roman Empire. Hungary's vast plains were the agricultural breadbasket of the Empire producing immense surpluses of grain and produce for consumption. Thirdly, being the most southeastern realm and essentially landlocked, it was an almost inaccessible bastion to an invading army from the north or west.

The Hungarian nobility's loyalty had saved Maria Theresa at her hour of maximum peril when she had appeared dramatically before the Diet on September 11, 1741, dressed in black, pleading for help with her infant heir, Joseph II, in her arms. With Prussia, Bavaria and France overrunning her inheritance, the Hungarian nobility rose to her summons, mobilizing an 80,000-man army that in an eighteen-month campaign, captured the Bavarian capital of Munich, drove the French out of Bohemia and brought Frederick the Great to agree to peace. Hungarian loyalty, despite everything, would be critical to the survival of Francis but that was yet to come.

This was exactly the sort of maddening jumble that Joseph II had despised and sought to break during his reign, but had failed to do. His attempts to bully, intimidate and, at times, force compliance to his will constituted the "centralizing" tendency of his reign and had been met with increasing resistance, hostility and finally rebellion described earlier in our story. Leopold II's tactical retreat, which mollified these constituent elements of the Monarchy, quelled immediate rebellion but returned government to the same kind of perpetual negotiation and partial anarchy that had vexed the Habsburgs for centuries.

The autocratic regime headed by Francis was largely a myth. It could not compare with the government of Louis XIV or even Louis XV, let alone Napoleon when it came to the ability to raise taxes and assert military power. Nor that of Tsar Paul or Alexander, nor the kings of Prussia. By comparison, the Emperor, no matter who he was, faced challenges and obstacles that most of the other rulers in Europe did not. No wonder the Habsburgs had relied for centuries on marriage and inheritance to acquire their lands, wealth and power. Military power was almost always used to hold what had already been acquired and not for conquest, with rare exceptions—usually involving the Turks.

The difference this time was that Francis increasingly faced the existential threat of France whose military potency would soon be in the hands of Napoleon, one of the greatest military geniuses in history. Given the precarious political structure just described, one can understand better the rather dismal performances sporadically rendered by the Imperial forces in the Napoleonic period. The fascinating thing about the Habsburg empire in this period is not how weak and badly it performed, but that it managed to perform at all.

The improvisational, last-minute, crash funding and raising of military force to defend the Empire and the hereditary lands would consistently hamstring what appeared on paper to be an equal or even superior opponent to France. Habsburg armies were chronically underfunded and often poorly trained since, between conflicts, pressure to lift the tax burden and conscription was so great. Even superior generalship could not make up for deficits in numbers, equipment and the quality of its troops and against France, Habsburg generals were as often as not, inferior as well with some notable exceptions. Paul Kennedy described the situation well:

> This potential military weakness was compounded by the lack of adequate funding, which was due partly to the difficulties of raising taxes in the empire, but chiefly caused by the meagerness of its commercial and industrial base. Although historians now speak of "the economic rise of the Habsburg Empire" in the period 1760-1914, the fact is that during the first half of the nineteenth century, industrialization occurred only in certain western regions, such as Bohemia, the Alpine lands, and around Vienna itself, whereas the greater part of the empire remained relatively untouched. While Austria itself advanced, therefore, the empire as a whole fell behind Britain, France, and Prussia in terms of

per capita industrialization, iron and steel production, steam-power capacities, and so on.[2]

By any measure, the intensity and extensity of industrialization within the Empire of Francis lagged that of any of the other Great Powers. This gap was disguised to a limited extent in the early days of his reign by the contributions of many of the lesser states of the Holy Roman Empire—the German States—to the military burden. This dissipated quickly after Campo Formio.

In the dark years between 1805–1814 when increasingly severe treaties carved off piece after piece of the Austrian Empire, and the revenue raised from them, the financial strain of mobilizing and maintaining an army in the field became virtually unbearable. The sinews of war were thin indeed and constantly weighed on the mind of the Emperor and at least some of his ministers. Unlike William Pitt and King George III in their island kingdom, the Habsburg monarchy was exposed to constant menace from all quarters of the compass and could not afford the wars into which it was pulled or, worse, through aggressiveness or mistake, began itself.

THE THUGUT MINISTRY AND WAR TO THE KNIFE

The actual governance of the possessions of Francis II and the Holy Roman Empire was, as we have seen, a confusing institutional muddle. As such, it was as important to his rule what individuals Francis placed in strategic positions, as it had been to his predecessors. Several individuals must be introduced at this point who guided the emperor in reaching his decisions.

The first of these individuals was a truly fascinating and perhaps dubious character, Johann Amadeus Francis de Paula, Baron of Thugut. De Paula was born in 1736, a commoner and son of a paymaster in the Imperial Army. Apparently, in his late teens he caught the eye of the Empress Maria Theresa who sponsored his education at the newly opened Academy of Oriental Languages. He learned Turkish and entered the imperial service in 1754 as a translator in Constantinople. He quickly became a paid agent for France, receiving an enormous annual income from the treasury of Louis XV. Kaunitz, apparently oblivious to this treason, recommended him for ennoblement for his services. Joseph II raised him to a baron in 1775 when Thugut managed to arrange the cession of the province of Bukovina to the Habsburg emperor. He continued to rise in diplomatic ranks, becoming ambassador to Poland in 1780. Between 1783–87 Thugut retired from the diplomatic service and lived in Paris.

Given Thugut's attitude toward France as the chief foreign advisor to Francis between 1793–1800, it is important to understand that until the Revolution, Thugut was a Francophile of the first order and had garnered a fortune in the pay of its kings. This he seems to have invested in France in the 1780s and then, to his horror, watched his investments shrink to nothing after the Revolution between 1789 to 1792. The loss of this fortune he blamed on the Jacobins in Paris for whom ever after he entertained an undying hatred and contempt.

Thugut seems to have impressed Francis upon his return to Vienna in late 1792 after witnessing the dismal campaign against the French revolutionary armies. He had been appointed a sort of ambassador at large with the army on the Rhine and watched the disintegration of the combined operations with Prussia after Valmy and the eventual retreat across the Rhine. Enraged and embittered by the failure of the allied armies to rout the French and restore monarchical government in Paris, his critique of the situation to the Emperor combined with the double shock of the Russo-Prussian annexation of large amounts of Polish territory in the Second Partition resulted in his being named the head of foreign affairs for Austria in March 1793.

Even higher office came to him the following year when he was appointed State Chancellor. He replaced Philip von Cobenzl. Francis was receptive to a more aggressive minister to advise him in a Europe increasingly unfriendly to his regime. He found one in Thugut.

The overnight success of this low-born diplomat disturbed the imperial court in Vienna. As state and foreign chancellor, Thugut occupied the very pinnacle of the civil service and aroused resentment and jealousy in the ranks of the nobility. The office had never been granted to an individual of such low social status, a fact that Thugut seems to have regarded with some degree of insecurity. He resented, in turn, the distain and cool contempt of other high-born civil servants.

He had a peculiar personality, we are told. Cölestin Wolfsgruber, writing in the Catholic Encyclopedia described him as "a kind of Jekyll and Hyde" personality.[3] Henry Fisher described him as a "dark spidery figure" in his book, *Remember to Tell the Children*.[4] Thugut never married and had no children. He lived as a sort of recluse for most of his life and worked alone or with the support of only a couple of trusted clerks. He avoided collegial discussion with other high Court officials about the issues of the day, which tended to encourage backstairs intrigue and criticism of him by the nobility of the Empire. Yet his influence with Francis was remarkable. His seven-year tenure exceeded that of any of the Emperor's other state chancellors, except Metternich.

Thugut's patron, Kaunitz, had imbued in him the eternal suspicion of the kingdom of Prussia and the dubious value of Russia as an ally, but to the head of the list would be added France. Britain was the only great power he trusted, and his pro-British attitude was reciprocated from London. In 1795, Thugut pushed his way into the negotiations involving what would be the Third Partition of Poland, eliminating it from the map of Europe for over a century, and gained the largest chunk of territory for his master.

The need for a show of muscular, military force on the frontiers of Poland in 1795 to impress Prussia and Russia with the seriousness of Francis' insistence to be included in any further land grab, however, resulted in the diminished ability of Habsburg armies to resist the French on the Rhine and in Italy, just as Prussia had done in 1783 after Valmy. Nonetheless, after being excluded the last time, Thugut and Francis would resist if Prussia attempted to shave off another prodigious chunk of Poland without corresponding compensation.

Surprisingly, even with limited support, the Imperial forces in the Rhineland area proved successful in combat against superior French forces. At Mainz on October 25, 1795, a Habsburg army led by Count Clerfayt defeated the French army of the Rhine-Moselle, relieving the besieged city. This was followed by another victory against Jean-Charles Pichegru at Pfedderscheim forcing the French entirely across the Rhine to end campaigning that year.

This acquisition of Polish territory, Thugut's second success in this way after the annexation of the Bukovina, seems to have solidified the trust and confidence Francis had in his first minister. Territory was something that could be seen on a map, and Francis liked maps. Especially maps that showed a significant, measurable gain in territory; something his father, uncle and grandmother had been unable to see in their reigns. Furthermore, revenue from the new provinces could be counted and money was in short supply and being consumed at a prodigious rate. Indeed, the reign of Francis II would be the last time in history that the Habsburg Empire gained territory and population with the small exception of the annexation of Bosnia and Herzegovina in 1907.

Regarding France, however, Kaunitz and Thugut would part ways. Kauntiz's belief that France could safely be left to its own devices and sink into chaos and confusion was not shared by Thugut but in any event, there was a war that had been declared by France that made Kaunitz' s advice immaterial. The issue of whether to conclude the war with France or persevere was the question and it was Thugut's advice to persevere in the long war with France after his appointment, to which Francis listened. Nonetheless, over time, the problem with Thugut's policy of war "to the knife"[5] with France was two-fold: the crippling cost of the war, even with British subsidies, and eventual catastrophic military defeats in Italy culminating in the disaster at Rivoli in January 1797.

The annual expenditures of the government in the later phases of the War of the First Coalition were essentially double the average state income which had to be financed by further debt or by simply printing money. Both methods were used but eventually some 200 million gulden (roughly $7.2 billion in 21st century money) were issued in paper money that, in turn, caused rampant inflation. By 1805, it is estimated that the cost of living in the Habsburg lands had tripled in just four years.[6] To keep Francis and his armies in the field by 1797, after the defeat at Rivoli and the fall of Mantua, the British government authorized another loan of £1.62 million; the equivalent of $50,000,000.00 in today's money.

The point was that the Monarchy was going bankrupt pursuing a war that consumed every penny of income and much more, month in, month out; year in, year out. Contrary to popular understanding, the Monarchy did not lack for manpower, nor talented commanders, nor equipment. It gave as good as it got with little help for four years but could not defeat a French nation-in-arms nor abandon its position in Germany and the Netherlands. Spread thin, the French made eventual headway, especially in the Netherlands. By 1795, the Dutch were defeated and out of the war. A new Batavian Republic became a French client state from that point forward.

Given the precarious financial predicament faced by Francis and his ministers, one might wonder how France with its enormous *levee en masse* could sustain them in the field? The answer was that its armies often plundered their enemies. In 1796, after the invasion and swift defeat of the kingdom of Piedmont, for example, it exacted an "indemnity" of 50 million francs in gold and silver.[7] This was the equivalent of $185,000,000.00 in today's money. From this fantastic sum, Napoleon paid his own troops and officers (and himself) first before sending the balance to an ecstatic French government.[8] There had been plunder, looting and indemnities forced upon the communities in the Austrian Netherlands and Rhineland states while occupied by the French earlier in the war. The Treaty of The Hague in May 1795 had imposed a crushing indemnity of 100 million guilders on the Dutch; the equivalent today of approximately $5 billion.

Francis and his Imperial army were never able to impose the costs of war on the French or other states because, after all, he was the ultimate defender of the territorial and political independence of the German and Italian kingdoms, duchies and smaller states. While the Emperor could and did seek "contributions" from his allies and the estates of his own lands, as we have seen, the response was often sporadic, stinting and, as the war went on, his allies simply left the field. War was not profitable for the Habsburgs, as it was for the French. It was a never-ending drain on its resources and ability to sustain the conflict. In fact, the amazing thing is that the Monarchy of Francis II could continue the war for as long as it did.

NAPOLEON AND DEFEAT IN ITALY

The war in Germany between 1792-96 had seen back and forth military victories and defeats, like most wars of the 18th century. There had been no colossal victories or defeats that had compelled one side or the other to concede. Battles lasted a day or two with casualties on both sides, some prisoners taken, one army withdrawing from the field in defeat, the other taking it in victory. Armies on both sides lived to fight another day, for the most part, licking their wounds or savoring the glow of success, only to march and maneuver again. The east bank of the Rhine had been invaded and cleared twice by the Emperor and his generals. The Austrian Netherlands had been lost and won and lost again. Yet the war ground on with seemingly no end in sight. The Emperor and his dwindling allies were often able enough to defend their ground, but not sufficiently powerful to bring the war home to the French, as the initial campaign in 1792 had sought to do. That chance never offered itself again until 1814.

With the invasion of Italy, a new front was opened in 1796 that would prove decisive in the grand chess game being played out by Francis and his British ally who continued to subsidize his war efforts but never landed an army on the continent. Furthermore, unlike the previous campaigns, this new commander, Napoleon Bonaparte, dealt knock-out blows to his opponents, often shattering whole field armies sent against him, compelling submission and eventual surrender.

The significance of Northern Italy to Habsburg and later Austrian security until the end of the Empire in 1918 arises from the simple fact of geography and terrain. The presence of the virtually impassible Alps between France and Austria had always presented a military challenge to Imperial and French military leaders over the centuries of warfare between them. Armies marching to Vienna from France or to Paris from Austria had to make a choice of going north of the Alps, through southern Germany, or south of the Alps, through northern Italy. In the early stages of the war, the contestants had battled in Germany and, for the most part, the Italian front lay quiet. In 1796, that changed. The soft underbelly received a gut punch from a military commander who would dominate his age and would rank with Alexander and Caesar in his almost magical talents on the battlefield.

The first to experience the Napoleonic firestorm was Piedmont. This small but rich Italian kingdom stood between Habsburg dominated possessions, such as Tuscany and Parma, and southern France. The king of Piedmont, Victor Amadeus III, had allied himself with the Habsburgs against the potential of invasion by his revolutionary neighbor to the West. In a lightening campaign, Napoleon's Army of Italy descended on Piedmont in March of

Figure 6.1. Napoleon, First Counsel, circa 1804. By Charles Meynier. Musée de la Ville de Bruxelles, Hotel de Ville.

1796. He defeated the Piedmontese at Montenotte, Millesimo and Mondovi in April, compelling the King to request an armistice. A peace treaty followed in May, with Piedmont compelled to withdraw from the First Coalition and ceding Nice and Savoy to France. Victor Amadeus now ruled as a puppet a satellite kingdom that required him to allow free passage of French armies through his lands and possession of several key fortresses occupied and held by French garrisons. The king died five months later.

A rampage through northern Italy and the Papal States followed that could not be stopped by the Imperial army. The small, weak and defenseless states of the peninsula were toppled and occupied one by one. They were, in turn, squeezed for treasure. The plunder of Italy was systematic and thorough. The French government sent art experts with Napoleon to Italy to ensure that the richest and best treasures were taken:

> The haul from Italy was commensurate with the extent of the treasures to be harvested: immense. In early May, Bonaparte had requested a list of the paintings, sculptures and other collections to be found in Milan, Parma, Piacenza, Modena and Bologna. The armistice with the Duke of Parma (May 1796) required him to turn over 20 paintings, to be chosen by the French commanding general. The Duke of Modena was obligated to offer 20 paintings plus 70 manuscripts from the library. Bologna lost 31 paintings, 115 prints, 546 manuscripts and some Etruscan antiquities. The treaty with Venice (May 1797) stipulated 20 paintings and 500 manuscripts. In addition, the French carried away the four bronze horses of St. Mark's cathedral and the lion of St. Mark's square, though the treaty had made no mention of them. Milan, Verona, Perugia, Loreto, Pavia, Cento, Cremona, Pesaro, Fano and Massa all rendered to Napoleon his artistic tribute. By the treaty of Tolentino (February 1797), Pope Pius VI agreed to hand over 100 treasures from the Vatican, to be shipped immediately to France.[9]

Priceless paintings, sculptures, and other art treasures enriched Napoleon, personally, his officers and in many cases, were used as gifts to corrupt French government officials in Paris to the rising ambitions of a military superstar whose exploits were magnified by Napoleon's masterful use of propaganda and self-promotion both in Italy and France. Not only that, but indemnities and contributions forced from Tuscany, Rome, Naples, Parma, Genoa and, eventually, Venice by December 1796 reportedly totaled some 45,706,493 francs in cash and another 12,132,909 in gold, silver and jewels[10]; a sum equivalent to approximately $214,000,000 in modern money. To put this in perspective, this was more than four times the amount of the British subsidy to Francis offered a few months later to keep him in the war of the First Coalition.

War had become quite profitable for those in power in France and for the officers of the French armies, with every incentive to continue it. France could continue the war with other people's money indefinitely. It was not, therefore, that the Imperial armies were exhausted; it was the treasury.

NOTES

1. The group included the three archbishops of Mainz, Cologne and Trier and six hereditary lay rulers: the Count Palatine of the Rhine, the Duke of Saxony, the Margrave of Brandenburg, the King of Bohemia, the Duke of Bavaria and, after 1708, the Elector of Hanover who was also King of England.
2. Kennedy, Paul. *The Rise and Fall of the Great Powers.* London: Vintage Books, 1989.
3. Wolfsgruber, Cölestin, "Diocese of Tarnow." *Catholic Encyclopedia, Volume 14.* New York: 1913.
4. Fisher, Henry, *Remember to Tell the Children: A Trilogy Book One; The Pioneers,* (Bloomington: Authorhouse, 2006) 707.
5. Roider, Karl: *Baron Thugut and Austria's Response to the French Revolution.* Princeton: Princeton University Press, 2014.
6. Ingrao 233.
7. Connelly, Owen, *Blundering to Glory: Napoleon's Military Campaigns*, 3 ed., (Lanham: Rowman & Littlefield Publishers, 2006) 26, 27.
8. Ibid.
9. Sandholtz, Wayne, "Prohibiting Plunder: How Norms Change," *European Journal of International Law,* (Oxford: Oxford University Press, 2007).
10. Nester, William R., *Titan: The Art of British Power in the Age of Revolution and Napoleon,* (Norman: University of Oklahoma Press, 2016).

Chapter Seven

The Second Coalition

The Treaty of Campo Formio and the Congress at Rastaat, as we have discussed already, failed to bring a true end to the conflict between the Habsburg Monarchy and France and, on the advice of Thugut principally, Francis girded himself for a resumption of the war with France in what would become the War of the Second Coalition. This time, in addition to Britain, Russia would be persuaded to enter the lists now that Catherine was dead and with the borders of Russia now abutting those of Prussia and the Monarchy.

Her son, Tsar Paul, believed that Russia must now involve herself more deeply in the affairs of the continent of Europe and was alarmed at the rapid expansion of a muscular French Republic that had by 1797 established new republics in the Netherlands, Switzerland and Italy. Tsar Paul's alarm at the ideological threat of the Republic had, of course, been shared years earlier by many of the crowned heads of Europe when his mother had steered clear of the affair, so far away. Most of those in central and western Europe had no intention of resuming a war with France or were now French allies, like Bavaria, or client states, like Piedmont or the Batavian Republic.

Emperor Francis, his new neighbor to the south and west, and his *Staatskanzler*, Baron Thugut, did share Tsar Paul's views. Like George III of Great Britain, Francis and Thugut agreed that France was a menacing and aggressive, if not rapacious Great Power that had to be put down.

AN ANTHEM FOR THE KAISER

George III had recovered from his famous bout with porphyria[1] and by 1799 was the longest-reigning monarch of any of the Great Powers, having become king of England on the death of his grandfather in 1760. He was now 62 and

Figure 7.1. Tsar Paul of Russia (1754-1801), son of Catherine the Great and the second of four Russian tsars during Francis' reign. By Vladimir Borovikovsky; State Russian Museum. St. Petersburg.

had been a constitutional but powerful monarch, especially when in partnership with his favorite and long-time prime minister, William Pitt. Strong-willed but sage, when not suffering from bouts of insanity, he had a life-long understanding of the existential threat posed by France to England, the most precious and richest of his kingdoms.

His early reign had been a lesson in just how much damage France could do when circumstances allowed. France had severely damaged Britain's overseas empire with its support of the American struggle for independence and practically bankrupted his treasury. That was mild, however, compared to the threat now rising off his shores.

George III and the British cabinet in London would be Emperor Francis' only, consistent ally throughout the coming decade and a half of peril. On every occasion that Francis found himself at war with France, Britain was too and often willing to help financially and at sea, if not with land forces until much later. The Anglo-French history of the Revolutionary and later Napoleonic wars are not the focus of this study, but this strong bond between the British and soon to be Austrian Empires that began with the First Coalition lasted long after the Napoleonic Wars were over. The close ties and trust would have a profound impact at the Congress of Vienna in 1815 and therefore on the Europe that would exist until the end of the Emperor's reign and long after.

Figure 7.2. George III, King of Great Britain and of Hannover, about 1799. Portrait by Sir William Beechey. National Portrait Gallery, London.

Joseph Haydn, the other towering musical figure, with Mozart in the late 18th century, was himself an Anglophile and traveled to Britain several times in his life to perform and compose. After the French declaration of war on Great Britain, Haydn had several occasions to watch English crowds sing "God Save the King" and the flush of patriotism that was aroused by the song. In 1792, the Marseillaise became the fiery anthem of the French resistance to invasion that swept the country. In a flush of patriotism of his own, he composed what came to be known as the *Kaiserlied*; the national anthem of the Austrian Empire.

It debuted on the Emperor's birthday on February 12, 1797, in his presence at the Burgtheater, where the audience was encouraged to join in the singing. The anthem was also performed simultaneously in Prague. The audience at the Burgtheater was reported to have enjoyed the song and sang it with great enthusiasm. The opening lyrics explicitly mention Francis—*Gott Erhalte Franz den Kaiser*—literally: God Save Francis the Emperor. The personalization of the music to this one Emperor, Francis, is unique and its rapid adoption across the Empire as a unifying, patriotic symbol speaks to the Kaiser's popularity at this time of trouble.

The anthem had an interesting history thereafter. It remained the Austrian national anthem until the fall of the dynasty in 1918. The melody was thereafter adopted as the anthem of the new German Republic in 1922 as the "*Deutschlandlied*" whose opening lyrics were "Deutschland, Deutschland, Über Alles" meaning, literally, "Germany, Germany above all." The interpretation of these lyrics, particularly during and after the Nazi period, was that it meant German superiority over everyone else. Since the conclusion of World War II, the third, more peaceful stanza is sung to the same tune, and the name was changed again to the *Lied der Deutschen* or "Song of the Germans" since 1952.

DEFEAT AND THE COLLAPSE OF THE SECOND COALITION

The Second Coalition and the war spawned by it saw the course of the French revolution come full circle from egalitarian revolution to dictatorship with the meteoric rise of Napoleon Bonaparte between Campo Formio and his *coup d'etat* on November 9, 1799. He had led an expedition to Egypt and Palestine after his Italian campaign against the Monarchy. The temporary victory and occupation of Egypt by the spectacularly successful Bonaparte had made him immensely popular in Paris and a latent political powerbroker. It had also aroused the Turkish Ottoman Empire against France particularly after the successful siege of Jaffa when Napoleon had permitted the massacre of more than 2000 Muslim defenders of the city. This was also despite the destruction of a large French fleet at the Nile by the British admiral Horatio Nelson. After essentially abandoning his army in Palestine, the opportunistic Napoleon Bonaparte returned to Paris and, in a lightening stroke, took power in a military coup d'état, creating a dictatorship with the neo-classical title of First Consul.

Slightly more than a month later, George Washington was engaged in some improvements to his plantation at Mt. Vernon, Virginia, on the morning of December 13. He had declined to allow himself to be elected president of the United States upon the expiration of his second term and in elections held in 1796 had been succeeded by his vice-president, John Adams. The weather turned rainy with sleet that day and by the time the former president returned to the house, he was seized with chills and nausea.

Bleeding and "blistering" were still regarded in 18th century Europe as mainstream medical treatment for a variety of ailments and had been a therapy used since the time of Hippocrates. It was based upon a belief that an excess or deficiency of "humors" was responsible for a patient's sickness. Blood was one of the four humors and bloodletting was thought to restore the "balance" within the body that physicians diagnosed responsible for symptoms they saw in a patient.[2] Within a day and a half, Washington was dead after having been bled four times. The exact diagnosis of his fatal illness remains unclear to this day. He was 67 years old.

The following year, in the hotly contested federal presidential election of 1800, the former ambassador to France, former governor of Virginia and principal writer of the American Declaration of Independence, Thomas Jefferson, defeated the incumbent president, John Adams. This would mark an end to the conservative, Federalist party with whom Washington had sympathized, although not been a member, and Adams had represented in the newly built White House in Washington. A Francophile with sometimes radical republican viewpoints, Jefferson's administration would pose interesting challenges to Britain, France and Spain on the North American continent.

It did not take Napoleon long to bring this war to an end that was even more advantageous to France and less to Francis and his monarchy than before. 1800 was the turning point for Francis and his army, being defeated in June by Napoleon at Marengo and in December by Jean Moreau at Hohenlinden. The second defeat, in which a Habsburg army under the command of the Emperor's brother, the Archduke John, essentially disintegrated, brought the French army within 80 kilometers of Vienna. When Archduke Charles took over command, he had to request an armistice. Francis found himself once again militarily defeated and compelled to accept a treaty, this one signed at Lunéville on February 9, 1801.

There would be no Congress to sort out the details this time. Francis accepted French gains that had been previously acquired after Campo Formio, and then some. All imperial lands west of the Rhine now fell to France "in complete sovereignty." The Grand Duchy of Tuscany where Francis had lived to age 16 was ceded to France as well, but in return the Republic of Venice which Napoleon had occupied was ceded to the Monarchy along with Salzburg and the Dalmatian coast. French puppet states in Italy and the Netherlands were also recognized.

So ended Francis' participation in the Second Coalition. It is difficult to see what else could have been done at this point, given the sharp military reverses sustained in the field and, as ever, the rather unsustainable cost of the war. The Treaty of Lunéville managed to salvage the integrity of the Monarchy itself with some territorial horse-trading, leaving Francis' empire entirely contiguous and more defensible. Nonetheless, it would be the last time that Napoleon would allow peace terms that were anything less than humiliating and immensely destructive to Francis and his dynasty.

Lunéville also marked the end of the Thugut ministry and its policy of implacable warfare with France. The baron had resigned on January 16, 1801 after Hohenlinden when it became obvious that peace would have to be negotiated with France. He was replaced by Johann Ludwig Joseph Graf von Cobenzl, cousin to the former *Staatskanzler* of the same name, who executed the treaty on behalf of the Emperor. Thus began a pattern that would repeat itself time and again with a new ministry being appointed after a disastrous campaign followed by a period of uneasy peace, another disastrous war and another resignation.

Cobenzl was joined in 1800 by Francis' old tutor, Franz de Paula von Colloredo as the chief advisors to the Emperor. This was a curious arrangement since Colleredo had little experience or knowledge of either international or military matters. Cobenzl, by contrast, came from a family of imperial counsellors, advisors and ambassadors and had long experience in international politics. It is not clear why Francis felt compelled to include Colloredo except as an old and trusted friend and advisor from his days in Florence. It is probable that Colloredo's influence was directed more toward domestic policy and reform in the post-Josephin era, that we will discuss in detail later.

Cobenzl marked the beginning of an evolution in Habsburg international, geo-political policy toward the menace of France on the continent. No longer was there any pretense that this was an ideological struggle against a 'revolutionary' opponent spreading the fever of republicanism since by this time, the revolution in France had been completely subverted, first by the Directory in 1795 and then by Napoleon's dictatorship.

Cobenzl viewed the continental situation pragmatically as a straightforward power struggle between the Monarchy and a dictator who retained the Revolution's awesome power to summon immense, conscripted "citizen" armies funded by booty and indemnities. The Habsburgs had a long history of rivalry with French kings—Louis XIV and the thirteen-year War of the Spanish Succession and Louis XV and the eight-year War of the Austrian Succession—for example. The peace negotiated at Lunéville was therefore widely seen as an intermission in the struggle for continental equality with France, but this time with a military dictator at the helm.

FRANCIS AND HIS FAMILY

By the year 1800, Francis was still relatively young at 32 years of age and yet had already reigned for eight tumultuous years, virtually all of them at war. As a man, he had begun to make his mark on the history of his homeland and the continent of Europe, as will be discussed further below, but he had also fathered a large and growing family, much like the one in which he had been raised in Florence.

Francis had been married to his second wife, Maria Therese of Naples, for ten years. By all accounts, his marriage was a happy one. His wife adored him and had now borne him six children between Marie Louise in 1791 and a one year old son, Joseph Franz in 1798. Francis and Maria Therese were openly affectionate with one another and when separated, corresponded regularly; sometimes twice a day.[3] Aside from the fact that the couple would go on to have twelve children together, the Emperor's personal correspondence to his wife left no doubt they had a robust sex life. In 1797 when forced to abstinence due to his wife's illness, he wrote that he had been "unable to sleep because of agitation and ardor . . . [t]his business of being alone is my greatest ailment, so that I am anxious to come to you, for I am not afraid of anything. . . . Try to find out how long the continence is supposed to last and write me about it, for if the time is too long I shall simply come to you. . . ."[4]

Maria Therese was an easy-going mother and consort and created a pleasant and fun home atmosphere for her husband and children. Life at the Habsburg court, often at the palace of Laxenburg, and despite the war years, was much more free and gay than it had been under Francis' father's or uncle's reign, thanks to the young Empress.[5] She loved entertainment, recreation and amusement and spent a lot of time arranging it for her husband, although without extravagance. She arranged a family orchestra in which she played the bass violin and Francis played the violin, calling her husband her "beloved fiddler." She liked to arrange simple plays, optical illusions and distortions, Chinese shadow-plays, and similar amusements as well as dancing, which the entire family enjoyed. The Viennese carnival and masquerades were also a favorite occupation with the Empress, who enjoyed

Figure 7.3. Francis the Emperor and his family, circa 1806.

changing her costume frequently during outings as soon as she thought she was recognized.[6]

Francis seems to have matured into a man whose personality characteristics alternated between several poles. One characteristic that emerges now is an almost self-effacing, affable charm that masked a more cautious, reserved and even skeptical inner mind. This affability or bluff surface charm would remain with him the rest of his life, mellowing to a sort of indulgent, grandfatherly persona still later in life. In the minimal, biographical portrayals of the Emperor's personality in this stage of his life, one grasps an almost stoic, pessimistic demeanor influenced, no doubt, by the difficult and unsuccessful consequences of his government's policy choices to date and conflicts within his own cabinet, as we will see. In a contemporaneous portrait of Francis of this era by Joseph Kreutzinger, the court painter, one can already see the beginnings of the long, oval face, receding hairline and increasingly stern facial expression that will harden further with time.

Another side of his personality that had emerged was a tendency toward micromanagement and over-work, the former quality one he no doubt inherited from his uncle who suffered from the same incorrigible tendencies. As Ingrao points out in his book on the Habsburg monarchy:

> In his first fifteen years as emperor Francis had issued twenty-four thick volumes of ordinances. . . . Yet his arduous work habits had singlehandedly slowed

the pace of government. He not only refused to delegate decisions to subordinates, but tended to agonize over even the most trivial matters. With as many as 2, 000 reports piled on his desk at one time, it was sometimes years before some matters were acted on.[7]

Also, like his uncle and unlike his father, Francis embraced frugality, simplicity and an aversion to pomp or ostentation. His own handwritten orders to subordinates all over the Empire during his life repeatedly admonished local officials to avoid expensive or showy ceremonials upon his arrival.[8] His frugality did not extend to charity, however. In 1793, his personal contributions to charity amounted to more than 80,000 florins or about $1,120,000.00 in today's money.[9]

The Emperor was known for his love of music and pleasure at playing the violin. He enjoyed making candy and gardening in his botanical hothouse. His collection of books was constantly growing and, at the time of his death, would reach 40,000 and form the core of the Austrian National Library.[10]

Francis' mother in law, Maria Carolina, Queen of Naples, visiting the family in 1800 had noted that Francis was "a devoted father who loved joking and playing with his children."[11] The family's love of dancing was well known and frequently, as noted by some contemporary observers, "the sovereigns, the musicians, the adjutants and the governesses all danced and frisked about together."[12]

Francis' domestic life was not, however, without disappointment and heartache. His oldest son and heir, Ferdinand, was seven years old by this time and was the source of much anxiety. Shortly after his birth, it was discovered that he suffered from severe epilepsy and hydrocephalus, with resulting neurological deficits and a speech impediment. It is reported that he could have up to twenty epileptic seizures per day. These serious neurological problems were congenital and probably due to the chronic inter-marriage between Habsburg family members, including Francis and Maria Therese who were 'double cousins.'

Given the primitive medical understanding of these conditions, Ferdinand was often regarded by contemporaries and earlier historians as "feeble minded" or mentally retarded, which was not the case. He kept an excellent diary his entire life and displayed great wit and humor among his family and intimates. Nonetheless, Ferdinand was slow to learn to walk or talk. In 1800, he was thought still too compromised to learn. His first formal education would not begin until 1802 when he was nine years old. We will return to Ferdinand later but his infirmities were kept secret from all but the most trusted servants and family. In the same portrait by Kreutzinger, the crown prince appears quite normal and handsome standing next to his younger brother, Joseph Franz, for example.

There were other heartbreaks as well. Francis' second daughter, Caroline Ludovika, born in 1795 died at four years of age in 1799. In all, between 1791 and 1807, Francis and Maria Theresa would have eleven children of which four would die in infancy or as a young child. Their last child, Amalie Theresa, born on April 6, 1807, would only live a day and her mother followed her to the grave a week later. The younger brother in the Kreutzinger portrait, Joseph Franz, would die as well in 1807 at the age of eight of a contagious disease; probably yellow fever. Another son, Johann Nepomuk would die two years later, at four years of age, in 1809.

The medical science of psychiatry and psychology did not exist then, but that does not mean, of course, that the mental afflictions later discovered and named did not. The great Viennese pioneer in this field, Sigmund Freud, would not be born until 1856 and would not publish his seminal work, *Die Traumdeutung (The Interpretation of Dreams)*, until 1899. Nonetheless, it is well understood today that the immense psychological impact of the death of a child can cause an array of consequences in its surviving parents including severe depression, anxiety, stress, and the risk of suicide. "Complicated grief disorder" is today a recognized diagnosis associated with such traumatic events and its symptoms are like post- traumatic stress disorder (PTSD) experienced by soldiers returning from war and combat.

Another author described the Emperor's appearance as one having." . . . a gaze as dreamy and blank as any ancient sculpture."[13] The personally catastrophic years of 1807–08 may have had something to do with this appearance and the Emperor's evolving personality. His increasing reserve in his interactions with others, including his own brothers and sisters, created the impression in many of a cold and taciturn man but may have come about as a result of these tragic personal losses as well as his seeming fate to be presiding over the end of the dynasty. The year 1809 would mark the lowest point of Francis' monarchy with the agonizing defeat of Wagram, which we will cover later.

The Emperor's brothers, the "Archdukes," became a source of persistent criticism and irritation to him. As one author has noted, "their royal blood also afforded them the luxury of criticizing the emperor's shortcomings."[14] Some of the Archdukes, several authors have claimed, were more talented than their brother, the Emperor, which gave them a sense of entitlement to criticize, and the Emperor irritation that would eventually result in their exclusion from all participation in political or military matters. Nonetheless, one has to search in vain for any objective basis for the supposed filial superiority of the Emperor's brothers, except in the military field and the case of the Archduke Charles.

Although the Archduke John was appointed as a commanding military officer, Charles had, by 1800, clearly demonstrated that he was the most talented and certainly the most successful Austrian commander in the field, bar none, at 29 years of age. John, only eighteen years of age, had been the nominal commander at Hohenlinden and had obviously been over his head.

Ferdinand, the next youngest brother of Francis had been given their father's sinecure and made Grand Duke of Tuscany after Leopold II had become emperor. The wars of the First and Second Coalitions had chased Ferdinand from his Tuscan throne and by 1800, he was essentially a refugee in Vienna.

Ferdinand had done nothing particularly to distinguish himself and would do little for the rest of his life except gain and lose ducal titles until his early death in 1824. Archduke Alexander Leopold had already died at the age of 22 in a tragic fireworks explosion at Laxenburg in 1795. Francis' fourth youngest brother, Archduke Joseph, had been the governor of Hungary (Palatinate) since 1796 and would remain his brother's keeper in Budapest until long after Francis' death, but as a benign civil servant. Anton Victor was another collector of titles and died childless the same year as Francis. And so it went. Any examination of the talents of the other male siblings of Francis reveal none with any particularly notable talents other than Charles. None had to contend with the sheer weight and responsibility of their eldest brother as ruler.

THE ARCHDUKE CHARLES AND MILITARY REFORM

Charles was a special case, however, and seems to have been recognized as such by Francis, beginning with his letter to his younger brother upon his accession to the throne in 1792. Charles had one interest and talent that Francis simply had never acquired, and that was in military command and the science of waging war itself. Francis had Charles, however, and yet it is between these two brothers that one finds the most evidence of filial rivalry and eventually mutual aversion. This was not in evidence in 1800, however; quite the opposite.

Hohenlinden and Lunéville ushered in a five-year period of peace which Francis used to reorganize the Empire and assigned his brother to reorganize and reform his army. Charles was appointed initially as president of the Court War Council or *Hofkreigsrat* but by 1801, this antique military command, hamstrung by the provincial estates and competing military organizations, was superseded, although not abolished, by a new Ministry of War. This ministry would be directed by Charles.

With actual military experience in the field fighting some of the best French generals, although not yet Napoleon himself, Charles understood better than his brother and most of his imperial advisers the uniquely grave threat posed to the Monarchy by France in general and Napoleon, in particular. This enemy was not the Sun king or even Frederick the Great, but a military mind of the highest order, galvanized by a capacity to generate massive numbers of motivated soldiers financed on the backs of tributary states which had grown in number. By 1802, even Britain had agreed to peace with France so that if war were to break out again, the Habsburgs would truly be on their own.

This was no time for pusillanimous reforms to bring the Imperial army up to Napoleonic standards, but for deep and far reaching reforms that would take diligence, money and above all time. Charles could supply the diligence, but not the other requirements which, as it turned out, were in all too short supply.

Charles' reforms, between 1801–1805, briefly put, involved an ambitious but incomplete reorganization of a peacetime army of about 330,000 soldiers and officers. Most importantly, recruitment and support of the army was wrenched out of the hands of provincial estates and levies. Command and financing would be from the top down, from now on. The army's regiments would each be tied to specific military districts, or *Hilfsbezirke*, throughout the empire. Providing manpower and the financial support to train, victual, and transport these soldiers, cavalry and artillery would be demanded from these districts from Vienna and overseen by a general officer or Conscription Director in each district. Lifelong service was abolished for a term of years, moving older soldiers into retirement in favor of younger but inexperienced troops.

These reforms were but a start. The command system of the Imperial army was still poorly organized by comparison with the French under Napoleon's superb chief of staff and sometimes war minister, Louis-Alexandre Berthier. The decision making and maneuvering of the Imperial armies remained slow, cumbersome and eventually fatal when the next confrontation arrived in 1805. Furthermore, reductions in recruitment of men and horses, equipment and weapons to save money drained the Austrian army of its military power. By 1805, the army was 160,000 troops below its supposed peacetime compliment of 367,000 and Quartermaster General Duka estimated that it would take six months to put the army on war footing.[15]

This narrative is not a military history, however, and so it will suffice to say that one school of historiography is that the Emperor's brother had insufficient time to implement the reforms so necessary to have allowed the Monarchy's military force to compete with Napoleonic France. A large standing army of the quality required to defeat a Napoleon involved equipping, training and drilling an army that remained chronically underfunded, under equipped and, in the event, poorly led. Yet another viewpoint is that the Archduke was slow to grasp how little time Austria had to get ready for the next fight and that he failed to conceive of and press home the necessary reforms and reorganization in four years' time. The Prussians and the Russians would also be found wanting in comparison to France when the time came. Yet it is in this struggle that the first differences arise between the brothers.

Charles, like most generals who must fight and win a war in the field, was invariably pessimistic about the Monarchy's chances on the battlefield and worried aloud about its survival. In memoranda to and personal audiences with his brother, Charles repeatedly warned against any conflict with France and, in the early years of the peace, he found a receptive audience. As time went on, however, the international situation and the Monarchy's position deteriorated in the face of new Napoleonic aggression.

In this Archduke Charles became increasingly at odds with a so-called war party that eventually included *Vizekanzler* Cobenzl and *Kabinettsminister* Colloredo. Neither of them were military men, but instead were far more attuned to changing European continental politics and diplomacy. Increasingly, they were forced to assume that, one way or another, and with allies, the military would, if necessary, have to improvise and blunder through. Pressed by a deteriorating situation for Austria by 1804, and prodded by one of the Emperor's councilors, Friedrich Gentz, Cobenzl came to realize by 1804 that war could not be far distant and like it or not, Austria would have to go along.

Charles' increasingly strident and negative advice to Francis became unwelcome enough that Charles was released as commander in chief of the Monarchy's army in favor of the "unfortunate" General Karl Mack von Lieberich, as he described himself in his own words after the decisive defeat and capitulation of an entire field army under his personal command at Ulm. Francis explained to his brother that in the event of war with France, he would require him, as Austria's greatest general, to be in the field and not in Vienna. Accordingly, he resurrected the *Hofkriegsrat* as the supreme council to direct the war that might be coming.

STORM CLOUDS GATHER—THE THIRD COALITION FORMS

The creation of the alliance that made the Third Coalition will be told very briefly. The short peace of Amiens between Britain and France lasted but a year when war broke out again on May 18, 1803 and would remain constant between them until Napoleon's abdication in 1814. In preparation for the war, on April 30, 1803, Napoleon agreed to sell New Orleans and the vast

Louisiana territory to the United States for $15 million; approximately $240 million in modern US currency.

Britain, always reluctant or unable to engage the French on land began a search for continental allies who could. This proved fruitless for a time, but with the execution of the Duke d'Enghien by the Napoleonic government in 1804, which again shocked the continent, Sweden agreed to join an alliance with Britain in return for a subsidy in December. Pitt then succeeded in negotiating terms with the new Tsar Alexander that brought Russia into alliance in April 1805. Yet the Russians could not strike at France without passing through central Europe, which meant that either Prussia or Austria would have to open its territory to passage. Prussia refused and Austria hesitated.

Austria hesitated because its government was divided, as we have seen. Francis still dreaded war, contemplating not merely the unpreparedness of his army, which Archduke Charles confirmed again was the case in January 1805, but also the invariably precarious financial condition of his Empire to wage another war with an enemy for which he undoubtedly, already had hard-bought respect.

The deciding factor was France's further penetration of Northern Italy. Napoleon, crowned Emperor of the French on December 2, 1804, decided to "accept" the crown of Lombardy in March 1805. The former Republic of Italy became a new Kingdom of Italy, comprised of the former Duchies of Milan, Mantua, Modena, the western part of the old Republic of Venice, part of the Papal States in Romagna, and the province of Novara. This placed Napoleon adjacent to the Habsburg half of Venetia and, from there, not far through the Alpine passes to Vienna. This was followed by the annexation of the Genoese Republic to France along with its capital and great seaport of Genoa. Finally, French military strength in Italy was increased to 30,000 which set off alarm bells in Vienna.

Combined with the increasing aggressiveness of France in Northern Italy was pressure which now came from the Russians for Austria to join the Anglo-Swedish-Russian alliance. Francis and his ministers had become aware of the existence of negotiations between Britain and Russia in March but had still not understood it to be an offensive, aggressive alliance to attack France. The terms were made clear to Vienna in April, requiring the Emperor to have to face the question of war or peace in short order. Cobenzl, Grentz and Colloredo eventually convinced Francis that Austria could not abstain from joining the Third Coalition in the face rising French power in Italy and Germany.

Francis is often criticized explicitly or implicitly for starting or becoming embroiled in wars with Napoleon that he went on to lose. The implication is of a leader who repeatedly, stupidly or foolishly could not face the fact that his empire and his armies were inferior to France until he was beaten into

Figure 7.4. Frederick William III, king of Prussia 1797-1840. Wilhelm Herbig. The Wellington Collection, Apsley House.

submission. The truth is that Francis and his empire were caught between immense and competing realities that offered no simple or guaranteed outcome. The situation before the War of the Third Coalition is a perfect example of the deadly dilemmas Francis and his ministers faced and one of the biggest ones of his reign.

Should Austria refuse to join the alliance and actively go to war, Russia would be unable to act and bring its military power to play. Russia required access to the central European theater one way or another—through Prussia or Austria—to confront Napoleon and attempt to defeat him. If Tsar Alexander's armies could not pass and join up with those of the central European powers, he could not play any significant part in confronting Napoleon and, perhaps, like his father, Russia would simply withdraw into itself and let France have its way.

Prussia's new king, Frederick William III, who had succeeded his father in 1797, had struggled with the same dilemma and decided under no circumstances to join the Coalition, but Prussia's situation was entirely different than Austria's. Prussia was not facing French encroachments into adjacent territory and a build-up of military power on its borders, as Austria was, among other things. British and Russian promises and threats poured in on the king and his advisors attempting to goad him into war, but he stood firm.

Nonetheless, as Archduke Charles pointed out to his brother, if Austria joined the coalition and were to go to war, geography and time would work against her. A French army of some 200,000 well drilled men who had been camped at Boulogne for two years facing Britain across the channel would be sent against Austria. French armies occupying parts of Germany and Italy would also be sent against Austria and all of them would likely arrive at the gates of Vienna before any Russian army came into the theatre of war. What then?

Alternatively, should Austria sit still? What would Napoleon do next? After having engulfed most of Northern Italy, Belgium and The Netherlands, what new depredations would be forced on Europe and, more particularly, Austria? The Holy Roman Empire stood, after the disgraceful Congress of Rastaat and the Treaty of Lunéville, tottering at the edge of disintegration with Francis at its head. With its proximity to France and the power of French armies led by Napoleon an ever-present threat, many of the surviving states within the Empire were now looking to Paris, not Vienna, to protect their interests and falling one by one to French influence. This included particularly Bavaria.

BAVARIA DEFECTS

A slight diversion of our story to discuss the situation presented by Bavaria is worthwhile at this point because it highlights the growing danger Francis faced by 1804 as Emperor of Austria and Holy Roman Emperor that would drive him to reject the advice of his brother and join the Third Coalition with disastrous results.

Bavaria's geographic position then and today comprises the eastern half of the most southern portion of Germany with the other, western half bordering Württemberg/Baden. Bavaria sat on the northern border of western Austria and the western border of eastern Bohemia. Indeed, there was no state whose location was closer to Vienna than Bavaria. Virtually all the northern and western passes and roads into Austria and to Vienna passed through Bavaria. Its strategic importance to Francis and the Austrian Empire could not be greater.

Bavaria, as a member of the Holy Roman Empire, had a fractious history with its neighbor to the south and east. The House of Wittelsbach was the only dynasty in Europe with a longer history and reign than that of the Habsburgs. The brief War of the Bavarian Succession in 1778, discussed earlier, was the last attempt by the Habsburg dynasty to absorb some or all of Bavaria into their collection of hereditary duchies. The Elector, Charles Theodore, whose attempt to trade part of Bavaria to Joseph II in return for part of the Austrian Netherlands had triggered the war, had fought as an ally of Francis until his death in 1799. His cousin, Maximilian, thought differently.

Maximilian was personally a Francophile and with one of his duchies occupied by French troops in 1800, his foreign policy changed Bavaria's alignment in favor of accommodation with France and Napoleon. Maximilian would eventually marry his eldest daughter to Napoleon's adopted son, Eugene Beauharnais, and would become Napoleon's most faithful ally until 1813. His hostility toward Francis became almost immediately a cause for alarm in Vienna upon his succession. By 1804, it was obvious that in any war with France, the Bavarian door would be thrown open to Napoleon's armies, to which Bavaria would add its own.

Therefore, in terms of geopolitics, Francis was not a reckless fool who threw in with the first passing car. On the contrary, by all accounts, he hesitated until at least in his own mind, he felt his hand was forced. Caught in a vice between French annexations and intrusions into Italy, which he had already reluctantly been forced to accept, and now increasing subversion of his German allies, passivity became itself an increasingly dangerous and, ultimately, unacceptable option. Francis gave his assent to preparations for war and assigned his brother, Archduke Charles, a subordinate position but commanding Austria's main field army in Italy. Overall command of the army in Germany would rest with von Mack who answered only to Francis and the Hofkriegsrat, not the Archduke.

NOTES

1. Hague, William, *William Pitt the Younger, A Biography*, (New York: Alfred A. Knopf, 2005) 219. George III suffered from the genetic disease porphyria. George III had a particularly severe form of porphyria. His first attack occurred in 1765, four years after his marriage to Queen Charlotte. Further signs of the disease showed up in 1788-1789. From 1811 to the time of his death in 1820 he became progressively insane and blind.

2. Seigworth, Gilbert R., "Bloodletting Over the Centuries," *New York State Journal of Medicine,* (New York: December 1980).

3. Langsam 159.
4. Langsam 161.
5. Langsam 162.
6. Ibid.
7. Ingrao 232.
8. Langsam 165–166.
9. Ibid., p. 166.
10. Ibid.
11. Vovk 289.
12. Langsam 162.
13. King, David, *Vienna 1814,* (New York: Random House, 2008) 11.
14. Ingrao 232.
15. Kagan 166.

Chapter Eight

Beethoven, The Third Coalition and The Birth of the Austrian Empire

It is difficult to imagine that the subjects of the Habsburg Empire between 1792–1815 could have been interested in much more than the on-going wars with France or the menace of another, impending war but this would not be a wholly accurate conception of the daily lives of Francis' subjects. Certainly, the burden and scourge of war could and did weigh heavily on high and low alike, but life did go on. The cultural heartbeat of the Empire and Vienna in particular, kept pumping and sustaining a stream of talent and achievement, especially in music. Indeed, the only comparison might be a similar outpouring from imperial Vienna at the sunset of the Empire in the late 19th and early 20th century.

Ludwig van Beethoven who had arrived in Vienna in 1792 with Joseph Haydn as his mentor had, by 1805, achieved immense fame and popularity in the city that he would never leave until his death. In the early years, between 1792–1800, Beethoven was unquestionably the most famous and dazzling pianist and performer in Vienna, the acknowledged center of music in Europe and therefore, the world. His passionate, some might say violent piano concerts were the stuff of legends. He was the successor of Mozart as a pianist but not yet as a composer.

He was not a handsome man. He was somewhat short, even by the standards of the day, at about five feet four inches. He had a pock-marked and dark complexion and wild hair. Some of his friends called him "the Sicilian." He had an eccentric personality, prone to fits of rage and condescension due, no doubt, to his brutal and alcoholic father's upbringing. As common born and a believer in the Enlightenment, he had a simmering resentment and contempt for the aristocracy who were born to wealth without any talent, in his view, that should entitle them to their privileged lives.

Yet he allowed the public to believe that he was, himself, of noble blood by changing the "van" to "von" in many publications advertising his concerts. He also subsisted on the patronage of several nobles who gave him generous allowances and gifts, Prince Lobkowitz and Prince Kinsky, among others. His impulsive and deeply emotional relationships with various women, many of whom were married, tortured his soul. None of the affairs lasted more than a year or two and a few of them left him devastated. He never married and had no children.

By 1800, Beethoven's contribution to Austrian culture reached a new high with the debut of his First Symphony on April 2 at the Burgtheater at which time his Piano Concerto No. 2 was performed. It was a stunner and received rapturous applause and celebrity. In 1801, he first began to experience the tinnitus that foreshadowed his eventual loss of hearing that gradually progressed in the following years. By 1802, he confessed to some of his closest friends and family that he feared he was going deaf and contemplated suicide. Nonetheless, by 1805, after producing more sensational pieces such as the Moonlight Sonata, his Second Symphony, and Third Piano Concerto, another bombshell was dropped on April 7, 1805 with the performance of the "Eroica" Symphony, his third, at Prince Lobkowitz's palace.

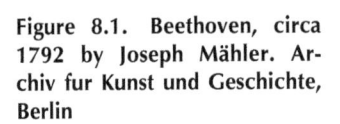

Figure 8.1. Beethoven, circa 1792 by Joseph Mähler. Archiv fur Kunst und Geschichte, Berlin

The Eroica was the bridge between what is known in music as the "classical" period and the "romantic" era in which emotion rises to the forefront in the creation of music. In 2016, BBC Music Magazine conducted a survey of over 150 orchestral conductors around the world and the consensus was that it is the "greatest symphony of all time." Leonard Bernstein called the first and second movements of the symphony "perhaps the greatest two movements in all symphonic music."[1] Already in the time of Joseph and Leopold II, Vienna had established itself as the trend-setting, cutting edge of music but the reign of Francis would have Beethoven and a new burst of creative energy and power that rippled across the continent. It would spawn the music of Schubert, Liszt, and Brahms, to name but a few.

The symphony would also have political overtones. Beethoven had admired the outburst of the French Revolution and the ideals of the Rights of Man stirred his idealistic inclinations deeply. The Eroica was composed as a tribute to Napoleon as First Consul and Beethoven intended to dedicate it to him. By 1805, however with the outbreak of war between his Habsburg and aristocratic patrons and Napoleon, Beethoven was sufficiently practical to realize, as a commercial proposition, that was out of the question. Instead, the work was given the more neutral "Eroica" name, although scores of the music in Beethoven's own handwriting make it clear that he had Bonaparte in mind when he wrote it. Anecdotal evidence by Ferdinand Reis has it that when Beethoven learned that Napoleon had crowned himself emperor, he recoiled in disgust and this was the reason the name was changed. There is evidence, however, that Beethoven continued to admire Napoleon later in life.

While there is no evidence of any significant personal relationship between Francis and the great composer, Beethoven was a regular performer at the Congress of Vienna in 1815 where he played before the Emperor and his guests. On the other hand, Beethoven had a very close relationship with the Archduke Rudolph, the youngest brother of Francis, and without doubt, the greatest patron the composer ever had.

In 1809, Jerome Bonaparte, as king of Westphalia, offered Beethoven 500 gold ducats per year to become his court composer in Cassel. When word reached Rudolph, he would have none of it. From 1809 onward, the 21-year-old Archduke gave Beethoven an annual salary of 4000 florins with the only condition that he never leave Vienna; equivalent today to $56,000.00 per year. This allowance made Beethoven financially independent for the rest of his life. Beethoven dedicated several musical compositions to the Archduke, including his Fourth and Fifth Piano Concertos.

Another future star we do know would have met the Emperor in 1808 was a young student named Franz Schubert who had won a spot in the Imperial Court's Chapel Choir as a singer. He was noticed quickly by Salieri who eventually decided that Schubert was a musical genius. The reign of Francis was a period of Austrian cultural preeminence on the continent of Europe, not merely in the war years, but in the Biedermeier period that would follow to the end of Francis' life. This is a fact that needs to be considered with the characterization of Austria as a police state; a subject we will return to again after the Napoleonic Wars ended.

WAR WITH NAPOLEONIC FRANCE AGAIN

It was in the summer of 1805 that Francis gave his assent to the newly created Austrian Empire joining the alliance that is known in history as the Third Coalition. Terms were negotiated and on August 9, Austria formally joined the alliance. Napoleon learned of the alliance a couple of weeks later and on August 26 ordered his army at Boulogne to strike camp, march across France and into Germany to attack the Allied armies at the earliest moment. Austria's war would be over in four months after two separate military disasters; one at Ulm and the second at Austerlitz on December 2, 1805.

This narrative cannot possibly give an account of this brief war in any detail, and yet it cannot be ignored because of the impact it had on the Monarchy and the responsibility of Francis and his government for the outcome. Once again, the lack of interest and knowledge of military matters on the part of the sovereign resulted in numerous mistakes and failures that predicated defeat and grave losses to the Austrian Empire. This defeat would not be like those of the last two wars in which, after protracted warfare, a tactical defeat that opened the door to Vienna resulted in an armistice, negotiations and loss of distant, peripheral provinces. In this war, an Austrian field army would be crushed quickly, Vienna would be occupied by the enemy, and another catastrophe would befall Francis' main ally and another part of his army at Austerlitz. Thereafter, very harsh peace terms would be imposed that would hobble and humiliate the Empire and its Emperor.

The first error committed by Francis was the appointment of Mack as the *de facto* commander of the Army of the Danube in Germany, which would be the main theater of the war, at least at the outset. The Emperor's irritation with his brother's hectoring and, worse, his naïveté, as he saw it, in geopolitical matters motivated an over-reaction. While the Archduke Charles was by then the best military commander Austria had available, he was demoted to field command in Italy—a theatre of war that would be inconsequential–but with overall command of the largest part of the Austrian army, a force of some 140,000. He would see conflict in only one unimportant battle, Caldiero, west of Venice, in which he would defeat Marshal Andre Massena on October 30.

The better part of the Austrian military, both in terms of numbers and leadership, would never get into the war in any meaningful way.

The second mistake was a consequence of the first. The unwieldy *Hofkriegsrat* was also resurrected, adding another layer of bureaucracy and inefficiency to the Austrian command system upon which he, the Emperor, stood as the final arbiter. To further complicate matters, Francis divided command of his army in Germany between his cousin, Archduke Ferdinand, an inexperienced 24-year-old commander but a member of the Austria-Este branch of the Habsburg family, and Mack whom he appointed, technically, as Quartermaster General but who usurped all real authority over the army, aided perhaps unwittingly by the Emperor himself. Ferdinand took an almost immediate dislike to the vainglorious Mack and his dismissive contempt for the Archduke's opinions. Eventually a major breach opened between them regarding the dispositions of the army which had to be settled by Francis himself. Ferdinand opposed the forward positioning of the army, as had Archduke Charles. Francis arrived in Munich on September 20 and sided with Mack to his everlasting regret.

Francis had known Mack from his days in the Turkish War and the successful siege of Belgrade under von Laudon. Mack had enjoyed a reasonably good military career since that time reaching general rank in 1794 and served well in the earlier French Revolutionary Wars. In 1797, he became a field marshal. His career seemed over, however, when he became commander of the army of Naples in 1798, was defeated, captured and imprisoned in Paris. He escaped, eventually, and returned to Austria but remained in semi-disgraced obscurity until he was recruited by the "war party" of Cobenzl as the only Austrian general who favored war with France and, therefore, as the one to replace the Archduke. His dubious career and talents, however secondary they had been politically, would have dire consequences on the military conduct of the war.

Mack seized the opportunity to become Austria's *de facto*, overall commander in the impending new war and supported an aggressive, attacking approach to this war with France rather than the defensive and cautious posture favored by the Archdukes. Francis accepted the dubious advice advocated by Mack rather uncritically, which fell in line with the war party of Cobenzl and the equally aggressive and naïve plans of the young Russian emperor, Alexander I.

This was the third mistake. Due to Francis' weakness in strategic military thinking, he casually squandered Austria's chance to direct the war on the strategic level as the *quid pro quo* for its participation. This would be a mistake Metternich would not make in 1813. Instead, in 1805, it would be the Russians and particularly Tsar Alexander and his entourage of young, inexperienced aristocratic toy generals who would largely call the shots, especially at Austerlitz.

Thus, in August and September, instead of concentrating their overwhelming numerical superiority under the command of two superior generals, Archduke Charles and Field Marshal Mikhail Kutuzov, the Austro-Russian plan divided their forces. A preposterous strategy of multiple attacks in multiple theaters of war that Tsar Alexander and his advisors thought would pressure Napoleon into defeat was adopted. Instead of a concentration of force to confront an invading French army of some 200,000 heading straight for the Austrian capital, there was a dispersion of force and, worse, a faulty timetable that, as the Archduke had warned, would result in Russia's first and most capable army under Kutuzov arriving only after the Napoleonic zephyr had swept into Austria.

Mack was regarded with contempt by virtually all the general officers who served with him. Archduke Ferdinand Karl Joseph would have nominal command over Mack's Army of the Danube in Germany and quickly became disenchanted with his seemingly senseless maneuvering and posturing. Mack exacerbated Austria's dangerous "first in line" position by advancing into Bavaria and establishing itself at Ulm, thereby increasing the marching time and distance between himself and Kutuzov with fatal results. Archduke Charles immediately foresaw the folly of the advance and penned a withering critique of Mack as a military commander emphasizing that his dispositions for the invasion of Bavaria exposed the Austrian army to great danger.[2] Yet Francis stuck with Mack.

On October 19, the hammer fell on Mack and his army of 40,000. Mack was not merely defeated but annihilated by 80,000 French under the personal command of Napoleon. His army was surrounded and suffered 4,000 dead in a two-day battle. Eighteen generals, sixty-six artillery pieces and 27,000 troops thereafter surrendered, including Mack himself. One of his commanders, Prince von Schwarzenberg, of whom we will hear much more later, and a few other officers escaped the ring of fire along with some other detachments under the command of General Keinmayer who would fight again at Austerlitz. All in all, the Battle of Ulm ranks as one of the worst and stupidest defeats in Austrian military history; not the absolute worst only in terms of scale. That was yet to come. Mack's incompetence resulted in a court martial, conviction and imprisonment for two years with loss of rank and honors.

Russian forces under Kutuzov, numbering some 50,000 and intending to link up with Mack, arriving at Braunau on the Austro-Bavarian border a few days' march away, were now exposed. Kutuzov turned around and began retreating into Lower Austria and eventually the fortress town of Olmütz in Moravia where he halted. Vienna was ignominiously occupied on November

14. Francis and his family were forced to flee the city. Francis joined up with the swelling Russian army there, having been joined by another 50,000 Russians under General Buxhowden and the remnants and scattered detachments of Keinmayer's forces. The combined Austro-Russian armies at Austerlitz would number about 85,000; the bulk of which were Russian. The French would muster around 65,000 on the day of battle.

AUSTERLITZ

The Battle of Austerlitz no less a person than Napoleon himself considered his greatest battle. It was given to him by the Tsar days earlier when the decision was made, over the objection of Kutuzov, to advance on Napoleon and give battle. Francis, apparently humbled by the debacle at Ulm and exiled from his own capital, passively listened and did nothing to support Kutuzov, the best allied general and one of the greatest Russian generals in history.

It was known to Kutuzov and the two sovereigns at the time that the Archduke Ferdinand had regrouped the remainder of Mack's dispersed field army of about 20,000 Imperial troops in Bohemia. The Archduke Charles, advancing through Hungary from Italy with another 40,000 troops was only a few days' march away. Moreover, due to violations of Prussia's territory by Napoleon in his maneuvering before Ulm, the King of Prussia had belatedly ordered the mobilization of his army of approximately 150,000 and intended to join the Coalition upon completion. Everything cried out for delay before giving battle under the best conditions. This was the reasoning Kutuzov advanced to Alexander and that was rejected in favor of a precipitous attack.

Austerlitz began at around 7:00 in the morning of December 2, 1805 and was over in four hours after a sudden, massive attack by Napoleon on the weakened center of the Russian lines broke through at around 9:00 am and all attempts to repair the breach had failed by 11. The shattered and dispersed Russian and Austrian armies retreated, leaving the Tsar, detached from his army with only a small guard, weeping in despair. Francis sped in his carriage to meet his wife at Olmütz and consider his options.

Here, in what must have been one of the lowest moments of his life, Francis gave in to despair and determined that further resistance to Napoleon was out of the question. He requested an interview with Napoleon. An armistice was granted on December 4 and the following day, December 5, 1805 at 2:00 pm for the first of only two personal meetings in their lives, Francis and Napoleon came face to face by a fire next to a windmill about 10 miles south of Austerlitz on the road to Hungary.[3]

... They embraced cordially and spoke for 90 minutes. 'He wanted to conclude peace immediately,' Napoleon told Talleyrand afterwards, 'he appealed to my finer feelings.' On getting back on his horse, Napoleon told his staff: 'Gentlemen, we return to Paris; peace is made.' He then galloped back to Austerlitz village to visit the wounded Rapp. . . . Napoleon refused to commit his thoughts about Francis to paper when writing to Talleyrand—'I'll tell you orally what I think of him.' Years later he would say that Francis was 'so moral that he never made love to anyone but his wife. . . . He was less charitable in his assessment of Tsar Alexander of Russia, who had not sued for peace. In a letter to Josephine he wrote 'He has shown neither talent nor bravery.'[4]

Talleyrand pressed Napoleon to treat Austria gently and turn her into an ally against the Russians but Napoleon rejected his advice. He believed that if he and France remained dominant in Northern Italy, Austria would remain forever hostile and must therefore be treated harshly.

The Peace of Pressburg, agreed on December 26, was harsh indeed. Austria was ejected completely from Italy, losing Venetia. She was also stripped of Tyrolea and the Vorarlberg, which were given to Bavaria, and other territories in western Germany which were given to Baden and Württemberg, now allies of Napoleon. Prussia was bought off by giving her Hanover in northern

Figure 8.2. December 5, 1805—Napoleon and Francis After the Battle of Austerlitz. Jean-Antoine Gros. Chateau de Versailles

Germany, at which point Prussia abandoned all thoughts of joining the British or the Russians and set about absorbing this enormous territory that was the hereditary dominion of the British king, George III.

Once again, Prussia profited from remaining neutral while Austria was diminished in Germany to its benefit. Francis also had to recognize the former electors of Bavaria and Württemberg as kings and release them and Baden from any further loyalty to the Holy Roman Empire or, of course, from himself as Emperor. An indemnity of 40,000,000 gold francs had to be paid to France as well, once again defraying the cost of Napoleon's military campaign but with the concurrent burden of adding crippling debt to Austria, on top of her own costs incurred in mobilizing and campaigning. At this point, Francis was now the Emperor of a gravely wounded, nearly bankrupt, second-rate power on the continent of Europe.

THE AUSTRIAN EMPIRE IS BORN

The Austrian Empire or *Kaisertum Österreich*, in German, had been officially declared a year earlier, on August 11, 1804. It had a population on that date of some 21,200,000 in round numbers and covered over 698,700 square miles making it the largest continental state in Europe behind France and Russia. No other state or empire in Europe other than the Ottoman Empire in the Balkans was remotely as large or populated as Francis' new, hereditary Empire. The new Empire consisted of the hereditary *Erblande* of the Habsburg dynasty. Uniquely, in history, for a period of two years, between 1804-06, Francis was Emperor twice over or "Double Emperor" of his own hereditary, Austrian Empire and the elective Holy Roman Empire.

In 1805, the Austrian Empire, as we have noted, lost population and territory. Hence, tax revenues were far insufficient to support a military establishment comparable to or superior to the French who were financing their army on the backs of subject states and defeated enemies. It was time to consider what had gone wrong, what to do now and how to do it. Francis, to his credit, now re-appointed Charles to become Commander-in-Chief of the Austrian army and President of the Council of War. Pride or jealousy could not ultimately separate the brothers at this time of defeat. A more petty or insecure man, as Francis is often attributed to be, especially with his brother, might not have made the decision to bring Charles back.

Francis also appointed Karl Phillip von Schwarzenberg, ambassador to Russia in St. Petersburg. Although he had not realized it yet, von Schwarzenberg would eventually become one of Austria's greatest military commanders. He had served at Hohenlinden and Ulm, by 1804, but missed Austerlitz.

Figure 8.3. Field Marshal Karl Phillip, Prince of Schwarzenberg. Artist Unknown.

In each military encounter, he distinguished himself as the best tactical general on the field for Austria. His prowess caught the eye of Archduke Charles himself who promoted him often both in title and as an able commander. He was made a Prince by Francis in 1806, but by then had retired from military service for diplomacy. We will hear much more of him later.

Another young star had caught Francis' eye as well; the 32-year-old ambassador to Prussia, Klemens von Metternich. This aristocratic son of another career diplomat, Franz George Karl von Metternich, was extremely handsome, charming and had grown up in privilege in the Rhineland. He was well educated at the Universities of Mainz and Strasbourg. He had attended the Congress of Rastaat as a secretary to his father, as we have seen. His family's land estates in the Rhineland had been confiscated by the French during the War of the Second Coalition.

He was also well traveled, having accompanied his father on some of his diplomatic missions but also on his own. He had traveled to England for a time in 1794, met King George III twice, had dinner with William Pitt and

Edmund Burke. He had even witnessed the departure and return of Admiral Lord Howe's fleet from its "Glorious First of June" victory over the French fleet, having dined with the Admiral before his departure. Metternich admired Britain and would remain an Anglophile for most of his life.

When Baron Thugut became State Chancellor, Franz George von Metternich's career ended out of favor and some might say, in disgrace. He had been the chief advisor to the Monarchy in the Austrian Netherlands and Thugut blamed him for the loss of the province to France. The failure at Rastaat did his career no help, nor did his relative poverty after the loss of the family estates. Klemens spent some time managing the lone, remaining family property at Königswart in Bohemia, located due east of Prague and west of Nuremburg. Years later, Metternich wrote to an American academic and linguist "When I was five-and-twenty years old, I foresaw nothing but change and trouble in my time; and I sometimes thought then that I would leave Europe and go to America, or somewhere else, out of the reach of it."[5]

Family fortunes changed for the better when Klemens' parents arranged his marriage with the Countess Eleonore von Kaunitz, granddaughter of the late State Chancellor, Wentzel von Kaunitz, in September 1795. This marriage vaulted Metternich into the first rank of society and no doubt advanced his career. Overnight, he became rich as well, after his family's disastrous fall in every respect after Rastaat. It was not an unhappy marriage, it seems, but Metternich would notoriously have numerous affairs and mistresses throughout his life and several "love" children with some them as well. He would also be widowed twice and have three wives in his lifetime.

During this period, while in Vienna, Metternich met Francis at social events on several occasions. In his autobiography, Metternich recalled Francis remarking to him "You live as I should be very happy to live in your place. Hold yourself ready for my orders, that is all I expect of you for the present."[6]

In 1801, Klemens von Metternich embarked on a diplomatic career of his own as ambassador to Saxony, posted in Dresden, and was then assigned as ambassador to Prussia in 1803. His diplomatic success seemed quite limited at first blush. He accomplished nothing of much consequence at the court in Saxony, but he did make quite a few personal contacts that would be important later in his life and career, the most important being the publicist Friedrich Gentz, with whom he would collaborate. He was at this time in his life, still much enthralled with and influenced by the policies and viewpoint of Kaunitz being, for example, deeply suspicious of Prussia. He saw his primary mission in Dresden to limit or diminish Prussian influence there.

In 1803, Francis re-assigned Metternich to Berlin upon the departure of Johann Phillip, Count von Stadion. This was a difficult assignment worthy of the talents of only a diplomat of the first rank, which Francis must have known when he sent Metternich there. The mission to persuade Prussia to join the Third Coalition in 1804-05, undertaken by Metternich and the Russian ambassador, Maximilian von Alopaeus, failed in time to prevent the disasters at Ulm and Austerlitz.

Despite these setbacks in his early diplomatic years, there was something about Metternich that Francis noticed, as he had with Schwarzenberg and other younger, newer personalities around him after Austerlitz. In April, while in Vienna, Francis' new foreign minister, Count Stadion, summoned Metternich to announce that he was appointing him ambassador to France, at Paris. Metternich, who had expected to be appointed as ambassador to Russia, at the request of Tsar Alexander, was stunned by the assignment. Napoleon had objected to Stadion's initial appointment of Philip Cobenzl. Due to Metternich's warm personal relationship with the French ambassador in Berlin during his assignment there, he had apparently been commended to Maurice de Talleyrand, the French foreign minister, and from there to Napoleon. Metternich described it himself this way:

> My French colleague in Berlin was M. de Laforest, before mentioned, a confident of Prince Talleyrand. At the moment of extreme tension, just before the conclusion of the alliance between Austria, Russia and Prussia, the position of M. de Laforest had become most difficult. It had, however, always been my habit not to mingle business affairs with personal matters, and so I endeavored to maintain relations with my French colleague on a footing of frank courtesy. These relations continued during all the different phases of the affair. This did not escape the notice of Talleyrand, whose policy was not averse to the establishment of good relations between France and Austria. The influence of Count Philip Cobenzl had become stale in Paris, a new man was wanted there: the choice fell on me. The change in my destination, when I learned it, fell upon me like a thunder-bolt.[7]

Metternich met with Francis after the Peace of Pressburg and his assignment had been made known to him and recorded the meeting:

> The task of representing Austria in France, immediately after the Peace of Pressburg presented so many difficulties that I feared I should not be adequate to them. The next day I waited on the Emperor Francis, and ventured to describe the embarrassment of my position. He received me with his usual kindness, praised me for my conduct in Berlin, and set before me the necessity of accommodating myself to what he called my destiny, with expressions which made it impossible for me to oppose his wishes.[8]

The maturing emperor that had survived the sharp disaster of 1805 was developing an eye for talent that had been absent in the younger man. Thugut and Cobenzl had been no Kaunitz and Stadion, who now became his principal advisor, while perhaps an improvement on the first two ministers, would still fall short of the mark, seduced by the siren song of war in 1809 with even more disastrous consequences, if that were possible. In 1806, however, this was unknown to Francis. What was apparent was the disintegration of Habsburg power in Germany.

Napoleon had rewarded Bavaria for its support and alliance against Austria with the Tyrol and Vorarlberg and by elevating Maximilian to a kingship, along with the Electors of Baden/Württenberg and Saxony. He now created the 'Confederation of the Rhine' with these western-most German states and thirteen others who announced their secession from the Holy Roman Empire on August 1, 1806. Saving face, Francis "released" these rulers from their oaths of fealty to him and to the Empire, which both they and he had broken since Lunéville. On August 6, he declared the dissolution of the Empire and abdicated his title which had been in his family continuously, with but a single interruption, since Albert II in 1438. There is no record of his personal feelings when these proclamations and acts of abdication were prepared and signed, but they must have produced profound depression and shame as he contemplated the portraits of his father, his uncle, his grandfather and other ancestors in their coronation robes at the Hofburg.

Yet even in this moment of supreme humiliation, the formal disintegration of the Holy Roman Empire declared by Francis, the last Holy Roman Emperor, may have thwarted Napoleon's usurpation of yet another crown, like the crown of the kingdom of Italy. French kings had long coveted the Holy Roman Emperor's crown and Napoleon surely would have "accepted" it, like the crown of Italy, had the newly minted German kings offered it to him. Now it was gone; beyond reach. Nobody could have it. Francis was now simply Francis I, Emperor of Austria, for the rest of his life and for posterity.

Indeed, Napoleon's growing power in Germany that year finally aroused Prussia to war. The Prussian habit of playing the waiting game to see how they could best profit from conflict between Austria and France, leaning one way and then the other while all the while aggrandizing itself with territory from Poland and then Hanover, would back-fire in a single stroke of madness when, on October 9, 1806, Prussia declared war on France. Prussia's treachery after Napoleon had bribed it out of the Third Coalition as recently as December of 1805 might account for the savage revenge he took after he and Marshal Davout utterly crushed the Prussian army five days later, on October 14, at Jena and Auerstedt. Berlin was occupied on October 27. Napoleon rode through the Brandenburg Gate to the tune of *La Marseillaise* at the head of his army.

The Prussian king and what remained of his army fled to the east and joined the Russian army and the Tsar. The war would go on into 1807. The inconclusive battle of Eylau was followed by the conclusive rout of the Russo-Prussians at Friedland on June 14 and the Treaty of Tilsit on July 7.

Francis was no longer alone. Prussia was reduced to a fraction of her former self. All territories in western Germany were carved off and created a new Kingdom of Westphalia which was given to Napoleon's brother, Jerome, to rule as king. Her eastern, Polish territories were lopped off as well, for the most part, to create a new, hostile Duchy of Warsaw. Aside from the natural hostility the Polish aristocracy felt for Russia and Prussia for the earlier partitions, Napoleon installed his ally the king of Saxony as the titular ruler although the French ambassador ruled in Warsaw.

This new and large state, a resurrection of Poland, was a client state loyal to France and embedded on the borders of both Prussia and Russia. The seeds of a future war were sown. In the meantime, King Frederick William III could ponder whether his fate and that of his kingdom was even worse than that suffered by the Austrians. Prussia would not enter the field against Napoleon again until 1813. Too late, the Prussian ministers and monarchy realized they had over-played their hand. To be sure, there was little sympathy for their plight in Vienna.

NOTES

1. Bernstein, Leonard. *The Infinite Variety of Music.* New York: Simon & Schuster, 1966.
2. Kagan 348.
3. The second and final meeting between the two came in May 1812, in Dresden when Napoleon invited (or summoned) all his client kings and allied powers there before the invasion of Russia.
4. Roberts, Andrew, *Napoleon—A Life,* (London: Penguin Books, 2014) 391–392.
5. Seward 27.
6. Metternich 27.
7. Metternich 64.
8. Metternich 65.

Chapter Nine

Conservative Reform in the Franciscan Era

We have discussed Francis at length as a war leader, but before going further into the course of the Napoleonic era, we will take a diversion to consider the internal, domestic reforms and character of the new Austrian Empire and how they reflect on the personality of the 'reactionary' Emperor we have come to know from so many fleeting accounts of him and his reign in other books.

Volumes have been written on the history of the Austrian Empire. Until recently, words like "ramshackle," "hodge-podge," "anachronistic," "teetering," "moribund" and the like were frequently applied to the Austrian and later Austro-Hungarian Empire. The weakness of the Austrian empire was back-handedly characterized by the Czech historian and statesman, František Palacký, who famously once said that if Austria did not exist, it would have to be invented. This was the view of Talleyrand and Castlereagh, both of whom viewed Austria as a benign bulwark against the aggressive Eastern monarchies of Prussia and Russia.

Against those contemporary and post-mortem evaluations after 1918, is the undeniable fact that predictions of the Habsburgs' collapse and that of their empire proved premature, to paraphrase Mark Twain, time and time again. This supposedly weak, multi-national, multi-cultural Eastern monarchy survived deadly blows that should have destroyed it in the Turkish sieges of Vienna in 1529 and again in 1683. A half century later, as we have seen, Maria Theresa faced partition of her inheritance to a host of enemies led by Frederick the Great and Louis XV. Francis had by now survived Rivoli, Marengo, Hohenlinden, Ulm, Austerlitz and lately, the Peace of Pressburg. The Austrian Empire and its dynasty would go on to survive another death struggle with France in 1809, revolutions, invasion and civil war simultaneously in 1848–49 and another death blow at Königgratz in 1866.

With all that, one should ask how did the Habsburgs and their Empires hang on if they were indeed so weak? So fractious? So riven by multinational conflicts and financial distress? By the same token, how was it that a single battlefield defeat, at Leipzig in 1813, would bring the Bonaparte monarchy to complete ruin and termination in 1814. Which empire had the glass jaw? Clearly not the Austrian Empire and definitely not Francis. Why?

For one thing, the modernization and reform of the era of Maria Theresa had brought the Empire into wealth, influence and power. While the hot and cold reforms of Joseph II followed by the partial retrenchment of Leopold II might have appeared awkward and ineffectual, they had staved off a revolution in Vienna, Prague and Budapest like the one that toppled the monarchy in Paris. Not all of Joseph's reforms had been rescinded and some of them only part-way. The aristocracy of the Austrian Empire had seen what the monarchy could do, setting free the serfs and peasantry, granting privileges to the bourgeoisie, limiting the power of the church and confiscating their property. True, they had rolled these liberal advances back to some extent, but the monarchy in Vienna was popular among the peasants and urban bourgeoisie, as Pieter Judson's new history describes in detail.[1]

When we last discussed the domestic outlook of the young Francis, we witnessed a man who had watched the "appalling ingratitude" of these very same classes toward his uncle, Joseph II, with whom the monarchy was now popular; the urban bourgeoisie and rural peasantry. Francis had assisted his father in re-balancing the more radical Josephin reforms, placating the aristocracy of Hungary, Transylvania, Bohemia and the Austrian Netherlands in the nick of time. He had watched the French Revolution execute his aunt and degenerate into mob violence and the Terror.

It would not be far-fetched to conclude, as Francis did, that the common folk were not to be trusted nor allowed liberties that could quickly flame into rebellion or revolution. In this sense, his reign could certainly be deemed a repressive or conservative one. This wary, cautious, some might say paranoid view of the *vox populi* would last until Francis' death in 1835. There is no getting around that fact, but if one compares him to the governments and institutions of other great states around him you find him at least in the middle of the pack, if not better placed.

The monarchies of Turkey and Russia were absolute in ways that the Austrian monarchy would never and had never approached. These autocracies remained rigid and unbending for another century and when compared to Austria, the police state of Francis is benign and even incompetent. The Prussian monarchy was likewise absolute with the added benefit or deficit, depending on one's viewpoint, of being remarkably thorough and efficient in its censorship and repression, as it was in most things. We will come to the infamous Carlsbad decrees in due course, but in terms of conservative, monarchical power and disdain for inclusion of the common man in government, even in the slightest, these monarchical states were second to none.

The French, of course, were completely subservient to a liberal and some might say beneficent Bonapartist monarchy until 1815 with laudable legal rights and liberties for its citizens, but there could be no doubt about the will and power of Napoleon on his ministers and his government. It was a dictatorship, pure and simple, whether clothed in pseudo-Roman togas of the Consulate or the imperial robes of Empire. Even after Bonaparte and the restoration of the Bourbon monarchy, the electoral franchise of the French parliament was tiny and comprised overwhelmingly conservative property-owners.

Even Britain, usually seen as the one democratic power among the Great Powers of Europe in the Napoleonic era was hardly one by modern terms. The British parliament was divided into a House of Lords with hereditary peers, unelected by anyone and from whom the king could choose ministers of state including his "first" or "prime" minister. The House of Commons was elected from heavily-gerrymandered districts with a miniscule franchise of less than 1% of the population. As late as 1831, Lord John Russell in Parliament said:

> Elections carried by money, treating and an appeal to low passions will produce such disorder, and such disgust, that an arbitrary monarchy will sooner or later be the consequence. Our object should rather be to place the power of choice in men of property and intelligence. . . . If you place the franchise too low . . . you run the risk of creating more evils on the one side than you put down on the other.

Only the United States of America had a radical constitution with universal (white) male suffrage.

The diets and estates of Francis' realm were hardly outside the norm and even ahead of the curve compared to many other states of Europe. Francis made no attempt to move toward an American model, although he was not unfamiliar with it. His father, while Grand Duke of Tuscany, had considered a constitution there based upon the model of the then-American colony of Pennsylvania. No European monarchies had the slightest intention of adopting what might be deemed liberal, American-style democracy at any time while Francis lived. Francis was no more a reactionary than any other monarch in Europe at this time. George III and Francis, had they ever met in person, would have had much in common in their views of government and the role of the monarchy.

The same could be said about some other odious aspects of life in the Austrian Empire while Francis ruled. Police spying and press censorship are usually held up for approbation, and deservedly so, but these were hardly unique nor invented by Francis. As we have seen, internal police surveillance and censorship had been used by Joseph II and enhanced further by Leopold II.

Given the wartime situation in which Francis found himself embroiled from the first day of his reign, surveillance, informers, agents-provocateurs, and the apparatus of a police state was no more nor less than the elaborate Napoleonic police network directed by the sinister Fouché in Paris. While it is true that the British would have had a far less intrusive police presence in their society than that of Austria, the subjects of Francis I were not more oppressed than that of any other continental state. It was taken for granted that in wartime, the *Geheime Staatspolizei* or "secret state police" would react immediately and harshly to conspiracies, treachery or treason, incitements to riot or rebellion. The rising resentment of police in Austria began after 1814 and the end of the war.

Francis indeed does not stand out as particularly reactionary or even conservative when compared with the political system and rulers in virtually any other European state. He does appear so when compared to twentieth and twenty-first century conceptions of liberal, constitutional democracy. That philosophical concept or point of view was not widespread among the ruling classes and monarchies of Europe of that time who had the land, the power and the money, for the most part.

LAW AND REFORM IN THE AUSTRIAN EMPIRE

Before he is judged reactionary for his belief in enlightened but autocratic rule, as Francis neared forty years of age, there are other marks that must be balanced in his favor. One was education. Another was the law and the judicial system which, for him, became the equivalent of a constitution. Another was equality in citizenship of all religions and nationalities.

Napoleon is rightly credited with the rationalization of ancient French, Roman and Canon law into the Code Napoleon. He is praised as a law giver, but Francis gave more to his people and his laws lasted just as long or longer. In 1803, Francis published a new criminal code that further rationalized Austrian law and formalized court procedures for the first time. Josephin criminal reform in 1784 had held for the first time that there was "no crime without a law," and thus, an act not defined as a crime was not a crime.[2]

While this might seem self-evident in modern, liberal societies, it was not at the time. *Ex post facto* criminalization of behavior had been a driver of the American Revolution, for example. Noble lords had heretofore exercised absolute judicial power over their peasants and villages on their estates and could punish or imprison them arbitrarily as they saw fit.

The criminal code of 1803 was both a penal code, which defined the elements of crimes but also a uniform, imperial code of procedure that was to be followed in all courts in the *Erblande*, except Hungary, and therefore what was to become the Austrian Empire.[3] It was the first ever criminal code with universal application in the Empire's long history and one of the first in Europe. It preceded the Code Napoleon by a year.

No one stood above the law, not even the Crown, according to Francis and the Code. Francis might have secret police but he also had courts. Convictions had to be obtained legally. His police might have read a defendant's letters but by law, this evidence could not be used against the accused. The conviction had to be obtained by some other means of evidence.[4] The *Geheime Staatspolizei* were used mainly to gather information on public opinion and prevent possible conspiracies, rather than to imprison political opponents. By 1804, the retiring Minister of Police, Johann Anton von Pergen, was convinced that the threat of revolution had long since passed.

This was followed in 1811 by an even more comprehensive law, the *Allgemeines Burgerliche Gesetzbuch* (AGBG) or General Civil Law Code. In it, the Code explicitly transformed all his subjects into citizens, equal before the law.[5] As such, the Josephin Edict of Toleration was enforced everywhere. As Pieter Judson points out one of the odd results was that:

> . . . only the Habsburg Monarchy and revolutionary and Napoleonic France conscripted significant numbers of Jews into the military. . . . The Habsburgs mobilized thousands of Jewish soldiers . . . between 15,000 and 19,000 of the half-million men conscripted in 1814. Altogether, 35,000 Jews may have served the Habsburgs during the twenty-five-year period of wars against the French.

Francis began a century long relationship between the dynasty and the Jewish community in Austria, particularly in Vienna and Budapest. In 1816 Salomon Mayer Rothschild was made part of the Austrian nobility when Francis awarded him the hereditary title of Baron. Aside from the longstanding relationship between the dynasty and the Rothschild banking firm, appreciation for relatively non-discriminatory acceptance, at least by the Monarchy, was returned by the Jewish communities in the Empire with robust loyalty to the crown and a steady influx of Jewish immigration from Russia, Poland and the Ukraine later in the century.

The correct, efficient and consistent application of the law and its enforcement in Austrian society was a core belief and interest of Francis throughout his reign. His legal and judicial reforms and codes were the basis for further refinements over the next two centuries. Much of his codes and, obviously, the concept of equality before the law, are very much part of Austrian law today as is the scrupulousness with which it is respected in Austrian society and culture.

The years 1804-1814 were the infant, formative years of the new Austrian Empire. It was during this time that the populations that made up the Empire embraced the concept that they were, indeed, citizens of a now well-defined imperium and that they were all equal citizens and not subject to arbitrary power.

> Together it seems that this common culture that celebrated empire constituted a different but equally important legitimation of empire, as did the many peasant communities that viewed empire—or the dynasty—as their protector against the arbitrary power of the local lords. The question remained, however, to what extent a defensive and conservative government under Emperor Francis would actively pursue the potential benefits of empire for peasants, the educated or the manufacturing classes. Would the common empire of Maria Theresa, Joseph and Leopold flourish. . . ?[6]

The empire could not flourish during the Napoleonic period due to the immense cost of the wars, the indemnities paid to France after Austerlitz and Wagram in 1809, and the increasing debt service imposed on the Austrian treasury. Taxation was heavy and still inadequate. Further loans and subsidies were used, on and off, to prop up a government staggering under the weight of it all with consequent inflation and *de facto* bankruptcy. It would take a long time for the Austrian economy to recover from the wars when they ended in 1815 at Waterloo with little or no help from the government itself. In fact, the continuing financial penury experienced so deeply by the Habsburgs continued under Francis to the point where his secret police, like everything else, were so understaffed and underfunded, they could not possibly carry out anything like the espionage network so often credited to them, as pointed out by Pieter Judson.[7]

EDUCATION REFORM

Educational reform was also a major policy pursuit of Emperor Francis I. Habsburg dynastic interest in education had been inaugurated by the Emperor's grandmother, Maria Theresa, who had in 1760 established a State Commission to consider the educational system in the *Erblande*. This eventually resulted in her decree in 1774 that there would be compulsory primary school education for all children within the hereditary lands.

This decree was not self-fulfilling, however, and often met resistance from local lords, communities, provinces and estates who would, naturally, have to provide the financial support for schools, teachers, books and other resources. Francis pushed this forward with renewed vigor to increase the productivity of the economy of the Empire, particularly after 1815. The vision of the Dowager Empress was pursued despite Francis' social and political conservatism and became far more of a reality in most areas of the Austrian state than ever before.[8] Where implementation and reform were weakest, the cause was the usual reason: lack of money from the government to fund its ambitious project. Nonetheless, education in the Austrian Empire was more advanced than most other areas of Europe if for no reason than that they had recognized it sooner, begun earlier and maintained a consistent policy in favor of broad, mainstream education of its population more than nearly any other European state.

The years right before and after Austerlitz were not a lost decade, nor should the Austrian imperium of Francis I be defined in this era solely by the Napoleonic menace and consequent wars, although these cataclysms, when they came, overwhelmed all else for a time. Too little time and scholarship has been spent on the day-to-day evolution of a new European empire on the Danube under its still relatively young leader. And what do these sociopolitical-economic measures reveal about the sovereign himself?

With respect to internal reform, Francis was undoubtedly more like his grandmother than either his uncle or his father. Far more cautious than Joseph II and yet more cautiously willing to permit further reform than his father, his careful, incremental management of reform from a conservative bedrock would undoubtedly have found favor with Maria Theresa. In truth, he was no more conservative than many of his contemporaries and more liberal than some. He pushed reform where he judged it was most needed; in law, in education, in equality of citizenship. He checked it where it had proved, at least in his lifetime, most dangerous: press freedom, police surveillance, and freedom of expression or assembly.

DEATH AND TRAGEDY

It was in the years after Austerlitz that the heavy blows of personal tragedy rained down on Francis with the death of his wife, Maria Therese, in 1807 after the birth and death of his last child, Amalie Theresa. Joseph Franz died the same year and Johann Nepomuk in 1809. Four deaths within a two-year period.

Figure 9.1. Maria Ludovica, Empress of Austria 1808-1816.

Francis did not wait long, however, after the death of his wife to remarry. Once again, he married a cousin, the 20-year-old Maria Ludovica, daughter of his paternal uncle, Ferdinand. He had just reached 40 and was now twice-over a widower. Francis and Maria Ludovica would have no children and she too would die just eight years later, in 1816, at the age of 28.

Maria Ludovica is significant in this history for her utter hatred of Napoleon and the French Empire, which she apparently imparted to Francis when her opinion mattered. She and her family had been forced to flee Milan in 1796 when it was occupied by Napoleon. This had made a very dire impression on the young girl, as did the relatively Spartan existence that followed, in exile in Austria. She had been raised in Milan where her father had been governor and apparently had received a good education. Like her husband, having been raised in a city of art and culture, she had sophisticated tastes and enjoyed indulging them. She was considered quite beautiful in her day.

Unlike Francis' other three wives, Maria Ludovica was quite political and outspoken. In the period before the outbreak of war with France in 1809, she was an avid supporter of the "war party" and openly advocated renewing hostilities against Napoleon. She had a poor relationship with Metternich following Wagram and vehemently opposed the marriage of Marie Louise to the French emperor that Metternich advocated. She was reportedly a devoted step-mother to Francis' children but became particularly fond and friendly with Marie Louise who was only four years younger than her. She would have a profound influence on Ferdinand, the heir to the throne, as we shall see. Finally, she would be quite active at the Congress of Vienna acting as her husband's consort and hostess, when required, and arranging entertainments for the assembled guests.

Francis had met her while he was still in mourning for the death of Maria Therese. He had sought consolation with his aunt, Maria Beatrice, and while at her residence in Vienna, met her beautiful daughter apparently for the first time. He was almost immediately smitten with her and within months sought her hand in marriage. They were married on January 6, 1808. Once again, the Emperor appears to have affirmed the adage "lucky in love, unlucky in war," as he genuinely loved each of his wives, including this one, while sustaining repeated defeats on the battlefield. His marriage to Maria Ludovica was undoubtedly, by all accounts, a consolation to him after the emotional losses he sustained and would yet sustain in the dark days after Wagram.

NOTES

1. Judson, Pieter M., *The Habsburg Empire, A New History,* (Boston: Belknap Press of Harvard University Press, 2016).
2. Winslow, Robert and Melissa Francescut, "Crime and Society: A comparative criminology tour of the world," (*San Diego State University*. www-roan.sdsu.edu/faculty/rwinslow).
3. Esmein, A. *A History of Continental Criminal Procedure With Special Reference to France.* London: Forgotten Books, 2012.
4. Ingrao 232.
5. Judson 54.
6. Judson 101.
7. Judson 106, 107, 131–134.
8. Judson 129.

Chapter Ten

Wagram

The ministry of Stadion that had picked up the pieces after Austerlitz and swept out the ashes of Austrian military incompetence had recognized in 1806, as much as anyone, that Austria was in no financial or psychological position to continue to engage in war with a triumphant France led by a man that many people considered a freak of nature. Napoleon's crushing defeat of the Prussians at Jena followed by the decisive defeat of the Russians at Friedland and the Treaty of Tilsit left Europe in no doubt that if Napoleon and the French Empire could be appeased, they should be. War with Napoleon, for Austria, seemed out of the question after Tilsit, even with continental allies. And yet, within three years, not only did Austria find herself at war again, but with no allies in the field with her. Why?

The answer lies in part with events in Spain and, in part, with the overarching bullying of Napoleon who simply did not know when to quit while he was ahead. Not content with dominance in the low countries, in Germany and in Italy, Napoleon now moved to subvert his one true Great Power ally: Spain.

French overreach began with the Berlin Decree of November 21, 1806 that established the "Continental System"—essentially an embargo by the entire European continent under Napoleon's control or allied to him. Britain had placed France under an effective and ever tightening naval blockade with the outside world, formalized by George III's Orders in Council on November 11. The annihilation of the Franco-Spanish fleet at Trafalgar earlier that year established British pre-eminence at sea and unquestioned ability to cut off French commercial ties to the rest of the world outside Europe. Napoleon's response in return sought to wreck Britain's trade with its largest market by far, the European continent.

The Berlin Decree would quickly cause many European states to chafe at French hegemony, most importantly Spain and Russia, while the Orders in

Council would bring the United States of America into war with Britain and renewed alliance with France by 1812. Portugal, one of Britain's oldest allies on the continent, refused to submit to the Continental System, thereby drawing the ire and attention of the great man himself after Tilsit in 1807.

At first, the idea was that France and Spain would jointly invade Portugal and divide the kingdom between them. This provided a pretext for movement of French troops in large numbers into Spain who were resented by the local population of the areas where they were quartered. In the meantime, after the defeat of their fleet at Trafalgar under French command, Spain began to reassess its position and a possible change of alliance to Great Britain. A pro-British party forced the Spanish King, Charles IV, to abdicate the throne in favor of his son, Ferdinand VII, in March 1808. Within a month, Napoleon had taken advantage of the rift in Spanish politics and deposed both father and son, making his older brother, Joseph, the new King of Spain. This interference and usurpation ignited a ferocious resentment among many in the aristocracy, but also among the Spanish people themselves.

Between 1807–14, the Spanish people and Ferdinand VII, increasingly aided by British military support, waged what became known as the Peninsular War against Napoleonic France. By 1809, the war was consuming vast amounts of blood and treasure with no end in sight. Napoleon himself took command of his armies there for a time but still could not vanquish the ongoing guerilla war that continued to rage. This protracted and increasingly frustrating military debacle slowly began to convince Stadion that there was a golden opportunity to overthrow French hegemony in Europe but, more importantly, to throw off the shackles that had been imposed on Austria by the Peace of Pressburg.

Stadion and Francis were also influenced by their ambassador to France, Klemens von Metternich, who had undertaken his assignment to Paris primarily as an opportunity to study in detail and in depth the mind of Napoleon. Metternich later wrote "I do not think it was a good idea on Napoleon's part to summon me to a post which, while giving me the chance to appreciate his brilliant qualities, also gave me the opportunity to discover the weaknesses which in the end ruined him and freed Europe."[1]

While Napoleon was away from Paris, Metternich returned to Vienna, arriving on October 10, 1808, at which time he met with Stadion and the Emperor. He described his observation of French public opinion and society that he had observed by that time, mainly during the campaign against Prussia and Russia that had ended at Friedland and Tilsit:

> A stupor then reigned in Paris, produced by a sense of the weight which the Emperor had laid on all classes of society. . . . The impression made on the public of Paris by the news of a battle won by Napoleon was certainly not that of joy;

it was satisfaction that France had escaped the consequences, and at seeing that her internal peace was not endangered. . . . The revolutionary elements were only smothered. The country had not one friend in Europe, and an immeasurable feeling of unrest reigned amid the rejoicings for a victory of the French army, for everyone knew that these victories made new ones necessary to complete the work, the ultimate extent of which no one could foresee. . . . With a few exceptions, the nation would willingly have exchanged glory for safety. . . .[2]

Metternich had detected the earliest, green shoots of treason among Napoleon's most trusted and high-ranking collaborators that included Fouché, a great number of generals and marshals, but above all, Talleyrand:

France felt the need of repose, and this feeling prevailed not only among the masses, but was shared by Napoleon's companions in arms. These individuals had been for the most part taken from the lower ranks of the army and raised to the height of military honor. . . . These men wished to enjoy their possessions, and objected to stake them on the chances of war. . . . The moral power of the Emperor [Napoleon] was too overpowering to be opposed openly, therefore intrigue was resorted to. . . . During the time that I was ambassador, I had many opportunities of verifying this fact. . . .[3]

As Metternich was departing Paris for Vienna, Napoleon met again with Tsar Alexander at Erfurt between September 27 and October 14, 1808. Among the agreements made were an alliance "in case" Austria and France should go to war. Nonetheless, anti-French sentiment within the Tsar's entourage was high again. Napoleon's object was to ensure Russia's peace and neutrality in the East while he turned his attentions to Spain. Metternich could not have known it at the time, but Talleyrand's first significant betrayal of his master occurred in secret at this conference when his Foreign Minister encouraged Tsar Alexander to resist Napoleon's blandishments. Yet Metternich correctly concluded as early as this time that Napoleon's seemingly irresistible power was already cracking and corroding on the inside.

Stadion and his own master had disagreed over the need to arouse popular, public opinion in Austria and Germany to overthrow the Napoleonic peace that had been imposed upon her. Ever wary and cautious about unleashing the genii of popular opinion and influence on the government, Francis had uneasily given way to the advice of his ministers that without popular support for a war of liberation, Austria could not succeed. After all, the world had witnessed what popular support had done for France in raising vast, motivated citizen armies. Stadion envisioned a harnessing of similar nationalist pride among the Germans.

By May 1808, Francis agreed to a limited, concerted effort by the government to arouse public support for resistance to Napoleon in preparation for

Figure 10.1. Johann Phillip von Stadion by Johann Ender

war. Austrian propagandists publicized the resistance of the Spanish people to French invasion and occupation in their homeland; the parallels to Germany being obvious. Austrian media and patriotic journals stoked a sense of national and imperial pride in the accomplishments of the new state, the rule of law, social mobility through ennoblement, and equal access to careers in the Austrian state civil service and the army.[4]

Francis and his new Empress left Vienna on tours in the countryside to encourage military enlistments and were greeted by patriotic displays of support. The Archduke Johann's conception of a national militia, the *Landwehr*, made up of citizen soldiers of all social elements, was created to supplement the imperial army. Large numbers of men joined the *Landwehr* including many students and others who were otherwise exempt from military service.[5] The exemplary role played by the Archduke, particularly in Tyrolea and the most western province of Austria, the Vorarlberg, remains alive to this day where he has achieved something like mythic status as a folk hero.

Special efforts were made among the German speakers both within Austria and Germany to arouse anti-French feelings. Friedrich von Gentz and Friedrich Schlegel both lent their talents to this cause. Yet Francis remained uneasy with this approach. In a famous anecdote at about this time, Francis was being advised by one of his councilors that a certain individual was known to be an exemplary Austrian patriot. "Yes, but is he a patriot for me?" came the reply.[6]

The Hungarians, always the wild card in the Monarchy's deck, were even more reluctant than Francis had been to arouse the common folk in favor of the cause. The semi-feudal, ultra-conservative Magyar nobility feared the consequences of populist nationalism unleashed within the kingdom. Yet even here, Francis reaped the benefit of the humiliation of Pressburg and indignation against French pretentions. When the Hungarian Diet was summoned at last, it rejected the idea of extending the *Landwehr* to Hungary, but instead offered Francis 60,000 troops for a period of three years.[7]

THE FIFTH COALITION AND THE BIRTH OF AUSTRIAN PATRIOTISM

On July 1, 1808, a French army corps of some 18,000 soldiers under General Pierre Dupont was forced to surrender to a Spanish army under General Francisco Castanos at Bailen. A British expeditionary force under Sir Arthur Wellesley, who would become the Duke of Wellington in 1813, then defeated another French corps under Junot in the first week of August. These twin defeats compelled Napoleon to transfer large combat formations from Germany to Spain; a process that would take months but eventually result in several decisive but temporary victories.

Metternich learned that Francis and his ministers were far closer to war than he had realized when he visited in October 1808. Even the ever-reluctant Archduke Charles had concluded by the end of August 1808 that war was unavoidable and submitted a memorandum to his brother regarding military preparedness. Encouraged by French defeats in Spain, and the transfer of French forces out of Germany, the likely theater of war, Stadion pressed the Emperor for a decision.

By October, Metternich found Francis in disagreement with his ministers only when it came to timing for the war. Over the winter of 1808-09, the Austrian government was encouraged at different times to believe that Prussia and Russia would join in a new coalition, goading it to making ever more deep and extensive preparations which, by now, began to be perceived in Paris. On December 23, 1808, the decision was made and Francis' assent given to Stadion to go to war in the Spring.[8]

Metternich himself was subjected to a belligerent outburst at a formal audience before the assembled diplomatic corps at Napoleon's palace at St. Cloud in August, 1808, when he was confronted by an obviously angry Napoleon who queried "Well, Sir Ambassador, what does the Emperor, your master, want—does he intend to call me back to Vienna?"[9] Anxiety about possible renewed war with Austria had prompted Napoleon to inveigle a hallow assurance from the Russian tsar of mutual assistance which, in the event, was not forthcoming. In December, Napoleon ordered the creation of a new Army of the Rhine to consist of some 100,000 men and demanded his German client states—Baden, Wurttemberg and Bavaria—call up their armies.

By January 1809, however, Napoleon himself had led his army in Spain and driven one British army under Sir John Moore out of northern Spain and scattered most of the Spanish insurgents. He returned to Paris on January 24, concerned about rumors and reports from Vienna suggesting war was imminent. Initial Prussian willingness to go to war with France and supply 80,000 men was withdrawn in March 1809 by King Frederick William III. Britain, ever willing to subsidize a continental ally against Napoleon, promised nearly £5 million, worth about $250,000,000.00 in modern money. On February 8, 1809, the *Hofkreigsrat* again reaffirmed its decision for war and four days later, Francis named his brother supreme commander of all Austrian field armies.

The pessimistic, manic depressive personality of the Archduke Charles, once given more authority than any Austrian military leader since Wallenstein, now welled up and overwhelmed him. He later claimed that he had "changed his mind because 'given the general conditions and the state of the military establishment our chances for success were minimal.'"[10] His gloomy pessimism sapped much of the energy out of the leadership of the army and within weeks of the outbreak of war on April 10, 1809, the Austrian field commanders were hoping to avoid defeat when victory over the French was required for Austria to regain its dignity and status in Europe.

Austrian historians of the post-Königgratz era tended to elevate Archduke Charles to heroic status to embellish the myth of the Habsburg dynasty for their own propaganda purposes. This historiography has been the subject of several authors and accounts, in part, for the dubious and invidious comparisons made between Francis and Charles, in favor of the latter. This was not the consensus opinion of earlier writers, however. As the German military historian, Hans Delbruck stated, in his estimation the Austrian monarchy "overestimated the capabilities of the man whom they placed in command."[11]

Close study suggests a man who was justly lauded for his intellectual prowess in military thought and organization and as a field general of the first rank. On the other hand, his chronic depression and black moods of despair marked him as a questionable supreme military commander, but he was at the time thought to be the best that Austria had. Schwarzenberg and Radetzky would disprove that in four years' time, but this was not known in 1809. Charles wavered between perhaps justifiable doubt in the capabilities of the army, for which he was much of the time responsible, and the necessities facing his country and his brother. He seems to have been very naïve about the position of Austria in Europe and the amount of time he had to whip the Austrian army into a fighting force that could contend with France, with or without allies.

The enthusiasm with which the Austrian people embraced the war this time was quite different than 1805 and even defeat would not relegate this cam-

Figure 10.2. The Tyrolean Rebellion of 1809 by Franz Defregger. Alte Nationalgalerie, Berlin

paign to the ignominy and shame that befell it after Ulm and Austerlitz. An uprising in Tyrolea led by Andreas Hofer began the war on a popular footing, for example. Unfortunately, however, Austria needed to inflict a major defeat on Napoleon, probably in Germany, followed by an invasion of France to restore itself and this simply did not happen. By April 22, the Austrians were defeated decisively at Eckmühl in Bavaria and forced to withdraw. Defeat at Ebelsberg followed on May 5.

Another famous anecdote about Francis occurs at about this time when the Kaiser and his family had evacuated Vienna at the approach of the French army. Clearly distressed at the course of the war, Francis was intercepted by Ignatz Franz Castelli, a poet, author and friend of Schubert. Castelli, caught up in the surge of popular support for the war had written several anti-Napoleonic poems and propaganda. Long after Francis' death, Castelli wrote his own autobiography of the encounter between him and the Emperor:

> The Emperor had already left the *Residenz*. . . . I made my way to him on foot and obtained an audience. His face showed clearly his grief at the tragic fate of his country, and this gave me hope.
> 'Who are you?' he asked, 'and what do you want?'

'A poor provincial clerk who has not even once drawn his full annual salary of 300 florins, because various taxes are still being deducted from him.'

'That is quite in order. I cannot help you there.'

'Majesty, I am asking for a very different kind of assistance. I have been proscribed by the French dictator. If I am found, I am to be handed over to a military court. I must therefore escape.'

'Of course.'

'But this is impossible, as I have no means to do so. I am therefore making so bold as to ask Your Majesty most graciously to deign to use me as an escort for one of your convoys.'

'You say you have been proscribed. And why is that?'

Humbly and sadly I handed him my work and said, 'It's all there. Please read it.'

The Emperor did so, shook his head, frowned, and then, handing me back the paper, said brusquely: 'So you have written a war-poem? And who, pray, ordered you to do so?'[12]

The distrust Francis felt for popular uprisings that could get out of control, even against a foreign enemy, can be understood in this exchange. Many in his government aspired to emulate in Austria the mass enthusiasm the French had displayed in 1792, but that example did not appeal at all to Francis. Aroused, armed citizen armies and militias with an abstract loyalty to Austria rather than specifically to its dynasty was a dangerous concept that by then Francis probably regretted having encouraged. He had no more faith in the masses of common Austrian folk than Alexander Hamilton did of average Americans.

VICTORY AND DEFEAT

On May 13, Vienna again fell to the French and was occupied. This time, unlike the occupation in 1805, when Napoleon was regarded as something of a celebrity by a passive Viennese population, the attitude of the Viennese was sullen and hostile. The Archduke Maximilian had rallied a militia to resist the French, who then subjected parts of the city to cannon bombardment. Armed resistance quickly collapsed, however, once the bombardment began and at 2:00 in the morning, the city surrendered. Then followed one of the most stunning and unexpected events in the long and usually dismal history of the Austrian army against Napoleon until then; they won.

Archduke Charles and the bulk of the Austrian army massed on the Marchfeld northeast of Vienna on the north bank of the Danube River with about 98,000 men and 262 guns. As the French took Vienna, the Archduke burned all the bridges between Vienna, on the south bank of the river, and the north.

Figure 10.3. Victory over Napoleon at Aspern by Johann Krafft.

Bridges were burned up and down the river to impede the French, while the Austrian army concentrated.

The Marchfeld was and still is an area steeped in Austrian military history. It was on the Marchfeld in 1278 that Rudolf defeated and killed King Ottokar of Bohemia, securing the Austrian heartland and the prize of Vienna by conquest. It is almost due east of the Vienna airport today and the topography of the land is quite different than it was in 1809. The Danube then was wide just downstream of Vienna where were located several islands, including one particularly large one known as Lobau Island. Today, much of the low land and water from the Danube has been silted up or filled, but this was the spot that Napoleon chose to cross the Danube to apply the coup de grace to the Austrian *Hauptarmee* around the small, outlying towns of Aspern and Essling.

On May 18 at 5 pm in the evening, General Gabriel Molitor's infantry division began crossing the very long pontoon bridge in Kaiser-Ebersdorf across a swollen Danube with very strong current that was still rising from melting Alpine snow. A second, much smaller bridge had been built from Lobau Island to the north bank of the Danube. The French first concentrated on the island and then filtered across the short bridge from the island as Archduke Charles, the Austrian high command and the Emperor watched. Approximately 24,000 French troops and 60 guns were mustered on the north bank by May 21. In the meantime, the Austrians launched a ship filled with heavy debris from upstream that smashed into the long bridge, isolating the French on the island. Another one knocked out the short bridge. This would continue for the next couple of days while French infantry, artillery and cavalry came across the bridges in fits and spurts, landing finally on the northern shore of the Danube.

Bloody fighting broke out on the 21st and continued the 22nd until the bridge to Ebersdorf was placed out of action for such an extended time that French reinforcements were unavailable to Napoleon. The weight of the Austrian army then fell on the French and by 2 pm on the second day of the battle, Napoleon ordered a retreat across the short bridge to Lobau Island, which was then dismantled to prevent the Austrians from crossing after him at 3:30 AM on the 23rd.

The story of the battle rocked Europe. For once, Napoleon's propaganda could not obscure the fact that the French army under the personal command of the Emperor himself had been defeated. The cost in blood had been enormous with some 20-23,000 casualties and 3,000 captured for the French and 19,000 casualties and 700 captured for the Austrians. Marshal Lannes, one of Napoleon's dearest comrades was gravely wounded and died nine days after the battle. The Austrians had also lost thirteen generals.

The French would not attempt another river crossing until July 4, but this time with much more preparation and deception to ensure that their entire army would get across the Danube to confront the Austrians; this time at Wagram, another small town on the north bank of the Danube across from Vienna. Another two-day battle ensued but in the end, was lost.

Wagram was the largest battle in history at that time. More than 300,000 men had fought for two days along a great front. For the Austrians, a figure of 23,750 killed and wounded, 7,500 prisoners and about 10,000 missing has been calculated; many of whom returned to their regiments later. In addition, the Austrians lost ten standards and 20 guns. Estimates of French losses also vary, but 27,500 killed and wounded, with an additional 10,000 for prisoners and missing. It is interesting to note that the French lost slightly more trophies than the Austrians, twelve eagles or standards and 21 guns. After the battle, Napoleon was reported as saying that, 'war was never like this, neither prisoners nor guns. This day will have no result.'[13]

THE TREATY OF SCHÖNBRUNN

A military defeat by Napoleon was certainly nothing to be ashamed of and it is not these two days for which the Archduke Charles can be justly criticized.

It was the intervening time between Aspern and Wagram that meant the difference between victory and defeat. After the victory at Aspern, Napoleon and nearly half his army were marooned on Lobau Island with no means of escape across the Danube until the long bridge was repaired. In the six weeks between the two battles, the Austrian army simply sat and waited in the ultra-cautious manner that Charles fell into in his campaigning. He had nearly 300 guns that were never moved into position to obliterate the French army stuck in the middle of the river with no escape. The point is that Aspern could have been an annihilating victory including the possibility that Napoleon could have been forced to surrender himself with his army.

Austrian historians in the latter half of the 19th century gloss over the monumental error made by the Archduke in this battle, instead focusing on the fact that he defeated Napoleon for the first time. But it was not the first time Napoleon had been defeated. He had been beaten by the Austrian Marshal Alvinczi at Bassano/Calliano in 1796 and by the Ottoman Army at Acre in March 1799. This was the first defeat Napoleon tasted as Emperor of the French, but it was not even the first time the Austrian army had defeated him.

Metternich, still ambassador to Paris, met with the Emperor at Walkersdorf on the evening of July 3, two days before the battle of Wagram:

> The Emperor received me with the hearty kindness which he had already showed me so abundantly.... Quiet and firm as ever, he was yet penetrated with the difficulty of the situation, daily expecting an event decisive of the war. The movement which I had observed in the enemy's army corresponded with this expectation. His majesty informed me that he intended to keep me with him during the rest of the campaign.... On the morning of July 5, I joined the Emperor on the battlefield, on which the fate of the Empire was to be decided. The battle was soon general.... About one o'clock in the afternoon.... Count Colloredo, a general-adjutant of the Archduke's, came with the information to the Emperor that his Imperial Highness had ordered the retreat of the army. Without losing his self-possession, the Emperor asked the messenger whether the Archduke had only determined on the retreat or whether it had actually commenced. When the Emperor heard that the army was already in full retreat, he turned to the adjutant, "Very well;" and added, turning to me, "We shall have much to retrieve."....[14]

On July 8, 1809, the Emperor summoned Metternich to announce to him that Count Stadion, Austria's foreign minister, had resigned in the wake of the military disaster. He informed Metternich that he was appointing him to replace Stadion as foreign minister. Understandably reluctant to accept the appointment under these circumstances and professing doubt at his capacity to reverse the misfortunes of Austria at this dangerous juncture, Metternich's objections were, in turn, rejected at this meeting:

> With the patience, which never left him in the greatest crises—and what monarch has gone through more than the Emperor Francis?—with a strength of mind and firmness of character which comprise all the gifts most valuable for princes who are called to govern, the Emperor answered. . . . "As to the difficulties which you raise about taking the office yourself . . . far from being deterred by the considerations you mention, I am confirmed by them in my choice. I am less afraid of men who doubt their own capacity than of those who think themselves fit for everything. I count on the knowledge you have of the difficulties of the position, and on your patriotism. Confer, then, with Count Stadion on the most suitable method of making the change of the ministry and come back and inform me when you have agreed what to do. . . ."[15]

Francis also dispatched General Johann von Lichtenstein to search out Napoleon and offer an armistice on July 8. In the meantime, the pursuing French caught up with the Archduke at Znaim in Moravia on July 10 and another battle began between him and a force of Bavarians under General Marmont. These were mauled and driven off but Marshal Andre Massena's corps and Napoleon himself arrived on the battlefield during the night with further reinforcements as soon as the location of the Archduke's army became known. Charles sent out emissaries to seek an armistice in the fighting and these reached Napoleon before Lichtenstein did. After another six thousand casualties had been sustained by both sides, a truce was called during the second day of fighting and an armistice was signed for four weeks between Napoleon and the Archduke.

In the wake of defeat, and after conferring with Stadion, another discussion between the Emperor and Metternich took place in the Emperor's carriage while on the way to Komorn in Hungary, about mid-way between Vienna and Budapest:

> I traveled from Znaim to Komorn in the Emperor's carriage and I made use of the time to lay before his Majesty my view of the present position of affairs. From this prince's calm and just line of thought, from the impression made on me by his strong and candid mind, I was convinced that in all important questions my views would always be in harmony with his, and that his great qualities would ever insure me the support without which a minister, be his views ever so good, can make no certain plan and carry out no project with the prospect of success. We examined the situation of the empire with thorough impartiality; we reviewed the prospects which the war still presented, as well as those promised by a peace concluded under the most unhappy auspices.[16]

The Treaty of Schönbrunn that followed simply piled on additional territorial losses and another indemnity to that which the Austrian Empire had been forced to accept at Pressburg after the debacle of 1805. Salzburg was ceded to Bavaria. Austria had to recognize Napoleon's brother Joseph as King of Spain. More territory in the East was ceded to Napoleon's client state, the Duchy of Warsaw. Austria was also bound to reduce the size of her army to no more than 150,000.

He did not know it, but Francis had now hit bottom. Nonetheless, with the appointment of Metternich as Foreign Minister, his fortunes were about to turn. He would henceforth depend upon and be assisted by a minister of Kaunitz's perception and penetrating intellect for the rest of his life. Surprisingly, when Francis and the Empress returned to Vienna from their refuge in Hungary, the people of the capital rejoiced:

> The return of the Emperor to his capital was like a triumphal entry. The populace there, as in the provinces, did not look beyond the present moment, satisfied with being relieved from the presence of an enemy who carried refinement in making use of all the resources of the country to the very highest degree. Napoleon, in the eyes of Europe, passed for an irresistible power, under the yoke of which all must bow. The feeling of the masses was no longer to escape this fate, but to lighten the burden as much as possible. . . . Under the load of enormous responsibility, I found only two points on which it seemed possible to rest; the immovable strength of character of the Emperor Francis and my own conscience . . . The results of the rising of Austria in the year 1809 were most destructive for the Empire. . . .[17]

Francis and Austria were isolated in Europe. Russia and Prussia had stood idly by, ignoring all attempts by Vienna to engage them in an all-out assault on Napoleon's system in Europe at a time when such concerted action would have stood a good chance of bringing him down. Austria alone had made a good run at it, but had failed in the end. Prussia, too frightened and debased to act, would endure another four more years of truncated existence. Russia would endure invasion and defeat before it expelled Napoleon in 1812 from its wintry desolation and only after Moscow was largely burned to the ground.

Even Britain held Austria in contempt for losing another war, chalking it up to another bad investment in Austrian arms. An article in a then-popular London periodical, *The Gentlemen's Magazine*, sneered in contempt at Austria's capitulation:

> This Treaty is certainly one of the most singular documents in the annals of diplomacy. We see a Christian King, calling himself the father of his people, disposing of 400,000 of his subjects, like swine in a market. . . . We see through the whole of this instrument the humiliation of the weak and unfortunate Francis,

who has preferred the resignation of his fairest territories to restoring to his vassals their liberties, and giving them that interest in the public cause which their valor would have known how to protect. . . .[18]

This from an empire who had suffered such a defeat in Spain that it had been forced to remove its expeditionary force under Sir John Moore in January 1809 and whose abortive landing at Walcheren after Wagram with 40,000 troops ended without accomplishing anything but the death of ten percent of its force from malaria.

Nonetheless, the Austrian capitulation in 1809 reduced her to a completely landlocked country, but which retained most of the core Habsburg possessions of Austria, Hungary and Bohemia/Moravia. She was saddled with another crippling indemnity of some 85 million francs. After four major wars against France with increasingly severe results, Francis would now conclude that, perhaps, collaboration was the only viable course. In this, he found comfort and fulsome support from Metternich, who had reached the same conclusion.

NOTES

1. Seward 50.
2. Metternich 72.
3. Metternich 85–87.
4. Ingrao 234.
5. Ingrao 235.
6. Taylor, A.J.P., *The Italian Problem in European Diplomacy, 1847–49,* (Manchester: Manchester University Press, 1970) 13.
7. Taylor 235.
8. Rothenberg, Gunther E., *Napoleon's Great Adversary,* (New York: Sarpedon Publishers, 1982.)
9. Metternich 80.
10. Rothenberg 160.
11. Rothenberg 161.
12. Castelli, I.F., *Memoiren meines Lebens,* (Milltown: Hansebooks, 2017)
13. Castle, Ian, "The Battle of Wagram," *The Campaign of 1809 Symposium.* (Vienna: 2009) 191–199.
14. Castle 100.
15. Castle 104.
16. Castle 106.
17. Castle 116.
18. Jefferies, F., *The Gentlemen's Magazine, Vol. 79, part 2,* (London: 1809) 1065.

Part III

Chapter Eleven

Metternich, Radetzky and the Policy of Collaboration

The character of Klemens von Metternich is a subject of intense controversy and cannot be avoided in this biography because of his immense impact on Austrian and European politics and history. His relationship with Francis also cannot be minimized. Yet viewing Austrian policy and practice in diplomacy and statecraft after Metternich's appointment in 1809 is made difficult by the vain, eccentric and often disingenuous nature of the Emperor's foreign minister and eventual *Staatskanzler*.

The publication of Metternich's Autobiography after his death by his son stirred intense interest and controversy. French historian Albert Sorel denounced Metternich's account of events and his role in the denouement of the Napoleonic Wars: "He makes himself the light of the world; he dazzles himself with his own rays in the mirror which he holds perpetually before his eyes."[1] Another historian wrote: "Totally vain, [Metternich] might just as well have entitled the memoirs he eventually left behind *The History of Me and the World* because, as he never tired of pointing out, the destiny of both marched together."[2]

Indeed, a fair reading of his book is to hear Metternich tell the story of his own pre-eminent role in the downfall of Napoleon in a narrative that sets it forth in the following manner. Francis had increasingly recognized the genius in his midst after having been repeatedly misguided and badly served by Thugut, Cobenzl, Colloredo, Stadion and even his own brother since the start of his reign. His appointment to Paris gave Metternich the unparalleled opportunity to study the mind and soul of the most dominant personality seen on the continent of Europe in centuries. He had cracked the code in these years and upon his return to Vienna, was sure he knew what to do. In the ashes of Wagram, he found a willing partner in the Emperor who shared his deeply conservative principles but was in desperate need of a minister of supreme

Figure 11.1. Klemens von Metternich, Foreign Minister, circa 1815. Sir Thomas Lawrence. Kunsthistoriches Museum, Vienna.

intelligence and guile to bring Bonaparte down. Using the unique insights he and only he had gained while in Paris, Metternich was able to maneuver Napoleon into his own destruction and liberate all of Europe.

Metternich and, posthumously, his son Richard, carefully cultivated the image of the supremely clever manipulator; that it was all part of a plan crafted by him that had, by careful and expert application, resulted in triumph. This egocentric view of history, aside from being false, obscures the true genius of Metternich; that of an unparalleled improviser with exquisite timing on a grand scale. A diplomatist with the full toolbox. A charmer. A flatterer. Ultra-perceptive and extremely intelligent. The life of a party who provided the snap, crackle and pop to any event. The man who knew just the right thing to say and exactly when to say it. In truth, a careful consideration of the facts makes it clear that it was not at all a preconceived plan; far from it. In 1809, Metternich believed that French hegemony over Europe would continue for the rest of Napoleon's life.[3] Rather, the improbable success of Austria and its Monarchy would arise from a partnership between Francis and Metternich and a policy of cautious, watchful, expectant waiting.

Metternich's assessment of Francis must be evaluated with knowledge of his own biases and prejudices. Indeed, more may be grasped about the

Emperor by Metternich's own policies and actions, taken with the Emperor's concurrence and approval and indirectly betraying the political mind of his master, than the direct pronouncements about Francis made by Metternich himself. Metternich was not the principal advisor to Francis as *Staatskanzler* until 1821, some six years after Waterloo, except in foreign affairs. Even after 1821, he would have competition for the Emperor's favor, and rivals too.

How does Metternich describe the personality of Emperor Francis? We receive only small vignettes in his Autobiography, but they are revealing nonetheless. One is after the disastrous 1809 rising in which hopes initially soared after the victory at Aspern, only to be dashed by the crushing defeats at Wagram and Znaim, described previously. Some of the character traits Metternich attributes to Francis include "hearty kindness," patience, calmness, self-possession, candor and strength of personality.

Francis' uncertainty and insecurity regarding military matters resulted in his having layers upon layers of military advisers including the *Hofkriegsrat*, the Army Commander, the Quartermaster Chief of Staff, and Marshals Bellegarde, Duka and Bubna revolving around him and dissecting every military issue with Francis. He was a man used to over-promises and under-performances, harried by lack of money to adequately fund a dwindling military resource he saw as his last and best hope for preserving his shrinking monarchy. Metternich, with absolutely no background or understanding of military matters, helped him not at all here.

The partnership that developed between Francis and his foreign minister was a collaboration that would have echoes a century and a half later between U.S. President Nixon and Henry Kissinger, a parallel Walter Isaacson noted in his biography of Kissinger.[4] In the aftermath of Wagram, Francis now held the reins of governance in his reduced *imperium* very tightly. No policy or plan of consequence was embarked upon without his knowledge or approval, no matter who the author, and only after much scrutiny.

> Defeat also brought the downfall of the war party. Although Stadion and Archduke Charles resigned voluntarily, Francis went one step further by prohibiting his *generalissimus* from participating in all public affairs. If the other archdukes were spared the humiliation, they also lost most of their influence over state affairs. For the next quarter century, Francis left no doubt about who was in control and what he expected from the men who served him. His determination was not lost on Stadion's successor.... Metternich also knew his place. Although he did not share Francis' rejection of the Enlightenment and the populist reforms it had inspired, he realized that the emperor would sooner change ministers than his policies. Having carefully climbed to the top of the ladder, he had no intention of causing his own fall by being out of step with Francis' domestic agenda.[5]

"We shall have much to retrieve," Francis had spoken to Metternich as they left the field of Wagram. In these words, and the black humor one reads from this time of his life, one can discern the kind of man Francis had become. A stoic. A steady hand. A man used to disappointment and unlikely to ever entirely trust the assurances or promises of anyone; especially in the military field. Hard working to a fault, pouring over his papers from morning to night, consulting with advisors and yet, and this is seldom mentioned, also granting audiences to common petitioners at his palace. It is a stoic, candid, hard-eyed pragmatic Emperor that one gleans from the pages of Metternich's own pen. It is this personality, alternately described by others as "dour and suspicious" or "cynical," that begins to emerge from this period and the wreckage of his empire.

Francis' changes in ministry were far more rapid than in the time of Maria Theresa, Joseph and Leopold II. As has been seen, all three were served by Kaunitz for decades, and served well. The change of ministries by Francis between 1792 and 1809, then, were relatively frequent and provide another clue to the mystery of this monarch. On the one hand, it could be inferred that Francis was looking for his Kaunitz and finally found him in Metternich. Indeed, in the great sweep of history, the bookends of Kaunitz and Metternich's ministries extend from 1753 to 1848; a nearly hundred-year period in which these two *Staatskanzlers* were the chief political officers of the Monarchy. On the other hand, by this method, he largely forfeited the credit he might otherwise have deserved.

SALVAGING A DEFEATED EMPIRE

The near-collapse of his monarchy and state from the one he inherited in 1792 was nearly complete by 1810. The great Austrian field marshal, Radetzky, about whom we will discuss more momentarily, concluded in December 1810 that Austria had become a "middle power situated between two superpowers, France and Russia."[6] The despair and humiliation Francis undoubtedly felt keenly might best be capsulized by skipping ahead for a moment to a description of his final face-to-face meeting with Napoleon at Dresden in May 1812. It was just before the invasion of Russia, which Austria had been forced to join by the terms of an alliance agreed between the two empires in March. The scene is described by author Adam Zamoyski:

> At nine every morning he would hold his levee, which was the greatest display of power Europe had seen for centuries. It was attended by the Austrian Emperor and all the German kings and princes. . . . He would then lead them in to assist at the toilette of [Empress] Marie-Louise. They would watch her pick her

way through an astonishing assemblage of jewels . . . trying on and discarding one after the other and occasionally offering one to her barely older stepmother, the Empress Marie Ludovica, who simmered with shame and fury. . . . Her distaste was magnified by the embarrassment and resentment she felt in the midst of this splendor, and that the poor condition of the Austrian finances allowed her only a few jewels, which looked paltry next to those of Marie Louise.

In the evening, they would dine at Napoleon's table off the silver gilt dinner service Marie-Louise had been given as a wedding present by the City of Paris, and which she had thoughtfully brought along. The company would assemble and enter the drawing room in reverse order of seniority, each announced by a crier, beginning with mere excellencies, going on to the various ducal and royal highnesses, and culminating with their imperial highnesses the Emperor and Empress of Austria. Awhile later, the doors would swing open and Napoleon would stride in, with just one word of announcement: 'The Emperor!' He was also the only one present who kept his hat on.[7]

"I cannot stand the creature," Francis remarked to Metternich at Dresden.[8] Leopold I had never been forced to such an extremity by Louis XIV, nor had Maria Theresa by Louis XV or Frederick the Great. The effort needed to disguise his personal revulsion at the pretentions and ostentation of his parvenu son-in-law on this occasion can only be imagined but, for the good of the Empire and of necessity, Francis swallowed his pride and indignation until he returned to Vienna to await events.

But to return to the narrative begun after Wagram, Francis and his foreign minister began to turn to profit some chances that came their way in the wake of defeat and debasement as 1809 turned into 1810.

The first bit of luck was Napoleon's granting of Austria's former West Galician territory that it had received in the partitions of Poland decades before, to the Duchy of Warsaw, enlarging this hostile state on the border of Russia while also moving 50,000 French occupying troops there to ensure its independence from Russia and Prussia as well as its dependence on France. The very existence of the Duchy was obnoxious to Prussia, who could do nothing, and menacing to Russia, who could, in time.

The second was the oppressive impact that the Continental System embargo had on Russian trade which Russia began to simply disregard in 1811 as relations cooled. For Napoleon's Continental System to work, it was an all or nothing proposition. If there was any significant breach in the wall opposing English continental trade, transshipment of manufactures and colonial raw material across the offending country combined with rampant smuggling made the adherence of all other states a mere hindrance to the flow of continental gold to London. By 1811, to add insult to injury, the Tsar began imposing tariffs on French luxury goods. More French troops were transferred from southern to northern Germany and the Baltic German states, nearer to St. Petersburg, the Russian capital.

The greatest piece of luck, however, amidst the gradually worsening relations between the Tsar and Napoleon, was the French emperor's decision to divorce the Empress Josephine in December 1809. Austria's ambassador in Paris, after Metternich was relieved of the post, was none other than Karl Phillip von Schwarzenberg who kept Metternich fully informed of the ongoing negotiations between Napoleon and Tsar Alexander and his eventual surprise when the Russian court turned Napoleon down, twice.

Schwarzenberg had gotten wind of the fact that Napoleon had sought to pressure the Tsar by implying that if Alexander did not consent to a marriage with one of his sisters, Napoleon would seek a bride in Vienna; a fact that Schwarzenberg conveyed to Metternich. Schwarzenberg was instructed that if the subject should arise, he should not under any circumstances, rebuff such an inquiry. By February 7, 1810, Schwarzenberg had executed a preliminary commitment to the marriage.

The use of advantageous marriage was a well-practiced Habsburg diplomatic weapon, but this one imposed a heavy personal weight on Francis and his eldest child. Before negotiations became serious in Paris, Francis directed Metternich that, while for reasons of state he would favor such a marriage, he would not force his daughter, Marie Louise, into a marriage with Napoleon.[9] Marie Louise herself had grown up in the oppressive shadow of Napoleon and the damage he had done to her family and her country, but she had never met him. The loathing the Empress had for Napoleon has already been noted and in the aftermath of Wagram and the Treaty of Schönbrunn, there could scarcely have been a man in Europe that might have repulsed the young Archduchess more.

The willingness of both Francis and Marie Louise to consent to the marriage speaks more loudly than almost any other fact to their acceptance of the reality of accommodation and a new policy of outright collaboration with France. The marriage would obviously be accompanied by an alliance; a fact that Metternich recognized and cultivated immediately. His short-term goal was to detach Russia from her alliance with France and to replace Russia with Austria for her own safety. The alliance between France and Austria came later, in March 1812.

When approached by Metternich, to his surprise and delight, the Archduchess quickly affirmed her willingness to serve her father and the country by consenting to the marriage, if that was what her father desired of her. In truth, unknown to her or her father at the time, the marriage between her and Napoleon, which was consummated at Compiègne on March 27, would be a very happy one on both sides. Whatever her misgivings might have been in

Figure 11.2. Marie Louise, Empress of the French 1810–1814. Francois Gerard. The Louvre Museum, Paris

Vienna, Marie Louise became a loving and devoted wife to Napoleon, whom she delighted a year later, on March 20, 2011, with the birth of a son and heir, Napoleon François Charles.

The importance of this dynastic marriage at the time is obscured by subsequent events that made it irrelevant. At the time, however, it was the first step toward a reconciliation and collaboration with France that Metternich and, reluctantly, Francis had concluded was the only viable path for Austria to take; certainly, in the short term and perhaps in the long run as well. Had Napoleon not wrecked his military empire and had he died on the throne of France, the next emperor of the French would have had Francis as his grandfather and Habsburg blood in his veins. It was a situation like the dynastic marriage arranged by Maria Theresa for her youngest daughter with Louis XVI, and made for the same reason; to cement a relationship and alliance between the two most powerful continental empires.

The dynastic marriage of 1809 did not produce immediate territorial concessions by France, but discussions between Metternich and Napoleon regarding the eventual return of Austria's coastal Illyrian provinces (now modern-day Croatia), Dalmatia and compensation for the loss of the Galician territories to the Duchy of Warsaw became a topic of discussion between them, especially in the event of war with Russia.[10]

Napoleon continued his provocation of Russia with the annexation of the Duchy of Oldenburg in 1811. The Tsar's sister, Catherine, who had been the object of Napoleon's initial interest as a second wife and whose hand in marriage had been rejected, had been married by her brother to the Duke of Oldenburg. This Duchy, next to Denmark, seemingly had little intrinsic value. The annexation therefore seemed a personal slap to the Tsar. The Tsar wrote his sister Catherine just before the annexation, on December 26, 1810, revealing to her that he believed war with France was inevitable.

RADETZKY VON RADETZ

On July 30, 1809, Field Marshal Johann Prince Lichtenstein was appointed commander of the main Austrian army. While Lichtenstein was an able commander, perhaps his greatest contribution was his recognition of the other great general to arise from the ranks of the Austrian military service, Joseph Count Radetzky von Radetz. Lichtenstein immediately requested Radetzky be appointed chief of the Quartermaster General Staff. While Radetzky was already a field marshal at that point, he initially declined, according to his memoirs, thinking he was not qualified for such an important assignment. Reportedly, Francis replied to Radetzky in a personal audience with his typical, back-handed, black humor: "Your character guarantees that you will not make stupid mistakes on purpose and if you merely make ordinary mistakes, that I am already used to...."[11]

Radetzky von Radetz would have a major impact not merely on Austrian military history but on the Austrian state's destiny, as we shall see, later in life. It is worthwhile therefore to pause for a moment to get to know this extraordinary individual for whom one of the most famous martial musical pieces in history was composed by none other than Johann Strauss. His name is also the title of one of the most famous pieces of Austrian literature depicting the late imperial era, *The Radetzky March*, by Joseph Roth in 1932.

An orphan of noble birth, Radetzky was raised by his grandfather, and began a military career early in life. He had briefly been educated at the Theresian Academy in Vienna and became a cadet in 1785. By the time of the Turkish War, he was an officer and served as an adjutant to Lacy and von Laudon, thereby having an opportunity to observe staff and command operations at close range by two of Austria's best generals at that time. Francis would have met him then as a young lieutenant. When war with France began, Radetzky was initially stationed in the Netherlands and then on the Rhine.

Nonetheless, and somewhat surprisingly, Radetzky never received a formal, military education. Rather, he was self-taught from experience and

Figure 11.3. Joseph, Graf Radetzky von Radetz. Carl Gutsch circa 1840.

observation and became one of the most astute and critical military thinkers in Austrian military history. To summarize his philosophy in a paragraph or two cannot do him justice. Nonetheless, his experience in battles of the Revolutionary period in Germany and Italy convinced him of the futility of the so-called "cordon" strategy favored by Austrian strategists, particularly the Archduke Charles, that involved dispersal of armies over wide areas to defend specific geographic points. Radetzky was the first and foremost Austrian military leader to grasp the lesson of Napoleon and his method of war that the great military thinker Jomini wrote about in retrospect: to concentrate force, seek out the main enemy army and defeat it in battle.

Radetzky was a highly skilled, tactical field commander but his personality and grasp of military strategy and logistics at the highest levels was what set him apart. After Wagram, it was Radetzky who reorganized the army between 1809–1813 and whose brilliance crafted the final campaign that defeated Napoleon once and for all in 1814.

His presence in this period was somewhat obscured by the cumbersome and frustrating structure of command at the highest level already discussed. In 1809, Radetzky, as Chief of the Quartermaster General Staff, was subordinated to the *Hofkriegsrat* and the army commander (Lichtenstein) and, before any major action could be taken, he was required to submit his recommendations and supporting documents to the Emperor's personal military advisors and Francis himself.[12] It was a frustrating and difficult process and early on, Radetzky wanted to resign. In a memorandum to Lichtenstein, Radetzky summarized his frustration and his view of the reason for Austria's record of defeat in the wars since the French Revolution. The reason, he wrote:

> . . . was Austria's chronic unpreparedness for war. Every defeat was followed by a great outcry for army reform, but at the same time there always was an ever-greater desire not to spend the necessary funds. As a result, our armies never were strong enough or adequately equipped. After every battle won by the valor of the troops, the means to exploit success were lacking, while after every defeat, the army had to look for salvation in retreat and a hasty armistice. Radetzky believed that the basic cause for this state of affairs was that the army never had been popular among the masses, while the higher classes too had little interest in a strong army.[13]

The complaint and his thoughts evidently had a greater effect than he might have realized when he penned them. In December 1809, Radetzky was made a full member of the *Hofkreigsrat*, which gave him much greater power to make reforms. Lichtenstein himself resigned in 1810, eliminating another bureaucratic obstacle, although the Prince had been supportive of Radetzky's proposals for reform. In 1810, Radetzky reorganized the Austrian general staff into functional sections, such as cartography, intelligence, and so forth.[14] Incompetent generals and officers were cashiered.

As ever, however, Francis' ability to maintain Austria even as a second-rate military power was hobbled by financial constraints of the highest order and this, in turn, limited what even Radetzky could do. The heavy expenses of four futile and increasingly disastrous wars, coming after Joseph's Turkish War, and the indemnities imposed on Austria by France had reduced the Monarchy to *de facto* bankruptcy. On February 20, 1811, the new finance minister, Joseph Count Wallis, issued a *Finanzpatent* due to the rampant inflation that had resulted from the government's methods of financing the latest wars and other government expenditures. The use of gold or silver coin had virtually disappeared years earlier in place of paper money printed by the government. The greater the need, the more money was printed. A six-fold increase in paper currency to 1.437 million florins had reduced banknotes to only a twelfth of their face value. Private credit was no longer available to the government either, after years and years of borrowing. The results of the war of 1809 had been a loss of another 3.5 million subjects and a debt that now reached 700 million florins.[15]

Austria's inflation had been further exacerbated by French counterfeit money that flooded the country in a deliberate action to undermine the Austrian economy. In 1810, the State had been forced to call in silver plate and other bullion in private hands. The *Finanzpatent* addressed the dire situation by undeclared bankruptcy. All existing paper money and small coins would be exchanged for new money at a rate of five to one. Taxes would be paid only in the new currency.[16] This would temporarily relieve the situation until 1813 when Austria began to re-arm for war and began printing money again to do so.

Relief also came, ironically, from the restriction of the size of the army imposed by the terms of the Treaty of Schönbrunn by Napoleon from a high of 253,202,864 florins expended on the army in 1809 to 47,795,343 florins in 1811.[17] While Austria never actually reduced her army to the 150,000-limit imposed by the treaty, it was reduced substantially in size and cost in these years. Field Marshal Bellegarde, as president of the *Hofkriegsrat* in 1811, improvised by freezing pay and allowances, hiring troops out for public and private labor, reducing rations, halting production of new weapons and depleting remaining stocks of uniforms and boots.[18] The British agent in Vienna noted to his government in 1812 that "The army has been so extremely reduced and what remains of it is so badly paid, clothed and equipped that 60,000 men would be the most that the Government could at the present employ on active service."[19]

The impact of Austria's financial and economic situation in these years was dire indeed, especially on those outside the land-owning aristocracy. The bourgeoisie of the Austrian Empire were essentially wiped out. Civil servants and soldiers, paid in the near-worthless paper money, were reduced to poverty while demands for their service and loyalty remained as high or higher than ever before. France and Britain, albeit for different reasons, prospered during the war; France due to the results of plunder and oppressive taxation and indemnities imposed on others, Britain due to its accelerating industrial economy that, heavily taxed though it was, increasingly could bear the strain. Austria had neither of these luxuries and languished in penury. As a result, her options and scope of maneuver were severely limited. Investment of any kind in infrastructure, military weapons or industry was virtually non-existent and the effects of this destitution would linger long after the Napoleonic Wars ended.

NOTES

1. Holmberg, Tom. "Metternich: The Autobiography, 1773–1815." *The Napoleon Series*. April 2005.

2. Dallas, Gregor. "Metternich: The Autobiography, 1773–1815." *The Napoleon Series*. April 2005.
3. Seward 75.
4. Isaacson, Walter, *Kissinger, A Biography*, (New York: Simon & Schuster, 2013) 143-144.
5. Ingrao 237.
6. Rothenberg 223.
7. Zamoyski, Adam, *Moscow 1812; Napoleon's Fatal March*, (New York: Harper Perennial, 2004) 109.
8. Seward 78.
9. Metternich 119–121.
10. Metternich 136–137.
11. Rothenberg 219; Radetzky, *Selbstbiographie*, p. 69.
12. Rothenberg 220.
13. Rothenberg 220.
14. Rothenberg 221.
15. Ingrao 237–238.
16. Rothenberg 221–222.
17. Rothenberg 222.
18. Ibid.
19. Rothenberg 223.

Chapter Twelve

Resurrection

The collaboration of Austria with Napoleonic France, as galling and reluctant as it might have been, had another side to it that became increasingly important by 1812 and would last into the Congress of Vienna after the war; the growing power of Russia and the possibility that it might succeed France in hegemonic power over the European continent. Austrian policy in 1812 was increasingly conducted with this fear in mind as much as the repeated defeats it had sustained in the wars with France.

A proposal by Tsar Alexander to form another alliance with Russia against France was presented in Vienna in the Autumn of 1810 and discovered by Metternich when he returned from a mission to Paris earlier in the year. The overture was rejected by Francis with Metternich's strong concurrence to maintain as much freedom of action as possible to maneuver with the current of events as they transpired in 1811 and 1812. The earlier mission to Paris involved discussions between Metternich and Napoleon about Austria's position in case of war with Russia and the possibilities of territorial gains by Austria in Dalmatia and in the Balkans, particularly in Serbia.

Francis gave Metternich an audience while in Gratz in October, 1810 in which it was agreed ". . . above all . . . to secure for Austria freedom in her political action when the moment came for decision with regard to the coming war."[1] Put another way, as the continent braced for a coming show-down between France and Russia, whenever war broke out, Francis would remain as neutral as possible, above all not disrupting the fragile but real relationship that had been cultivated with Napoleon, until events made clear which way Austria should turn. As Metternich put it, "the fate of Napoleon's undertaking . . . will give us the direction which we shall afterwards have to take. . . ."[2] In the meantime, Bellegarde, Radetzky, von Wallis, Metternich and the Emperor's other ministers would do what could be done to strengthen Austria's financial and military situation to be as ready as possible when the moment came.

This tilt toward France and away from Russia was not popular at Francis' court. His brothers, the Archdukes, hated it. His wife opposed it as well. The Hungarian nobility balked at providing necessary subsidies when its Diet convened which, given the desperate need for capital resulted in Francis taking the extreme step of dismissing the Diet and taxing the Hungarians anyway. Francis would not budge, this time, having been goaded into war in the past by his family and impetuous members of his court. Caution and biding his time was now the watchword.

Due to the tendency, in hindsight, to assume inevitably what did happen was bound to happen, it is often believed that Austria was implacably hostile to Napoleon and was simply waiting for the right moment to strike and bring him down. This common belief has also been fanned by Metternich's later writings that attribute to him a certain clairvoyance:

> I foresaw that neither [Napoleon] nor his undertakings would escape the consequence of rashness and extravagance. The when and the how I could not pretend to determine. Thus my reason pointed out to me the direction I had to take in order not to interfere with the natural development of the situation and to keep open for Austria the chances which the greatest of all powers—the power of circumstances—might offer, sooner or later, under the strong government of its monarch, for the much-threatened prosperity of the Empire.[3]

Until 1809, implacable hostility and opportunistic waiting was the overarching policy urged upon Francis and upon which he had acted time and again. The great humbling of 1809 and the marriage of his daughter altered the equation. Between 1810–13 Francis, and therefore Austria, would just as easily have formed a dynastic and diplomatic pact with Napoleon, junior partner though it might have been, to survive and prosper as best it could in a new continental European order. Napoleon's defeat in Russia and his stubborn refusal to compromise thereafter, and only that, pushed Austria increasingly in the other direction, but not without misgivings.

The state of Austrian military preparedness for war in 1812 was as parlous as ever. The British agent, King, reported that in assembling an imperial army in the last extremity, the Hungarians could not be counted on and that "the ill-will of the Hungarians is deeply rooted."[4] In March of 1812, a bizarre, formal alliance with France was reached that demonstrated the lengths to which Francis would go to placate both France and Russia in a balancing act without parallel. Napoleon demanded an Austrian "auxiliary corps" of 30,000 to join in the invasion of Russia. Francis agreed, but it was stipulated that Austria would not declare war on Russia and that the territory of the Austrian Empire would remain inviolate to both Russia and France. This worked to Russia's advantage because with French armies unable to pass through Austria, Russia would not have to defend a large swath of its southern territories.

A DELICATE BALANCING

In June, the war began with Napoleon at the head of an immense army of French and allied troops, including an Austrian contingent on the farthest, right flank led by Prince Schwarzenberg. On August 12, the Austrians engaged and defeated a Russian army at Gorodetshna. Napoleon was sufficiently impressed with Schwarzenberg's command that he suggested to Francis that the Prince be made a full field marshal. Francis complied and granted the honor, but not until August 1813 when Schwarzenberg would take the field against Napoleon.

Napoleon received another, not entirely unexpected gift on June 18, 1812 when the United States declared war on Great Britain, making herself thereby an ally of France and posing an immediate threat to British Canada and its Caribbean possessions. Military operations would take some time to get underway, but invasions of Canada were undertaken from Michigan and New York in 1812–13. These were beaten back by British regulars and Canadian militia, but Britain was too distracted and weak to undertake any offensive

Figure 12.1. Napoleon, Russia–1812. Adolph Northen.

of its own in this corner of the world and had to content itself with a naval blockade of the coastline, which devastated American agricultural exports. By 1814, however, a British landing in the Chesapeake Bay and victory at Bladensburg resulted in the occupation of Washington and the burning of the White House, the Capitol and the Navy Yard.

By November, with Napoleon's army decimated by disease and cold and in full retreat to Smolensk, Schwarzenberg reached a verbal cease fire with his Russian counterpart and withdrew his troops to winter quarters near Byalistok. On January 30, 1813, Schwarzenberg was allowed to sign a formal convention with the Russians "neutralizing" his corps which was then removed to Galicia. Metternich informed the French military command that Austria was now withdrawing from a war it had never declared. Napoleon was forced to accept this *fait accompli*, as he was now facing the widening Sixth Coalition that included Russia, Prussia, Sweden and, of course, Britain. Austria was the only remaining great power not at war with him and still his nominal ally, at least.

This narrative is not a military history, but before passing on to discuss the Austrian role in the eventual downfall of the French Empire and Napoleon, it is worthy to consider for a moment the curious attribution of leadership given to Russia and Tsar Alexander as the main force that conquered Napoleon. This myth begins with the commonly held misconception that the Russian army defeated the French during the five-month long campaign between June and November 1812. This never happened.

The one major battle fought between the Russians and the French during the entire invasion, from start to finish, was Kutuzov's last great battle, at Borodino, on September 7, outside Moscow. The battle was a tactical defeat for Russia and a bloodbath, although the Russian army withdrew in good order.

The defeat of Napoleon was a matter of logistics and weather; the long supply lines from Central Europe, the destitution of the Russian countryside that provided no nourishment or support, the enormous demands of such a large army so far from its base for food, ammunition and supplies and, of course, the increasingly harsh Russian winter. It was the retreat from Moscow, defections from nominally allied contingents, horrific attrition from cold and starvation on the way out and effective harassment by Russian cavalry on Napoleon's straggling rear-guard that ruined him.

In fact, it comes a surprise that, apart from Alexander Suvorov's Italian campaign in 1799-1800 while Napoleon was in Egypt, the Russian army never had any particular, significant success against the French, unless it was in combination with Austria. Russian generals suffered several ghastly defeats, including Austerlitz and Friedland, as well as a number of bloody, tactical defeats such as Eylau and Borodino. Between 1800-1815, the Russian army never won any single, significant battle against Napoleon or any of his marshals except when subordinated to the command of Austrian generals.

Prussian generals fared no better. The stunning and catastrophic defeat at Jena was an all-Prussian affair and ranks as dismal a defeat as Austerlitz or any other battle in the long list of military catastrophes of the Revolutionary or Napoleonic wars. Prussia's military prowess in history rightly stems from the era of Frederick the Great—before Napoleon—and from the mid-19th century brilliance of Helmuth von Moltke—after Napoleon–not in this era. As late as the battle of Waterloo in 1815, which was actually a series of four battles, the legendary Marshal Blücher was defeated at Ligny by Napoleon on the way to his confrontation with Wellington.

By contrast, the Austrians—so often derided for their military weakness or incompetence—defeated Napoleon himself no less than three times before the end. Russia had no military commander who ever defeated Napoleon. Austria had four: Alvinczi, the Archduke Charles, Schwarzenberg and Radetzky. Moreover, as we have already seen, Austrian military commanders, especially the Archduke Charles before Wagram, regularly inflicted defeats on subordinate French generals in the Revolutionary and Napoleonic periods. Until the Austrians took the field against Napoleon in 1813, the other two Eastern monarchies fared no better against Napoleon than they had ever done. Once expelled from Russia, as we shall see, Napoleon would rally and continue to inflict stinging defeats on the combined Russian and Prussian armies in Germany.

To be sure, Austria too had suffered humiliating defeats at the hands of Napoleon but in and among them were flashes of success. In truth, Austria was Napoleon's most proximate and dangerous military opponent, as Napoleon himself knew well. For all its financial and economic deficiencies, Austria remained a subdued but potent potential enemy. The credit so casually given to the mercurial Tsar Alexander or even to Wellington obscure the eventually decisive role that Austria, Francis and, by 1813, his highly talented military commanders had on the outcome of the wars. While history rightly credits each of the Great Powers in their own way with contributing to the end of Napoleon, as we will see, the greatest came from his most persistent continental adversary in Vienna.

AUSTRIA AS THE FULCRUM OF EUROPE

Immediately a chorus of voices in Vienna urged war on France but here the diplomatic skills of Metternich, supported by the will of the Emperor, achieved consequences nothing short of remarkable. Francis rejected the calls for war within his own court and set Metternich to play the French and the forming Sixth Coalition for all they were worth, while a new army was mobilized and fitted for war as best it could be. His will to remain neutral in early 1813 to maximize Austria's advantage extended to his brother Johann who tried to arouse the *Alpenbund* in the Tyrol, Salzburg and Carinthia to rise against the Bavarians who were still allied to France. The main conspirators were easily discovered by the *Geheime Staatspolizei* and arrested. The Archduke Johann was banished from court.

The period between Austria's withdrawal from the war in January 1813 and its entry into the war in August, was a period of "armed neutrality". Metternich was directed to attempt to mediate between the Sixth Coalition and France while, at the same time, pursuing Austria's own interest, leveraging the defeat of France and swelling Coalition forces, to secure restoration of Austria's lost territories in Croatia and Dalmatia.

Some might argue that the following months of negotiations and policy making were Metternich's finest hours. His historic last meeting with Napoleon on June 26, 1813 in Dresden brought Austria's carefully saved diplomatic and rapidly rising military strength to bear with decisive results for Francis, his empire and for Europe. The "fate of Napoleon's undertaking", obscure in 1810, was now increasingly apparent in mid-1813. Yet neither Francis nor Metternich foresaw the total collapse of Napoleon and his empire just yet. That would occur a year later, brought about by Napoleon's towering hubris in rejecting anything less than continued French dominance on the continent of Europe.

Rather, the possibility of a humbled, constrained Napoleon as a counterweight to the burgeoning power of Russia with Austria balancing between the two would have been as welcome an outcome as any to Francis with his grandson, Napoleon II, eventually inheriting the French imperial throne. The moment of truth had arrived and all Europe watched to see what Vienna would do.

If Austria maintained its alliance with France and did not join the Coalition, Napoleon might well hang on. Remarkably, since the retreat from Russia, he had cobbled together another mighty army that was massing in Germany. Less than 100,000 men out of the Grande Armée of over 600,000 that had invaded Russia, had walked out alive. With these as a core, Napoleon built up the Army of the Main to 140,000 and, combined with the Army of the Elbe, brought his strength in Germany up to over 200,000 by April 2013.

On April 30, his army crossed the Saale and on May 2, defeated Blütcher and Russia's Prince Wittgenstein (Kutuzov's successor) at Lützen, in Saxony, near Leipzig. Both Tsar Alexander and King Frederick William III were pres-

Figure 12.2. Tsar Alexander of Russia by Franz Kruger, circa 1837. The Hermitage Museum, St. Petersburg

ent and watched as their armies retreated once more before their very eyes. On May 22, Napoleon inflicted another defeat on the Russo-Prussian armies at Bautzen. There was no guarantee that the Russians and the Prussians would drive to Paris and depose Napoleon. In fact, several Russian commanders had voiced their misgivings to the Tsar about further operations against the French after Napoleon had been driven from Russia into central Europe.

On the other hand, should Austria renounce its alliance with France and join the Coalition, logic counselled that Napoleon would have no choice but to submit. Again, it was not necessary for Napoleon and his regime to go at this point; merely be forced back into its old boundaries and allow the other Great Powers to re-draw the map of Europe with Austria the fulcrum of the new order.

It was in this atmosphere that Francis and Metternich proposed an armistice which France, Russia and Prussia immediately accepted at Pläswitz on June 4. The armistice would last, with an extension, until August 10. It was the first sign of the resurrection of Habsburg power in Europe. Both sides now set about courting Vienna.

Francis and Metternich would not be rushed into playing their cards too quickly this time. Shortly thereafter, in conversations with the Russians, Metternich learned that among the terms of the Russian-Prussian alliance was that after the peace, Prussia would have Russia's support in annexing the kingdom of Saxony. Prussia would compensate by ceding Polish territory to Russia. This confirmed the suspicions and fears in Vienna that Prussian power in Germany, backed by Russia, would threaten Austria's own security as much as Napoleonic France. Further, the contemplated exchange would move Russia ever closer to the center of Europe.

As Francis pored over his maps in conferences with his ministers, a plan took shape in the Hofburg, as more information became known, that had at its heart minimizing the influence of both France and Russia, but in no way contemplated the overthrow of Napoleon. A balance was to be sought with Austria at the heart of it. By then, Metternich had also learned that, aided by British subsidies, Prussia and Russia had agreed not to seek a separate peace with Napoleon. Further, the terms of the Russo-Prussian alliance also included the dissolution of the Confederation of the Rhine, and withdrawal from (and independence for) Spain, Holland and Italy.[5] As can be seen, precipitously throwing in with the Coalition would have been very foolhardy indeed.

Negotiations and conversations were continued with Metternich holding the trump card of Austrian intervention or abstention. It was Austria's plan that was eventually agreed by the Russians and Prussians at Reichenbach on June 27. It was a more minimalist plan that required the end of French control over the Grand Duchy of Warsaw and its partition, Prussian expansion westward, not into Saxony or the Rhineland, the return of Dalmatia to Austria and the independence of the Northern "Hanseatic" cities in Germany. With this more moderate proposal, France would remain a powerful state and counterweight to Prussia and Russia on the continent.

The Tsar, and therefore the Prussian king, agreed reluctantly, but in return obtained a promise from Francis that if Napoleon could not be persuaded to accept this program, that Austria would join the Coalition and the harsher terms contemplated in the Russo-Prussian alliance would be sought. Once again, however, there was no program for "regime change" in Paris, merely a victory on the field of battle and the imposition of terms on Napoleon that he could not resist. The Russians and Prussians authorized Metternich to speak on their behalf and conduct the negotiations with Napoleon alone.

THE END OF COLLABORATION

Francis now dispatched Metternich to Dresden on June 26 to treat with Napoleon. It would be the last time the two men ever met. It proved to be a dramatic test of wills and diplomacy. Metternich provided some details of the meeting in his memoirs and in a letter to his wife immediately afterward. So did Napoleon's secretary, Baron Fain, and his aide-de-camp, Armand de Caulaincourt. As might be expected, their recollections and account of a six-hour interview vary to some extent, but the broad outlines of the conversation can be and have been discerned.

True to form, Napoleon, after being informed of the proposed peace terms reacted with cold contempt alternating with rage. Metternich, on the other hand, remained imperturbably calm, weathering each storm, then returning to the fray attempting to reason with and persuade the French Emperor to accept Austrian mediation and peace. These two men, who had come to know one another so well in other circumstances when Napoleon held all the cards, grappled with intensity as each sought to bend the other. This time, however, it was the Austrians who held the cards.

Whether feigned or genuine, the possibility that Austria might defect to the other side was felt by Napoleon, incongruously considering his harsh treatment of Austria, to be the unkindest cut of all. After years of flattery by Metternich, the dynastic marriage, the submissive collaboration of Austria after Wagram, the prospect of what Napoleon saw as betrayal by his father-in-law now loomed before him. By one account, the conversation reached a crescendo on this very point when Napoleon reportedly exclaimed "Three times have I replaced the Emperor Francis on his throne. I have promised always to live in peace with him. I have married his daughter. At the time I said to myself you are perpetrating a folly, but it was done and today I repent of it." [6]

The intransigence of Napoleon toward Austria, begrudging the cession of even the meaningless province (to him) of Dalmatia/Illyria seems inconceivable, in retrospect, had that been all that was required to have secured Austrian neutrality. Having defeated the Austrians in four wars, Napoleon could not bring himself to accept that this time, without a friend on the continent, he would be opposed for the first time by all four of the other Great Powers of Europe, if he spurned Austria's mediation. His rage alternated with almost pleading, and by all accounts, a candid explanation for his belligerent rejection of the Reichenbach proposals:

> "Your sovereigns who were born to their thrones cannot comprehend the feelings that move me. To them it is nothing to return to their capitals defeated. But I am a soldier. I need honor and glory. I cannot reappear among my people devoid of prestige. I must remain great, admired, covered with glory."

Here from Napoleon's own mouth is what made the Habsburgs what they were, what they had been, and what they would be for another century. Time and again, Francis and his dynasty could and did absorb defeat and the humiliating treaties that followed, but there was no revolution or coup that unseated him. Napoleon was prophetic. Defeat would be the end of Napoleon. But the Habsburgs lived on and survived, as Maria Theresa had done after defeat by Frederick the Great. It was the sheer weight of centuries upon centuries of legitimacy and deft exercise of often illusory wealth and power that enabled Francis, his ancestors and his heirs to return to their capital defeated and yet never be overthrown.

Yet Metternich turned the tables and reportedly replied "but when will this condition of things cease in which defeat and victory are alike reasons for continuing these dismal wars? If victorious, you insist upon the fruits of your victory. If defeated, you are determined to rise again." The menace of Napoleon's overbearing, aggressive imperial policies had run their course and now everyone would be against him. "You are lost, sire. I am sure of it," Metternich said after the interview, perhaps with equal parts of sorrow and dismay. "We shall meet again in Vienna," Napoleon replied.

In the end, Napoleon would not or perhaps could not accept the terms Metternich had brought to him and now Francis gave his assent, reluctantly, to join the Coalition and trust his fate to the fortunes of war against an enemy he had never beaten. Historians have taken different views of the conference, but when the objective facts of Austria's position are considered, the failure of the Austro-French alliance was more a defeat than a victory for Austrian policy. Francis and Metternich would nevertheless return to the concept of

Figure 12.3. Metternich and Napoleon, Marcolini Palace, Dresden. Woldemar Friedrich.

a balance between Napoleonic France and Russia time and again before the end.

LEADER OF THE SIXTH COALITION

Francis and Metternich, however, continued to extract concessions from his allies. The supreme commander of the Coalition forces would be Austria's Karl Philipp Schwarzenberg, former ambassador to Paris and the commander Napoleon had recommended to Francis be made a field marshal only a few months before. Francis bestowed the title of *Generalfeldmarschall* on Schwarzenberg upon his appointment. The field marshal immediately chose Radetzky as his chief of staff and it would be Radetzky, already a field marshal, whose strategy and planning formed the backbone of the military campaign that would culminate in the entry of the Coalition armies into Paris in 1814 and the abdication of Napoleon.

In this way, Francis had maneuvered his impoverished, exhausted Austrian Empire from the shadows of a defeated dependency of Napoleonic France into the leadership position, diplomatic and military, of a multi-state alliance and, indeed, of continental Europe. It was a position that Francis would occupy with growing confidence and power for the rest of his life. What is not clear is the relative contribution of Francis to the course of Austrian policy, as compared primarily to Metternich.

Most authors, in discussing this period and, for that matter, the role Austria would play in post-war Europe, reflexively attribute all credit to Metternich. This may be due to Metternich's own propensity to promote himself as the source of the system that would eventually bear his name in his own writings and those of his heirs. Conversely, there exists apparently very little in the way of notes or transcripts of the meetings, discussions and decisions taken by the Emperor, his other ministers or generals. Yet it would be inconsistent with Francis' meticulously, sometimes painstakingly slow, deliberative style to assume he had little to do with it all.

Francis had been at the pinnacle of European power politics and war far longer than Metternich. He had been baptized at the outset of his reign with war and its consequences. He had absorbed painful and deep lessons in over 21 years on the throne, not merely military ones, but political and diplomatic lessons. And not merely with Napoleon, with whom Metternich was intimately familiar, but the other players on the chess board of Europe, particularly Russia and Prussia. His fiercely controlling, workaholic personality, when it came to major decisions affecting his dynasty and the state he had created, cannot be ignored. It is nearly preposterous to believe that he was simply a passive by-stander in the formulation of one of the most remarkable come-backs in European history, as most historians seem to have assumed without bestirring themselves further. Perhaps this is because, in the end, Austrian state policy was what it was and it was of little concern to these authors to whom credit was due.

More likely than not, Metternich probably was one of the greatest contributors to a strategy and policy that grew and evolved in discussions with the Emperor and his ministers. What is incontestable is that Metternich was the supreme and public executioner of the emerging policy. His diplomatic gifts would be put to the test by Francis, but Metternich was nothing without Francis. The reverse was not the case. Certainly, the brilliance of Metternich's application of Austria's strategy cannot be doubted, but by this time, not a clock chimed in Vienna without the Emperor's knowledge and consent.

The issue of rising Russian power, represented by Tsar Alexander had not and would not diminish in the months and years ahead. Given the state of Austrian finances and military strength, concealed as best it could be, Francis and Metternich grasped that the only means by which they could avoid becoming a Russian-dominated client state, after the defeat of France, was with the help of other powers. This would gradually evolve as a bedrock principle of Austrian policy, not merely during the reign of Francis, but ever more so with his grandson, Franz Joseph, for the rest of the existence of the Habsburg monarchy. It began here and would flare up in crises of varying degrees; most notably at the Congress of Vienna, as we shall see. The double-headed Habsburg eagle, iconic symbol of the dynasty, had forever looked both east and west, but after the fall of Napoleon, increasingly east.

NOTES

1. Metternich 150.
2. Metternich 140.
3. Malleson, George, *Life of Prince Metternich,* (Philadelphia: J.B. Lippincott, 1888) 63.
4. Rothenberg 225.
5. Leggiere, Michael V., *The Fall of Napoleon: Volume 1, The Allied Invasion of France, 1813–1814,* (New York: Cambridge University Press, 2007).
6. Seward 185.

Chapter Thirteen

Triumph and Redemption

On August 12, 1813, Francis declared war on his son-in-law. His proclamation added some 300,000 troops from its Army of Bohemia to the Coalition. Austrian territory immediately became a base of support contiguous to the main theatre of operations in Saxony, around Dresden. Radetzky had by now raised and equipped two major armies; one in Bohemia and one in Northern Italy making Austria's contribution of over 500,000 troops total the largest of the continental powers. Combined with the armies of Russia, Prussia and Sweden, Coalition numbers were daunting and yet, Napoleon's defeat would take the better part of a year of careful, methodical campaigning with many setbacks and pitfalls along the way.

As usual, Napoleon took the initiative on August 26–27, defeating a Coalition field army of about 214,000 with 135,000 of his own. Casualties of about 3:1 in favor of the French were sustained, but the Coalition forces could bear it more. Since the campaign in Russia, France had lost enormous quantities of horses and had extreme difficulty fielding any meaningful cavalry arm. This meant, in turn, that victories on the battlefield were unlikely to be decisive because there could be no rapid follow-up and ravaging of a retreating army that broke contact. At Kulm, two days later, the verdict went the other way with the loss of an entire corps by Napoleon and sent the French reeling into retreat to Leipzig with something like 175,000 soldiers remaining. For the next month and a half, each side would gather its resources for a show down battle around Leipzig. Time would favor the Allied Coalition, however, and not Napoleon.

In the meantime, an Austrian diplomatic blitzkrieg began conceived, no doubt, in the weeks between Metternich's meeting in Dresden and the declaration of war. Bavaria, long one of Napoleon's most loyal allies, and who had been rewarded with elevation to kingdom status and territory taken from

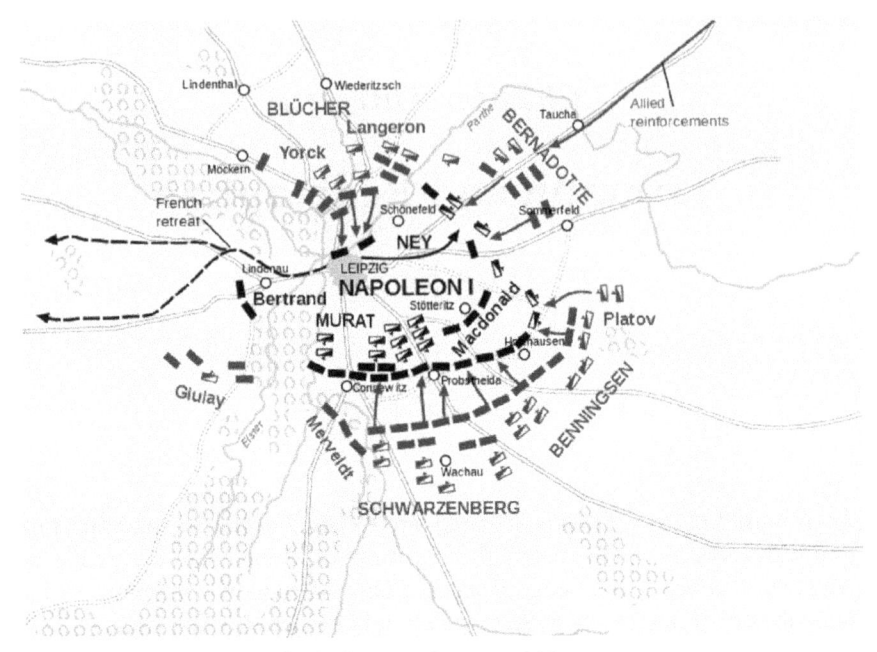

Figure 13.1. The Battle of Leipzig—October 18, 1813

Austria, was contemplating the consequences of the collapse of French power in Germany, the Confederation of the Rhine, and delaying too long in making amends with its neighbor to the east. Without French bayonets, the Bavarian king, Maximilian-Joseph, had few illusions what his long collaboration with Napoleon, particularly against Austria, would bring. He signaled his agreement to preliminary, secret discussions with Austria.

Austria used its immensely enhanced leverage with Prussia and Russia to come to an agreement known in history as the Teplitz Accords or the Treaty of Töplitz on September 9. This treaty was the formal alliance between the three powers against France. Right away, the price of Austrian admission was to place the private agreement between Russia and Prussia that divided Poland and Saxony between them on hold. The issue would come back later with a vengeance, but inserted into the Treaty was that Allied war aims included "the entire and absolute independence" of the German states. While the phrase was ambiguous, from the Austrian point of view, it was a shot across the bow of Prussian ambitions of aggrandizement by annexation of smaller German states like Saxony. It was also used to reassure the lesser German states that after Napoleon, it was Austria who would look to uphold their independence and interests particularly against avaricious Prussian designs.

Austria engaged Bavaria in direct negotiations a day later, on September 10, and a week later, Bavaria and Austria signed an armistice. Austrian policy toward Bavaria appeared surprisingly mild, but was part of a larger diplomatic mustering of the small German states against future Prussian hegemony, and was seen for what it was by the Prussian cabinet. "The arrangements made with the Bavarians tie our hands and are harmful to the general measures to be taken," wrote Prussian minister Heinrich Baron vom Stein, one of the first advocates of a united Germany under Prussian leadership.

Francis was not interested in mere territorial annexations in Germany, although there would be adjustments in Bavarian acquisitions at Austria's expense from the earlier wars. Francis, and therefore Austria's German policy, was the long-game: to leverage the other German states against Prussia in general and her annexation of Saxony in particular. On October 8, 1813, Bavaria signed an alliance with Austria alone. Bavaria thereby became Austria's ally until 1866 against Prussian ambitions in Germany. Württemberg signed a similar alliance with Austria on November 2, followed later that month by Hesse-Kassel, Nassau, Baden, Hesse-Darmstadt and Coburg.

Metternich soothed anxious, recently minted monarchs of these kingdoms with assurances they would have Austrian support against any attempt to retract the honors, privileges and territory Napoleon had awarded them not eight years earlier. While on the surface, these alliances and understandings appeared to be for the general purpose of rallying them beneath the banner of defeating Napoleon and France, their bi-lateral nature with Austria tacitly revealed their secondary purpose for a later date. The picks had been set for what Francis and his ministers foresaw would be a battle to the knife with Prussia once the dust had settled.

Swedish forces now arrived in Saxony in early October, numbering some 30,000. All in all, by the time the Coalition forces reached Leipzig in October, their numbers had crested to some 430,000 as against 191,000 French and allied troops, mainly from Poland and Saxony. The battle that followed was the largest fought in Europe until World War I and lasted four days, between October 16–19. Leipzig, often called The Battle of the Nations, was attended by the crowned heads of every major power in Europe but Britain and Spain. During the battle, the Saxon army defected to the Coalition and the king of Saxony was captured by the Coalition forces.

After the first day of fighting, Napoleon failed to break through or defeat the Coalition forces and the day ended in a bloody stalemate. The second day saw largely a pause in the fighting, but the far greater numbers of the Russian, Austrian, Prussian and Swedish armies now began to be felt as they began to encircle the French army to the south and east of Leipzig. The third day, Napoleon realized that if he did not withdraw, his army would be completely

Figure 13.2. Baron vom Stein, Prussian Minister, circa 1804 by Johann Rincklake. The Westphalian State Museum of Art and Cultural History

encircled and defeated, probably resulting in his own capture. He offered an armistice, which was refused. Napoleon concluded that the battle was lost and during the night, much of his army silently and secretly escaped the closing trap. Nonetheless, due to the premature destruction of a bridge out of Leipzig, 30,000 French troops were stranded and ultimately taken prisoner.

It was a catastrophic defeat unparalleled in the history of the Napoleonic Wars of Europe. History records some 100,000 French soldiers killed or wounded compared to about half that for the Coalition. The route of retreat would pass through Erfurt where it was estimated that the French army had only some 70,000 men organized and under arms with perhaps 30,000 stragglers on the roads. This defeat could not be blamed on the weather or sugar-coated in the French press. The skeletal force remaining would have to continue marching west and evacuate Germany while an enormous Coalition Army continued to pursue it. Worse still, Wellington's defeat of the French at Santa Vittoria and again at Sorauren preceded his crossing the Pyrenees and entering southern France on October 7. The invasion of France had be-

Figure 13.3. Victory at Leipzig by Johann Krafft, circa 1839. The Deutsches Historiches Museum, Berlin. Tsar Alexander I, Emperor Francis I and King Frederick Wilhelm III at center right receive the news of Napoleon's defeat from Field Marshal Karl Phillip von Schwarzenberg, center left.

gun and most of the major battles for the remainder of the war would be on French soil.

Furthermore, while the Austrian and Russian contributions in men were about equal, the battle was managed and won by Schwarzenberg and Radetzky which made it the third time Austrian commanders had defeated the great Napoleon in the field. Austrian prestige, in a matter of months, had vaulted into first among equals of the Allied Great Powers. Even Britain, who opposed anything less than the removal of Napoleon from the face of Europe as a matter of principle, agreed to defer to Austrian insistence upon exhausting all possibilities of a negotiated peace with him. Perhaps this was due to British belief that the Napoleon known to them was unreasonable to a fault and that Austrian attempts would fail. Later, however, its chief diplomats, Castlereagh and Wellington, came to fully understand the Austrian fear of Russian hegemony as we shall see.

While France remained a formidable opponent led by the greatest military commander of his age, it would not be like 1792. Then, an aroused population, who saw themselves as liberated from the *ancien regime* of the Bourbon dynasty, massed armies to repel the foreign invaders on every front. Many had felt then that they were fighting for themselves and their own freedom. That patriotic, self-interest would be absent in 1814. Instead, the French were weary of war, sullen and moved to the defense of *la patrie française* largely by fear. Fear of foreign invasion. Fear of the consequences of avoiding impressment, conscription and service in the French army. Fear of what would happen to their country if and when it collapsed.

Nor would it be like the glory days of the Napoleonic empire when France was able to impose itself on the rest of Europe to finance its war machine through "contributions" and indemnities, not to mention outright pillage and looting. This time, the French treasury would have to bear the cost of the war, imposing it on the French people themselves as the shrinking areas of French control and declining population made the cost ever steeper to the nobility and common people. The army's well-deserved reputation for "living off the land" would now be directed toward French land and Napoleon himself would admit that his army ". . . instead of being their country's defenders, are becoming its scourge."[1] In November, Napoleon ordered the doubling of taxes on tobacco, postage and salt to raise 180 million francs. The French treasury was down to 30 million francs. He also ordered that all payments of pensions and salaries be suspended.[2]

The Napoleonic edifice would fissure and crack under the strain in the coming months with treason arising within. Talleyrand and Fouché would openly discuss surrender terms with the Allies shortly and even plan a coup.[3] But it was the marshals who became increasingly hostile to the rejection of peace terms, again and again, by Napoleon and who would, eventually, force him to abdicate.

FRANCIS, THE SILENT PARTNER

The history of the ultimate decline and fall of France has primary relevance to the story of Francis of Austria, though, and certain aspects must be studied in some detail to catch glimpses of the power and influence of this mysterious monarch. As ever, due to the lack of his memoirs and historiography in the two centuries since this time, much of what we know today must be gleaned through indirection, rather than direct evidence through transcripts, contemporaneous documentation, letters and other, normal sources of information.

These silent, neglected wellsprings of knowledge, to the extent they still exist, have given no answer to the popular attribution given to Metternich for virtually every aspect of Austrian statecraft during this period and beyond. Yet it is telling, perhaps, that this celebrity with a famously narcissistic personality had this to say about his partnership with Francis in the creation of his own memoirs, specifically about this period in 1813:

> ... We have also been influenced by another feeling, and this we will confess with the utmost candor. Few monarchs have conferred more honor on their throne than the Emperor Francis. His people knew his value as a man. A true father to his subjects, he was not honored so much as he ought to have been by many of his contemporaries in regard to the qualities which distinguished him as a sovereign ... Of pure morals and simple manners, averse to every kind of parade, he disdained even the distinctions which dazzle the crowd and often make Princes appear what they are not. In everything loving and seeking only the truth, firm in his principles and just in his opinions, this Monarch nevertheless often played what seemed to his contemporaries a subordinate part, exactly at those times when the extraordinary results were due only to his energy, his determination and his virtues. The materials which we shall leave to an impartial posterity will not contradict this assertion....[4]

And again, regarding the Teplitz Accords, so vital in launching Austria's essential take-over of leadership in the Coalition:

> I will here give in a few words the views and feelings which the Emperor and I, in the most perfect harmony, laid down as invariable rules for our guidance in the immediate as well as the more remote future. The object we must keep before us was the re-establishment of a state of peace, firmly based on the principles of order.... The points already elsewhere mentioned, which arose between the Emperor and myself on the question, determined us to give up the idea of a restoration of the old Empire, and to keep to the form of a Confederation. That this determination would meet with opponents from different and quite opposite quarters was to be expected, and we did not deceive ourselves in the matter. We were well aware that many desires for conquest would have to be checked, many individual interests would have to be restrained. All considerations of this kind were subordinate to the aim and intention of the Emperor Francis, to secure to Europe and his own Empire the blessings of political peace for as many years as possible....[5]

These statements by Metternich in his Autobiography might be suspected of being motivated by flattery of his sovereign, upon whose support he depended over his entire career. Or gratitude, perhaps, for the favors and titles bestowed upon him by Francis. But Metternich never published his memoirs in the lifetime of Francis, nor even in his own lifetime. He did not begin writing what he thought would be entitled *Materials for the History of my Public Life* until 1844; nine years after Francis' death. It was his son, Prince Richard Metternich, who, after heavily editing his father's papers and drafts, first published the Autobiography in 1880 during the reign of Francis' grandson.

There may be another reason for Metternich's perceived predominance not merely in executing Austrian policy, in which his preeminent place in history cannot be doubted, but in its conception and design. This has to do with the rise of the Austro-Russian rivalry within the Coalition that would continue until the fall of both empires in 1917–18.

As we have already seen, Austrian power and influence skyrocketed in 1813 and Austria would remain the dominant diplomatic power in continental Europe for the rest of Francis' reign. Time and again, alone among the Coalition members, Austria held out for a negotiated peace with Napoleonic France against opposition from Russia, Britain and Prussia. The fact that at several crucial points, the other powers deferred to Austria, accepting the possibility of a negotiated peace, is stark testimony to how far Austria's star had risen, but it came at a price and that price was rising animosity from the Tsar of Russia, Alexander I.

It becomes apparent by the time of the Frankfurt Proposals toward the end of 1813, that a clever tactical approach was agreed between Francis and Metternich in dealing with the mercurial personality of the Russian tsar.

Figure 13.4. Gebhard Leberecht von Blücher, Prussian Field Marshal. Sir Thomas Lawrence. Waterloo Gallery, Windsor Castle

Metternich, the ultra-diplomat whose skills had already won him the title of "Prince" by Francis after Leipzig, would be the one bearing the consistent and often unpleasant opposing position of Austrian policy toward Napoleon and France. When it got increasingly warm between Alexander and Metternich, Francis would intervene. Francis' bluff, hearty but firm personality was completely disarming to Alexander, time and again. In effect, Francis played the "good cop" to Metternich's "bad cop." It had the unintended effect, however, of giving Metternich, the "front man," all the glory at each phase of the game. Francis, who deliberately stayed in the background as part of a tactical plan, has been wrongly judged a non-entity.

There is no basis, in fact, to the factitious repetition by many historians of the nineteenth and twentieth centuries that Metternich was the progenitor of all Austrian strategic, operational and tactical thought since he accepted his ministry in 1809. It is far more likely to have been a collaboration in which the diamond-hard, analytical genius of Metternich was partnered with the sober, deliberative, seasoned mind of the veteran Kaiser from which both men derived immense satisfaction and Austria, incalculable benefit.

NOTES

1. Roberts 687–688.
2. Roberts 698.
3. Ibid.
4. Metternich 174.
5. Metternich 201, 202.

Chapter Fourteen

Finis Napoleon

The period between Leipzig and the occupation of Paris on March 31, 1814 lasted five months. From a military point of view, it compares to the fate of Germany in 1945, with some unexpected, brilliant, local checks but overall, overwhelming might applied to a crumbling structure until it collapsed. Napoleon's military brilliance in late 1813–14 in staving off immediate defeat after Leipzig is often remarked, but his colossal errors in judgment when he repeatedly rejected peace terms is the real story. On the military aspects of the period, the signal fact is that at several points, the Tsar challenged Austria's supreme command of the Allied armies.

Soon after Teplitz, Alexander summoned Metternich to visit him at Saxon Altenburg. Schwarzenberg and Radetzky had just assumed supreme command. It was after the initial reverse at the Battle of Dresden after the armistice had just ended on August 27, 1813. Alexander peremptorily raised the issue of supreme command over allied forces with the statement that in his view, the present arrangements could not continue. He proposed replacing Schwarzenberg with the recently defected (French) General Moreau but, acknowledging the possible impact this might have on the army—replacing an Austrian with a Frenchman—he proposed that he, Alexander, take the title of *Generalissimo* with the assurance that he would always follow the advice of Moreau, however. Metternich responded:

> I at once declared that if his Imperial Majesty meant to insist on this arrangement, the Emperor, my master, would withdraw from the Alliance. . . . After a long pause, during which he seemed lost in profound thought, the Emperor at last broke silence, saying 'Well and good, we will postpone the question, but I make you responsible for all the mischief which may arise from it.'[1]

Alexander I is often given credit as the Russian tsar who defeated Napoleon and, in a sense, this is true, but not in the sense most people think. As a supreme autocrat, his determination to resist Napoleon's invasion in 1812 to the utmost, leading to Napoleon's epic military collapse in the wastelands and snow of his Empire cannot be denied to him, but he was not an able military commander. Quite the contrary. His personal intervention in the operational command of the army in 1805 had been nothing short of disastrous and he contributed nothing, in a military sense, to the eventual victory.

He had virtually no military experience prior to the battle of Austerlitz, yet twice overruled Mikhail Kutuzov, before and during the battle that directly and substantially wrecked the Third Coalition's opportunity to have crushed Napoleon in that campaign, eight years earlier. Kutuzov, by contrast, had decades of military experience and is thought, even today, to be one of the greatest Russian generals who ever lived. Goaded into a precipitous engagement at Austerlitz by an entourage of equally inexperienced, young, military pretenders and thirsting for personal glory, he compounded the operational mistake of giving premature battle to Napoleon with misguided tactical command on the battlefield itself that might single-handedly have been responsible for the worst defeat of the Napoleonic wars. He was found by his *aide-de-camp* after the battle weeping in despair.

Alexander was ambitious to have "the Great" appended to his name, like his grandmother Catherine and his great ancestor, Peter, by leading his Russian army to victory without the temperament, experience and military training required to accomplish it. In his own country, he was surrounded inevitably by sycophants and flatterers in whose adoration he basked. Opposition to his word was virtually unthinkable and unknown and, when encountered, was simply overridden. He could use his imperial power as sovereign to bully and intimidate in his own court, but in the presence of other sovereigns of equal rank, he shrank back from confrontation.

He was awed by Napoleon, whose real military talent could not be questioned and in whose presence, at Tilsit or later Erfurt, he was mute and deferential. King Frederick William III of Prussia had been an exception. The Prussian king was so fearful of Russian power and so dependent on Russian support for his very existence, especially after Jena, that he submitted to Alexander's personality as if he were a member of his court. Francis, however, was another personality altogether.

Francis was almost a decade older than Alexander, in the first place. Of the three leaders in 1813, Francis was the most senior at 45 years of age. He had also reigned the longest; more than five years longer than Frederick William and eight years more than Alexander. His dynasty, however, was by far the oldest and most prestigious in continental Europe. Since the time of Peter the

Figure 14.1. Francis I on campaign by Johann Krafft, circa 1832. The Hermitage Museum, St. Petersburg.

Great, the Romanovs had pushed forward, trying to establish themselves as part of the European royal landscape and their arrival as major actors on the European scene was recent compared to the Habsburgs.

The Russian imperial court was also viewed with some distain due to its dark and violent history. Peter the Great had emerged as Tsar in 1682 after the culmination of several bloody palace coups and murders. Catherine the Great came to power in 1762 upon the murder of her husband in which she was undoubtedly complicit. Her son, the Tsar Paul I ruled for less than four years between 1796–1801 when he too was murdered in a palace coup that had placed Catherine's grandson, Alexander, on the throne.

Tsar Paul, Alexander's father, was strangled in his bedroom of St. Michael's Castle by a group of military conspirators headed by General Levin August Bennigsen. Alexander was in the castle at the time. Bennigsen had been cashiered by Tsar Paul. Alexander reappointed him to the active service and maintained him in active military command after the murder of his father. Bennigsen was eventually awarded the Cross of St. Andrew by Tsar Alexander after the battle of Eylau; the highest military order of the Russian Empire.

The extent of Alexander's knowledge and involvement in the murder of his father has never been established by direct evidence, but it was widely assumed in Europe that he was, from circumstantial evidence such as this. For example, the French general Dominique Vandamme, who was captured after the battle of Kulm, was brought before Tsar Alexander who accused him of being a brigand and a plunderer. Vandamme replied with some heat, "I am neither a plunderer nor a brigand, but in any case, my contemporaries and history will not reproach me for having murdered my own father."[2] This unsavory history of murder and intrigue gave the Romanov dynasty an aura of barbarity, especially when contrasted with the continental monarchies and even more so, the Habsburgs.

Where Alexander was mercurial and impulsive, Francis was deliberate and steady. Where Alexander meddled in diplomatic and military affairs, Francis held back and rarely intervened directly. Alexander was a sexual libertine, a sensuous lover of luxury, pomp and deference to his majesty while Francis was sexually conservative, and disdained ostentation and obsequiousness. Francis was mature and taciturn in public while Alexander was voluble and changeable. As described by one author, Francis was an Austrian George III.[3]

All these factors seemed to combine to have created a sense of insecurity and unease for Alexander in directly confronting and opposing Francis if and when the Kaiser chose to directly involve himself. As we have seen, Francis seems to have taken the measure of his younger ally on several occasions and devised the perfect means of handling him by using Metternich as an intermediary and a foil. As Alexander's social inferior, Metternich could be used as a sounding board for Alexander's ever-changing and conflicting ideas, many of them killed on the spot, as was the attempt to co-opt supreme command of the armies. Alexander's tantrums and outbursts, unthinkable in the presence of Francis, could be indulged with Metternich to test how far he might be able to push the Austrians since both knew that whatever Alexander said or did would be reported by Metternich to his sovereign.

In 1813, Alexander felt certain that victory was imminent. He wanted to be at the head of the Allied armies when the final battle brought Napoleon to his knees, prostrate before him. He wanted to be the one leading the Allied armies into Paris on a white horse as the liberator of Europe. He was not an evil man, but a vain and inconstant one. Yet his meddling and attempts to dictate the course of the military campaign to Schwarzenberg and Radetzky were blocked due to Francis' cool but inflexible opposition. Francis was as much a rock of support to his generals as he was to his foreign minister and they were just as grateful. Without his unflinching support, they were nothing.

FRANCIS AND TSAR ALEXANDER

By December, the Coalition forces had reached Frankfurt, crossing almost the entire breadth of Germany, and paused there to consider when and how the invasion of France would be accomplished. The Austrian plan involved, among other things, an invasion of Switzerland for several reasons that are unimportant but one that was. Austria had a second army operating in northern Italy. Austrian territorial ambitions for postwar expansion were, at minimum, to seek restoration of former Habsburg possessions in Italy and, perhaps, a little more. The Tsar adamantly opposed Schwarzenberg's plan and then abruptly left Frankfurt where the councils of war were taking place in late December 1813. Alexander was overruled by Francis, who had purposely stayed out of direct participation in the discussions, leaving matters to Schwarzenberg and Radetzky in the Tsar's absence. Francis then authorized the Swiss incursion on December 21, 1813.

Metternich informed Alexander of the decision and, indeed, the Swiss invasion when the Tsar returned to Frankfurt the following day, and described it this way:

> The emperor was very much agitated by this news; when he had collected himself, he asked how the army had been received. 'Amid cheers for the Alliance, your Majesty. The Confederate troops in a body have joined our flag, and the people came in crowds from all sides to bring provisions to the army, for which we paid in ready money.' I could easily read in the Emperor's features the conflicting feelings which this news excited. After a longer pause, he took

my hand and said: 'Success crowns the undertaking: it remains for success to justify what you have done. As one of the Allied monarchs I have nothing more to say to you; but as a man I declare to you that you have grieved me in a way that you can never repair.'[4]

Again, Metternich: "And in fact, we did not talk any more about it, and the Emperor Alexander never mentioned the subject to the Emperor Francis."[5] Had Alexander reversed the decision, it would have meant that he, not Schwarzenberg, was *de facto* the supreme commander and that the issue had not been settled at Teplitz. This was how the jockeying for power between Russia and Austria was handled by Francis and Metternich and invariably, successfully. By deliberately placing Metternich or Schwarzenberg "out front," Francis held his own power and prestige in reserve, but again, deprived himself of the historical limelight in the decades and centuries to come.

The other significant military fact about the campaign from Leipzig to Paris was the fact that it was fought in an operational manner devised by Radetzky, almost without deviation. The principle was that the armies operated in parallel lines, as closely as logistics would permit, as they crossed Germany and into France. The mass would remain largely a whole, although individual engagements and battles would break out across the wide arc of the Allied army. When the engagement was against Napoleon, the local commander would avoid direct battle and simply halt while the rest of the army moved on. Engagements with any of Napoleon's subordinates were encouraged and fought. In this manner, the incoming tide of an overwhelmingly superior army avoided being divided and conquered, as Napoleon had done so many times in the past. It was an Austrian strategy, conceived by Austrian marshals and backed by the Austrian Kaiser against occasional challenges by Alexander that won the war this time.

It should be noted that for the entire campaign, Francis was with his army, day and night. The entry of the former Holy Roman Emperor into Frankfurt on November 6, 1813, was described as "very moving and extremely solemn" by Schwarzenberg.[6]

> ... 'Red Breeches,' the popular nickname for Kaiser Francis, entered the former imperial city where he had been crowned Holy Roman Emperor twenty-one years earlier. Frederick William was absent, having returned to Berlin following the battle of Leipzig. 'We were well-received [wrote Sir Robert Wilson] ... although Bonaparte warned the inhabitants not to commit any follies, since he would reappear in the spring. ... *Te Deum* followed his entry, and for two hours we froze in a cold church. The troops then filed by the sovereigns, and this ceremony was almost as chilling. We then went to dine with Mr. Bethmann who gave a *grande fete*. Afterwards we passed to the opera, where *Titus* was

performed before the emperors and an overflowing house by some very talented actors.' [7]

Given the depredations visited on the German Reich—the Confederation of the Rhine—by the Napoleonic regime and the humiliating subservience of the German people to the arrogance and demands of French domination–whether through puppet kings set up by Napoleon, by members of the Bonaparte family, such as his brother Jerome who was made king of Westphalia, or by direct military privations enforced by the French military authorities—the mood in Germany in general and Frankfurt in particular was ripe for revenge. The image, as Francis solemnly rode his horse through the ancient medieval streets, must surely have been one that recalled to many who lined the streets that day of another era; of a much softer and gentler rule from Vienna by the Habsburgs.

The French emperor, again at the insistence of Francis and Metternich, was given yet another chance to end the war as the Allied armies ensconced on the Rhine with the sovereigns and their ministers in Frankfurt in early November 1813. The "Frankfurt Proposals," conveyed to Napoleon on November 9, two days after Francis had entered the city, would allow Napoleon to remain as Emperor. France would have to return to her so-called "natural frontiers," but could also retain Belgium, Savoy and the lands west of the Rhine River. At first, Napoleon signaled that it might be acceptable as a basis for a final peace agreement, but quickly began negotiating, treating the Allies' conditions as a starting point, rather than the end. The negotiations collapsed and now Britain added its insistence that Belgium be evacuated as well to permanently remove the menace of future French control of its ports directly across the Channel.

It must have seemed inconceivable to Francis and Metternich that Napoleon would spurn such an offer and they must have despaired at his delusional intransigence. Napoleon's regime had only months left to live, at this point. The invasion of France began in January. Napoleon fought on, winning several brilliant victories, but on a small scale against an ever- advancing avalanche of Allied formations. In all, Napoleon was commanding an army of about 80,000 as against an Allied army of 400,000.

There would be one last attempt on March 19 pursuant to the terms of the Treaty of Chaumont. In this proposal, France would have to give up everything and return to her pre-Revolutionary War boundaries of 1792. Napoleon rejected the proposal the following day. Nonetheless, the Treaty contained several other important agreements among the Allies. These included turning Belgium over to the new Kingdom of the Netherlands, the division of Italy into several independent states and the restoration of the Bourbon monarchy in Spain.

On March 30, 1814, Paris fell while Napoleon's army was near Fontainebleau. The French Senate issued a decree on April 2 announcing that Napoleon was deposed. His decision to march on Paris was overruled by his marshals who, essentially, mutinied on April 4. Napoleon abdicated on that day in favor of his son, but this was rejected by the Allies. On April 6, he abdicated unconditionally and on April 11 signed the Treaty of Fontainebleau in which he agreed to go into exile.

The Senate of France, which had deposed Napoleon, resolved to recall the exiled brother of Louis XVI as the new sovereign, Louis XVIII. In the meantime, Talleyrand, Napoleon's former foreign minister, and Charles, the Count of Artois, who had been so active in stirring up the First Coalition to save the Bourbon monarchy, negotiated the terms of the Treaty of Paris on May 30. The Treaty brought a formal end to hostilities and provided that the remaining details regarding the restored French monarchical state and the rest of Europe would be decided at a conference which would take place in Vienna. The War of the Sixth Coalition was over.

MARIE LOUISE

A telling personal aspect of the fall of Paris and Napoleon is that Francis did not join his allies in their entry into the French capital. Alexander and Frederick William on horseback basked in the moment. Paintings depict their triumph at the head of their soldiers, but Francis was missing. Instead, he nominated Schwarzenberg who is often mistaken for the Emperor in paintings depicting the scene. Instead, Francis parted company with his fellow monarchs and his ministers to go to his daughter at Blois.

The triumph of his arms had brought down Marie Louise's husband and cast her fate to the wind. Her marriage to Napoleon had turned out to be a happy one, and there was the matter of her infant child by him. Marie Louise had fallen from the dizzying heights of being an Empress of the most powerful European state and married to one of the wealthiest and most powerful men in the world to a state of complete uncertainty. To Francis, it was a matter of state that had been decided with the best interests of the monarchy and the Empire foremost, but now that the defeat of France was complete, he turned to his daughter and away from Paris.

As part of the abdication treaty of Fontainebleau, Marie Louise had been granted the Duchy of Parma and two other smaller Italian provinces, but it remained to be seen if this would be modified or abrogated at the Congress. On April 14, 1814, after the fall of Paris, Francis arrived in Blois, where Marie Louise and her son had fled. There they discussed what she should do.

Marie Louise's initial impulse was to join her husband in exile with their son. She loved Napoleon and believed it was her duty as his wife to share his fate. Francis, meeting his infant grandson for the first time, had more to consider.

The diplomatic position of Austria at the then-upcoming Congress, after having invested so much in the repeated attempts to save the Bonaparte dynasty over the grudging acquiescence of his allies, would be placed in an embarrassing position if the daughter of the Austrian Kaiser were to remain with Napoleon. Her Italian possessions, Parma, Piacenza and Gaushala, were important to the reestablishment of Habsburg power and influence in Italy and would perforce have been ruled by Napoleon *in absentia* and then, presumably, by his son. This was a prospect that would have evoked mixed feelings in the Emperor, but opposition from every other Great Power. Francis could not have failed to consider as well that if ever there was a chance of a Bonaparte restoration in France, the custody of Napoleon II would be a trump card that he would want in his hands.

Francis forbade her rejoining Napoleon in Elba in what was, apparently, an unhappy conversation. It is possible that Francis' relationship with Marie Louise was forever chilled by this affair, probably more to his regret than hers. Nonetheless, upon parting with his daughter, their relationship had been sufficiently affected that Francis was evidently suspicious that she might defy him. As a precaution, he instructed Metternich to assign someone to escort Marie Louise back to Vienna. Metternich obliged by appointing a military attaché and confidant from his own entourage, Adam Albert von Neipperg. In a very short time, von Neipperg became her lover; a fact that could not have long escaped the notice of her father.

Yet there is no evidence that Francis ever made any serious effort to break up the liaison, which he could easily have done. Perhaps he viewed it as the price he was prepared to pay for denying Marie Louise her wish to carry on a marital relationship with her husband. Perhaps it was a tacit admission that, after her agreement to serve the state in 1810 by marrying Napoleon, she could now do what she wanted. Francis' toleration of what he certainly regarded as a sinful and immoral relationship was highly inconsistent with his conservative, Catholic views on sexual morality, especially within the family. As we shall see, Austrian civil servants would be fired for lesser moral lapses, although not Metternich. This seems to confirm even more that at some level, he indulged her this unique, special *quid pro quo* for the sacrifices she made for him and the state.

When Marie Louise returned to Vienna, her arrival created something of a sensation among the gathering diplomats and courtiers who were frequenting the salons and balls. She was immediately the subject of intense gossip. Her relationship with von Neipperg was either guessed or assumed, much to her chagrin. She gradually became aware of the fact that she was perceived generally in Vienna, as being an unfaithful wife and an indifferent mother to her son, causing her to become increasingly isolated and depressed. Her grandmother, for example, criticized her for "deserting" her husband. By August, she wrote: "I am in a very unhappy and critical position; I must be very prudent in my conduct. There are moments when that thought so distracts me that I think that the best thing I could do would be to die."[8]

In due course, Marie Louise was confirmed by the Congress as Duchess of Parma, but only for her life. Her Bonaparte son would not inherit. Furthermore, her son would have to remain in Vienna under the watchful eye of his grandfather. She and von Neipperg soon left Vienna for Parma. By then, Francis' relationship with his daughter had cooled exceedingly. They saw little of each other in Vienna and virtually never once Marie Louise took up residence in Parma. In 1821, Napoleon died and Marie Louise immediately married von Neipperg with whom she had several children. He died in 1829 and she married a third time, dying herself in 1847. The fate of her son in Vienna is another interesting story that we will take up later.

NOTES

1. Metternich 206, 207.
2. De Marbot, Jean Baptiste, *Memoires Du General Baron de Marbot, Vol. 2*, (Charleston: Nabu Press, 2010) 375.
3. Seward 66.
4. Seward 222.
5. Seward 223.
6. Leggier 21.
7. Ibid.
8. De Saint-Amand, Imbert, *The Happy Days of the Empress Marie Louise*, (Miami: HardPress Publishing, 2010).

Chapter Fifteen

The Congress of Vienna

The reign of Francis can almost be divided evenly in half. The first half, between 1792 and 1815 was dominated by the wars with Revolutionary and Napoleonic France. The second half, between 1815 and the Emperor's death in 1835, was known in central Europe as the Biedermeier era. This time was one of international peace, relative and growing prosperity, especially of the middle classes and, in the case of Austria, two decades of recovery from the ravages of war. But first, peace in Europe depended on a settlement among the Great Powers now that France had been vanquished; a peace that would be difficult to arrange among allies whose divergent interests, mutual suspicions and rivalries had been sufficiently difficult to overcome that it had prevented them from uniting and defeating France for over twenty years.

On his return from Blois through Germany, Francis was hailed with triumphal arches, banners in the streets and on houses as the prince of peace, liberator, and even German Emperor.[1] Indeed, as Pieter Judson points out in his book *The Habsburg Empire*, the defeat of Napoleon was a unifying moment in the history of the young Empire that was meticulously chronicled at the time by Joseph Rossi, a Viennese civil servant, who documented the celebrations in a two-volume book.[2] News of the final defeat of Napoleon was received throughout the Austrian Empire with unrestrained exultation.

> Rossi's second volume recounted in comparable detail the quasi-spontaneous celebrations and illuminations that broke out in the rest of the empire, not only in cities and towns, but also in the tiniest of villages. These celebrations were not created, designed, imposed or even suggested by the central state, which had in any case long ago run out of the kind of money such an undertaking would have required. Instead, local businessmen, civil servants, and landowners initiated and financed these ceremonies. . . . At the very least they reflect the

Figure 15.1. Triumphal Entry of Emperor Francis. Johann Krafft, circa 1828. The Belvedere, Vienna.

existence of a common legitimating understanding of empire shared by thousands of regionally dispersed Austrians. They also demonstrate the existence of a distinctive and shared culture of imagery, slogans, and ritual practices around the idea of empire.[3]

On June 15, 1814, Francis reached Schönbrunn and the following day, he made his way into Vienna through the Carinthian Gate where he was met by the mayor and a mass of young girls and boys wearing Austrian colors of red and white. After this greeting, the Emperor passed through the ancient streets of the inner city to St. Stephens Cathedral where a *Te Deum* was held. Bonfires, fireworks and illuminations in the windows of the houses in Vienna greeted the returning Emperor. A drama was staged at the Kärntner Theater dedicated to the Emperor.[4]

Yet even in this moment of supreme triumph and vindication, the fate of Francis' empire hung in the balance. The bankrupt finances of his treasury, the looming and unresolved threat of Russia and Prussia's ambitions on his borderlands and the failure to have set a counter-weight in the form of a tamed but still powerful France were unquestionably on his mind. The prospect of war with one or both Eastern monarchies was unthinkable, and yet something had to be done.

It had been in the wake of the Battle of Leipzig when Tsar Alexander had suggested Vienna as the site for the future gathering of nations where the fate of Europe would be decided. Francis had immediately agreed and it was formally designated as the place where the Peace would be decided in Paris. Initially, the conference was supposed to begin in July, but in deference to the Tsar who wanted to return to St. Petersburg before attending, it was set to begin in October. Delegations began arriving in late September. Francis would be the host of the gathering and it was not lost on him that the Congress would afford him a golden opportunity to impress and perhaps even awe his guests. No matter that the Empire could little afford it.

Francis would use every advantage the city could provide, including the network of spies and informers who would be waiting for the arriving dignitaries in the form of cooks, valets, housekeepers, maids and gardeners who would report to Baron Franz von Hager and who, in turn, reported directly to Francis. The highest-ranking guests, such as the Tsar, the King of Prussia and various kings of the German states would be given lavish apartments in the Hofburg itself, the rambling Habsburg seat of power within the walls and behind the guarded gates of the inner city. So much the better to keep an eye on them. Instructions from von Hager to his agents were unequivocal:

> Since a certain number of representatives of the different powers attending the Congress have already arrived in Vienna and the rest will be following in a steady stream, you should not only keep me informed of the arrival and address of each one, but by virtue of a secret watch intelligently maintained you should also make it your business neither to lose track of their whereabouts nor of the company they keep.

Lavish entertainments would be provided, not merely to the royalty, but their ministers, retinues and members of their courts who accompanied them. Vienna was quickly bulging to overflowing with foreign guests and courtiers, driving rents and rates even for attic rooms out of sight. Viennese salons, gathering places for evening meals, champagne and conversation, were a favorite place to conduct informal diplomacy. Viennese aristocratic society opened their palaces and mansions to a veritable *glitterati* of European royalty and nobility. Metternich was, of course, a prominent host but other prominent ministers were as well. Castlereagh, at his mansion in the Minoritenplatz, Talleyrand at the Kaunitz Palace, and many other salons were places to see and be seen, gossip, drink, eat and flirt. The most famous of all, however, was the Palm Palace where the Duchess of Sagan and Princess Catherine Bagration both held court. These two wealthy aristocratic women were both lovers of Metternich and Tsar Alexander which fueled the still growing hostility between the two men.

A NEW ORDER FOR EUROPE

The Congress of Vienna was unprecedented. As Talleyrand emphasized to Castlereagh, "the present epoch is one of those which hardly occur once in the course of several centuries. A fairer opportunity can never be offered to us. Why should we not place ourselves in a position to answer to it?"[5] Since it had no precedent, the format and protocol had to be established at the outset and proved to be one of the first contentious issues of the conference. Naturally, the "big four" of Austria, Britain, Prussia and Russia—the conquering powers—had assumed that the major decisions would be decided among themselves, but this reckoned without the talents of France's ambassador, Maurice de Talleyrand, who promptly objected.

A formal document, excluding France, was prepared by Metternich for agreement on October 4 and shown to Talleyrand that evening. The following day, he appeared at Metternich's summer villa where the Big Four was meeting and submitted a protest. He threatened to take no part in the deliberations of the major powers unless France were allowed an equal voice. He pointed out that were the other Great Powers to decide everything in advance of the Congress and impose it on Europe, they would be no better than Napoleon and that it would never preserve the peace they wanted so badly.

On October 8, Talleyrand had a private meeting with Metternich. At that meeting, it seems, the French minister played a card that struck home with the Austrian. Talleyrand asserted that France and Austria ought to be united when the issue of Russian expansion into Poland and therefore Europe was concerned. Talleyrand also revealed that the newly restored Bourbon France had, as its governing policy, the idea of a post-war Europe based upon "legitimacy," meaning the rule of international law based upon tradition and custom. Legitimacy meant also maintaining the king of Saxony and that the Prussian appetite for additional territory should be opposed and curbed. Metternich, at this point, is supposed to have grasped Talleyrand's hand and exclaimed "we are much less divided than you think."[6]

As the conference went on, Francis was heartened not only by the support of France but by a hardening British position toward the Russians as well. By October 13, British opposition to Russian annexation of Poland was openly expressed to Alexander by Castlereagh in a personal meeting between the two at his embassy. Britain, after over twenty years of near continuous war, had not yet embarked on its isolationist foreign policy that would evolve in the late 1820s and last until the first years of the 20th century. The Britain represented by Castlereagh was very interested in continental affairs and, above all, in a "balance of power" arrangement that prevented any single Great Power from gaining hegemonic status. It was this over-arching philosophy

Figure 15.2. The Congress of Vienna by Jean Isabey, circa 1819

that motivated the British government and, at Vienna, the fear was of Russia being that power.

Metternich's views on the world of the early 19th century were expressed in his own autobiography and clearly corresponded with those of Emperor Francis and with the British:

> In the ancient world, policy isolated itself entirely, and exercised the most absolute selfishness, without any other curb than that of prudence. The law of retaliation set up eternal barriers and founded eternal enmities between the societies of men; and upon every page of ancient history is found the principle of mutual evil for evil. Modern history, on the other hand, exhibits the principle of the solidarity of nations and of the balance of power, and furnishes the spectacle of the combined endeavors of several states against the temporary predominance of any one to impede the extension of this principle, and to constrain it to return to the common law.[7]

This guiding philosophy was unknown to Alexander who pointedly inquired what business Poland was to Great Britain and the fact that his army already occupied the country and could not realistically be expelled by anyone. Castlereagh replied that any settlement that hoped to preserve the peace could not be based on conquest alone and that in this, the Tsar would have to decide "whether the present Congress shall prove a blessing to mankind, or only exhibit a scene of discordant intrigue, and a lawless scramble for power."[8]

Francis, as was by now his practiced method, remained in the background leaving the day-to-day negotiating to Metternich, whose talents and advice he trusted in this extremely tense and vital conference on which the fate of his dynasty and Empire balanced on a knife's edge. His work began every morning when he read the detailed and copious reports on the previous day's espionage prepared by von Hager. He would confer with Metternich and his ministers and then prepare himself for the entertainments or activities of the day, often with his fellow sovereigns. Balls, hunting, riding, military reviews and the like were organized almost continuously, day after day, to occupy the time of the very highest royalty of Europe and their courts. This was particularly so with the German royalty whose fear of an aggressive Prussian program of aggrandizement they suspected would be at their expense.

The question of Saxony became increasingly important, as the Congress went on, with Prussia pressing for the deposition of the king and complete annexation backed by Russia. Saxony, although small, was one of the richest states in Europe and included the cities of Dresden and Leipzig. It abutted Poland, Prussia and Austrian Bohemia; a perfect country for a "buffer state" between all three. It is inconceivable that Francis, at the pinnacle of his intelligence network, would not use the information he was receiving daily in his discussions of Austrian diplomacy with Metternich. He alone received the reports that he shared or kept to himself, as he saw fit. It was Francis who gave Metternich an incriminating piece of intelligence that would prove decisive with the Tsar in the denouement of the Saxon issue.

The Congress of Vienna lasted until the Final Act brought it to an end on June 8, 2015. The complex undercurrents eddied and flowed throughout and in the middle of it all was Napoleon's dramatic return from Elba between March 20 and July 8, 2015. Francis had foreseen the problem of Russia and Prussia long before the Congress but now it had to be faced. The question was whether it would be resolved by war or peaceful negotiation, and it is a tribute to all the participants that it was eventually resolved by negotiation and a settlement that forestalled another general European war for a hundred years.

The showdown came in January. On December 24, 1814, representatives of the United States and Great Britain had agreed to peace terms at Ghent, ending the war between them that had begun in 1812. This meant that the British navy and military forces that had been fighting across the Atlantic Ocean could now be brought home. Canada and Britain's West Indian colonies were no longer under threat. This event was conveyed to Castlereagh within days in Vienna. Emboldened, he reached out to Talleyrand and proposed consideration of an alliance against Prussia and Russia. Talleyrand responded enthusiastically and quickly informed Metternich.

Francis agreed immediately to join the proposed defensive alliance and on January 3, 1815, the pact was agreed. Each party agreed to support the others in case of an attack from any other power and contribute 150,000 troops. Austria, which had tried to the utmost to save Napoleon and maintain a strong France had succeeded in the end with a Bourbon France and Britain to boot. The steady, patient maintenance of her position together with a willingness to improvise and take advantage of the mutual interests of new allies forced a compromise. With his hand now strengthened with the knowledge that Austria would not be alone, Francis authorized Metternich to display to the Tsar a letter carelessly written by the Prussian minister, Hardenberg, that candidly admitted that Prussia was only supporting Russian policy to advance its own interests and because, with Saxony, "it would make Russia weaker."[9] The letter had undoubtedly been intercepted by Francis' secret police and, when revealed, served as a convenient pretext for Alexander to withdraw his former support from Prussian annexation of Saxony when the time came.

Alexander had also begun to hear rumors of the alliance against him, which had been negotiated in secret. At one point, he directly asked Castlereagh if it were true. Castlereagh did not deny it saying only that if the Tsar acted with pacific intentions, he had nothing to fear. Russian policy softened at that point and without its support, Prussian ambitions sank. In the end, Russia agreed to accept what had been Napoleon's Duchy of Warsaw, which would not be incorporated into Russia but ruled by the Tsar as a separate kingdom with himself as king. Another piece was ceded to Prussia and Austria retained Galicia. The ancient city of Cracow was also detached as a free city, although in the Austrian zone. Prussia settled for only a part of Saxony, with the Saxon king returned to his throne. Saxony would remain a staunch ally of Austria until 1866, fighting with Austria against Prussia in the Austro-Prussian war of that year.

In the meantime, Austria's main ambition had been in the lands of the Kaiser's birth: Italy. Venetia, which had been occupied and incorporated into the Empire after the War of the Second Coalition would be returned to Austria. Further, the kingdom of Lombardy with Milan was added to the lands of the Austrian crown. Tuscany was also returned and Habsburgs archdukes and archduchesses returned to their thrones in Parma and Modena. Except for the kingdom of Piedmont-Sardinia, bordering France, Austria would be the dominant power in Italy. The kingdom of Naples was restored to the Bourbons but their defense and independence would depend, in the years to come, on Habsburg arms.

Austria renounced all claims to Belgium which was made part of a strong kingdom of the Netherlands. The other German states were re-affirmed in their independence and territories and the Austrian Emperor would now be the perpetual President of the new German Confederation, of which Prussia was a part. These kingdoms would also look to Vienna for protection against Prussia and France, just as in the old days of the Holy Roman Empire, and would also fight with Austria in the Austro-Prussian War half a century later.

To further cement the settlement at Vienna, two alliances were signed; the Quadruple Alliance and the so-called Holy Alliance. The first included Austria, Russia, Prussia and Britain and called for the continuation of a "Congress" system to resolve international issues without resorting to war. It was a precursor to what the victorious powers would do after the Versailles Treaty of 1919 (the League of Nations) and in 1945 (the United Nations), except that there would be no standing institution. The foreign ministers of the Great Powers, who would be joined by France at the Congress of Aix-la-Chappelle in 1818 creating the Quintuple Alliance, would meet annually at a designated location.

The Holy Alliance was created for restraining or suppressing republican, liberal and secular movements—revolutions—throughout Europe. This alliance included only Austria, Prussia and Russia. It committed the signatory powers to acting in concert and providing one another mutual support in effecting its purpose. Due to Russia's geographical position and Prussian reluctance, it provided Austria with support in challenging and confronting, with military force if necessary, dangerous agitation or revolution in Italy and Germany.

The Austrian Empire was now at its maximum territorial position; a contiguous sprawling mass that ostensibly made it the largest and most powerful continental state in Europe. This was an illusion, as we shall see, but what made Francis and his Empire so powerful was its soft power as the pivot point and fulcrum of the European balance of power. This was a position it would maintain for the rest of Francis' life.

The Congress was in its final months of life when word reached the Great Powers that Napoleon had escaped from Elba and, shortly thereafter, that he had reached Paris and proclaimed the re-establishment of the Bonapartist Empire. On March 13, 1815, all the Great Powers declared war on Napoleon himself and began mobilizing their armies to remove him once again.

While the Battle of Waterloo, fought on June 18, 1815 is perhaps the most famous battle of the Napoleonic Wars and retains pride of place in the annals of British and German military history, it was in truth little more than a farcical encore to the drama that had convulsed the continent for fifteen years. Nor was it comparable to the denouement of the dictator's reign in 1813–14, nor the scale of the Battle of Leipzig that had fatally crippled Napoleonic France.

In the first place, there was no diplomatic coalition building as had taken place when Francis and Metternich had so brilliantly played their cards to establish an irresistible tide of intractable power and resistance to Napoleon. The Great Powers in Vienna declared war in a single day without the slightest negotiation or hesitation. Even if Napoleon had managed to defeat the Anglo-Dutch-German forces in Belgium, rather than the other way around, Austria, Prussia and Russia were mobilizing and would have invaded France with another stupendous army that would not be parlayed or bargained with for anything less than what actually happened after Waterloo: the abdication and imprisonment of Napoleon Bonaparte.

Nonetheless, in the English-speaking world, the Battle of Waterloo has retained an almost mystical status that eclipsed the methodical and complete annihilation of Napoleonic France before the Congress of Vienna when Napoleon still had enough cards to play that he could have preserved his dynasty and France as a viable power. Napoleon in 1815 had no chance to preserve his empire or dynasty and few resources to fend off even a fragment of the coalition that had instantly been called to arms the moment word of his return had reached Vienna.

NOTES

1. Rossi, Joseph. *Denkbuch für Fürst und Vaterland, Herausgegeben von Joseph Rossi*, 2 vols. Vienna: J.B. Wallishausser, 1814–1815.
2. Ibid.
3. Judson 98, 99.
4. Judson 97.
5. King 91–93.
6. Ibid.
7. Metternich, 37.
8. Metternich 106.
9. King 197, 198.

Part IV

Chapter Sixteen

After the Congress—Biedermeier Austria

For the next twenty years, Francis would preside over half of what became known in history as the Biedermeier era that would last until 1848 when revolutions, civil war and foreign invasion would roil the Empire inherited by his son, Ferdinand. The Biedermeier period is today a relatively obscure historical era, largely remembered for its furniture and art and less for its historical or political significance. The Biedermeier period describes a time unique to central Europe and most particularly to Germany and Austria. In Britain, it corresponded to the Regency period of 1795–1837 and shared some of the same characteristics insofar as a flourishing of the arts, architecture, and cultural achievement.

The era got its name essentially from a cartoon character, "Papa Biedermeier," whose über-bourgeois lifestyle and antics were humorously caricatured by Ludwig Eichrodet in a Munich tabloid. Herr Biedermeier was an amalgam of middle class values and tastes that arose in the early years of peace and growing prosperity after decades of war. The era is considered to be one of contented living when not much happened, but this in retrospect is inaccurate. It has some parallels with the 1920s "return to normalcy" in the United States when, after the First World War, people wanted to forget about the bad old days and move on to happier and carefree times with new fashions, new music and changing attitudes toward old values. The imperial government's paranoid fear of liberalism and nationalism would also find parallels with the US government's obsession with communism seen in the "Red Scare" and Palmer Raids of the early 1920s.

Francis' new and sprawling Empire, now only nine years old, had much to repair in the aftermath of the wars. Austria's debt was little short of stupendous. Demobilization of the army and drastic paring of the state budget regarding military expenditures was imperative and unavoidable, and yet service of interest on state debt alone remained a heavy burden. A French indemnity, for once paid to Austria, helped to some extent, but the Austrian treasury would remain a constant source of anxiety and constraint for the rest of Francis' life.

In the immediate aftermath of the Napoleonic Wars, Austria was not alone in facing massive state debt. All the Great Powers were in the same boat as were, for that matter, the smaller states of Europe who had also endured the depredations of French occupation and plunder. The difference in the long run would be Austria's limitations, relative to the other powers, to rejuvenate and create a robust economy. This was due to several reasons but in a sense, Austria was a victim of her own success and her new-found role as the fulcrum of the Concert of Europe.

As Francis gazed at his empire on one of his great maps at the Hofburg, of which he was so fond, his position looked impressive and powerful. Only Russia ruled a larger mass of territory in 1815 and much of that was sparsely populated and impoverished. In population, Francis could count some 32 million subjects, exceeding that of France and second only to Russia. Its geographic position allowed it interior lines to potentially project military power into every sector of Europe. Finally, in the Biedermeier period, its role in maintaining the peace—so vital to every one of the states of Europe after two decades of war—was generally supported by at least one or two of the other Great Powers, but most of all by Great Britain, the undisputed winner and greatest of the Great Powers in the decades ahead.

Austrian bayonets would check French expansion into Italy, if need be, where it now exercised unquestioned dominance and with the kingdom of Piedmont-Sardinia as a convenient buffer between Austrian Lombardy and French Provence. As the leader of the German Confederation, Austria was once again the protector of the small, weaker German states along the Rhine against French penetration there and could count on Prussian, if not British and Russian support, if necessary. But Austria also checked further Prussian expansion, supported by the other German states and, in Francis' time, by Russia and probably France. Austria also guarded against Russian expansion into the Balkans or toward Constantinople, very much supported by France and Britain. Finally, Francis was now opposed to any further expansionism and, indeed, opposed strongly any changes at all to the *status quo* of Europe after 1815, as we shall see, with force if necessary.

The happy geopolitical situation in which Francis found himself has been described as a "complex five-sided checkmate"[1] It is no wonder, then, that Francis, of the post war sovereigns, had the greatest interest of all in preserving and enforcing the Vienna settlement of 1815 and would do so rigorously to the end of his life. Metternich would carry it on after he died to 1848 and his grandson, Franz Joseph, until his armies were literally driven out of Italy and Germany in 1859 and 1866.

Austria appeared to be a colossal military power but, even better, with the balance of power as it was until Francis' death in 1835, Austria could count on leveraging her own somewhat illusory military power with that of at least one and perhaps two or more other Great Powers. Intimidating as Russia might be, uninvited Russian aggression at any point in Europe would almost certainly bring France and Britain into alliance with Prussian neutrality, at the very least. In its time, from a purely geopolitical, power-politics viewpoint, one would have to be a fool not to take advantage of this position and to maintain it for as long as possible. And so, Francis did with the brilliant cunning of Metternich, whom he elevated to *Staatskanzler* in 1821.

FRANCIS THE CONSERVATIVE

The "reactionary" role played by Austria as the enforcer of the Vienna settlement is but one source of the dour and forbidding personality attributed to Francis by latter-day critics but it seems largely, although not entirely, off the mark for a couple of reasons.

In the first place, not to mince words, but the very term "reactionary" refers to those who wish to turn back the clock and return to "happier times" or an "idyllic past" that is inevitably illusionary. Francis was conservative but not reactionary. A turning back the clock to earlier times would have meant a renewed burst of Habsburg state reformism and Enlightenment thinking that had so distinguished the eras of Maria Theresa and Joseph II during the dynasty's rise to renewed geopolitical prominence. This was not at all what Francis had in mind, and is to some extent a pity because his conservatism was to retard Austrian receptivity to increasingly vital economic and technological improvements, such as those taking place in Britain.

Francis' grandmother and uncle, however, had not seen and endured what Francis had seen and endured for more than two decades. Francis believed that the natural and logical conclusion of too much liberal thought and devolution of power was mob violence, revolution and war, with all that they entailed. How could he not? To have suggested otherwise to Francis in his fifth decade of life would have evoked a blank look of incredulity from the Emperor, as if to say that he was talking to an idiot or a fool. Those genii were not going to be let out of the bottle again, come what may. In this, he was more conservative than Metternich who had his own ideas about reform of the Monarchy that were ignored or rejected by his master.[2] With this in mind, we must consider the Carlsbad Decrees of 1819.

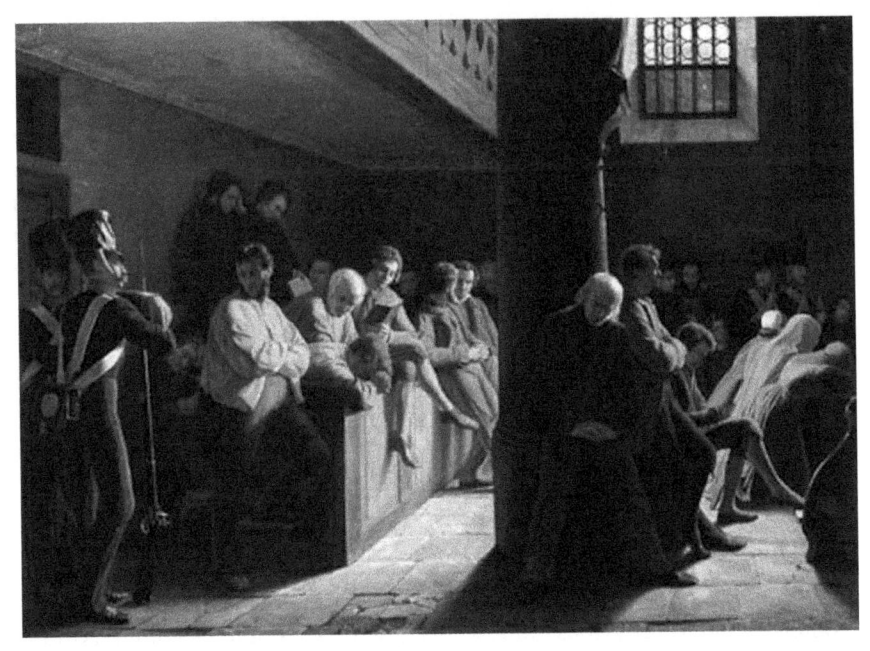

Figure 16.1. Wilhelm Joseph Heine's Inmates at the Prison Church, 1837. Deutsches Historiches Museum, Berlin.

On March 23, 1819, Karl Ludwig Sand murdered the publisher, August von Kotzebue in Mannheim by stabbing him to death in his house, before one of his children. Sand was a veteran who had fought at Waterloo, but thereafter attended several universities. He was soon an advocate for liberal ideas and helped form or joined at least two nationalist student fraternities—*Burschenschaften*—to promote the ideas of a liberal constitution in the German Federation as well as German political unity.[3]

These ideas and organizations were increasingly spreading within Germany and Austria in the immediate aftermath of the Napoleonic Wars, particularly in the universities. Von Kotzebue was the publisher of a conservative, weekly gazette in Weimar that opposed and ridiculed these increasingly popular notions and for this, he was deemed a traitor by many students, intellectuals and urban *cognoscenti*. Von Kotzebue's murder was an overnight sensation and crystalized the simmering conflict between conservatives and liberals in German society. Another murder was attempted on July 1, 1819 on Karl von Ibell, the President of the state of Nassau by a 28-year-old pharmacist connected to another radical republican student association.

There could be no doubt which side Francis was on. The representatives of the German states (*Bundestag*) were called to Carlsbad where Metternich presided as minister for Francis in his role as President of the Confederation between August 6–31, 1819. The reactions of the German kings and rulers to the two incidents and the perceived rise of revolutionary ideas were scarcely different than those of the Austrian Emperor. In three weeks, the Bundestag enacted the so-called Carlsbad Decrees, effective on September 20, 1819.

The decrees essentially fell into three major sections. The first applied to universities, banning the student associations outright and embedding a "representative" of the monarch or government of each of the 39 states into the university administration to ensure the suppression of any publications, agitation or teachings inimical to the honor and dignity of the Confederation and its member states.

The second section provided for universal press censorship of the same kinds of vaguely described writings that impugned the honor of the Confederation, the safety of individual states or the maintenance of peace and quiet in Germany. Advance approval was required for all newspapers, or other publications with heavy penalties, including a ban on further publication for five years, with no right of appeal. The last section set up a permanent, intrusive "central investigating Commission" to root out the "origin" of the "revolutionary plots" directed against the "internal peace" of the union or the individual states.

The Carlsbad Decrees would be the legal authority for censorship and surveillance not merely in Austria, but throughout Germany for the next three decades, until the Bundestag repealed them in 1848. Liberal university professors were fired, students who were deemed active in the former Burschenschaften were blacklisted from ever holding governmental or military office and untrustworthy publications were shut down. The result was a suppression of open expression of liberal or nationalist opinion that was now forced underground but would never die. These ideas and the oppressed parts of the subject populations who supported them would erupt with a vengeance in 1848.

The other source of potential disruption of the European scene after 1815 was tribal nationalism, especially in central Europe, but this would not be a major factor for Francis during his reign. In the Habsburg hereditary lands, for example, feelings of national identity were largely missing, except in Hungary, and there mainly in the aristocracy and wealthy landowners. Judson describes the Austrian dilemma in Francis' time as unrealized potential that existed in nascent form at the outset of the imperium:

> The elements of cultural diversity mentioned by Rossi also tend to reinforce a larger common framework of social and cultural unity. In Rossi's depiction, the emperor's subjects may worship differently and they may use different languages in some regions of his realm, but they use their different languages

to convey unified feelings of loyalty to the Austrian state and to its dynasty in surprisingly similar ways. This sense of unity is thus reflected in the common culture of celebration shared in the diverse regions of Habsburg central Europe. . . . Together, it seems that this common culture that celebrated empire constituted a different but equally important legitimation of empire, as did the many peasant communities that viewed empire—or the dynasty—as their protector against the arbitrary power of the local lords.[4]

What Judson describes echoes the musings of the Austrian essayist Hugo von Hofmannsthal in the late imperial era of the early 20th century that became known as "the Austrian idea." It was a subject that preoccupied and bedeviled Metternich and later Austrian ministers; the role of Austria with respect to Germany and, simultaneously, toward the non-German peoples ruled by the Habsburgs in the East and, for a time, in the South.

Metternich realistically once described the Austrian Empire as a "Slavic" one. It could not possibly Germanize its other subject peoples, as Joseph II had once dreamed, nor, alternatively, remain a Great Power of the first rank if it had to accept rejection from the German nation, now represented by the Confederation. As A.J.P. Taylor remarked:

The problem was, in essence, simple: the Habsburg monarchy and nationalism were incompatible; no real peace was possible between them. . . . Metternich saw this more clearly than many of his successors. . . . [He] explored, too, all the remedies, and despaired of them. . . . Metternich's suggestions anticipated all the constitutional developments of Austria in the second half of the nineteenth century. . . .[5]

The Austrian idea was, like most Habsburg concepts, an improvisational compromise that sought in a unique Austrian destiny the role of the fulcrum or flexion point between the Germanic and non-Germanic peoples of Central Europe. It was an idea that was never attained in Francis' time, nor any later era, but whose spectral allure continued to dance before the eyes of Francis' grandson and his ministers, always just out of reach, always beckoning them on.

The vast mass of Francis' empire was made up of peasant farmers who had little interest or knowledge of any national identity. Few ventured very far from the towns and villages of their birth or met individuals speaking a language other than their own vernacular. At most, for these masses of peasants and rural townsfolk, there might be some limited interaction with those of other religious faiths. To the extent that they credited themselves with any distinct identity, it would be their religion, as was discovered as late as 1919 with the break-up of the Austro-Hungarian Empire.

Ironically, to the peasantry, the Habsburg monarchy and Francis in particular were still regarded, as Hohenwarts had taught Francis long ago, a "visible deity . . . well-nigh infallible . . . the guardian spirit of security, property and liberty." They still looked to the monarchy, now augmented by its laws and courts, to protect them against the overbearing and sometimes arbitrary power of their local nobility. Francis was a heroic figure to them and would remain the "father" of his people for the rest of his life.

In the countryside, especially in Hungary, it was the aristocracy and landowning gentry whose opinions mattered during Francis' reign. Their loyalty was bought and maintained in the same way that governments to this day ensure it; low taxation or exemptions and a conservative political establishment that viewed radical change with suspicion or repression. Francis' own moralistic, Catholic, social conservatism, which would be a hallmark of the dynasty right through 1918, also served to reinforce the regime's ultimate legitimacy among a largely, but not exclusively, Catholic nobility. The income of the aristocracy, in Francis' day, largely based upon rent from their lands and local taxation of villages, was secured by an imperial army that could and would be dispatched, when necessary, to put down unrest wherever it occurred.

In urban areas, the story was a bit different but again, over the vast expanses of the plains of Hungary and Galicia, in the isolated mountain towns and villages of Bohemia, Moravia, Transylvania, Tyrolea and Dalmatia, there were no cities of any significant size. The big cities of the Empire were Milan, Venice, Trieste, Budapest, Prague and above all, Vienna. It was these urban areas that, like Paris, posed the greatest potential for a mass uprising and it was the urban elites who were watched. It was in urban areas where newspapers and printing presses—the social media of its day—could rapidly spread inflammatory ideas and news that might arouse a densely-packed population. It was logical, therefore, that it was there censorship would be pervasive and most vigilant.

So, it was that mainly in the cities where the "police state" would operate long after the various delegations left Vienna after the Congress. The internal network of informers and press censors made little impact on most of the population of the Empire but were increasingly resented in its urban centers as time went on. The merchants, bourgeoisie, university students and professors, artists and intellectuals were the ones who felt the weight of the *Geheime Staatspolizei* as an oppressive, intrusion into their lives and work.

CENSORSHIP AND REPRESSION IN AUSTRIA AND GERMANY

Here again, the question of whose policy was being pursued arises. There is reason to believe that Metternich himself believed in a more liberal regime, at least in terms of the political structure of the Empire, than did the Kaiser himself. Robert Waissenberger, in his book *Vienna in the Biedermeier Era*, remarks on this very subject:

> Without it having been obvious, it is nevertheless remarkable how well Francis I managed to keep his name and his person clear of any association with the oppressive nature of Metternich's system. In his habits of mind and in the whole way in which he conducted himself, the emperor contrived to appear to the middle classes as "one of them"; the quiet gardener—which indeed he was—fitted the Biedermeier idyll as nicely as did the irritation we know him to have expressed over the country's censorship: "Our censorship really is silly." People seem to have been very ready to believe that the emperor himself was a prisoner of the system—though it would have lain within his power to alter the way it operated . . . the emperor was able to feel secure in the veneration of his people, a people who failed to see that, in reality, he held absolute sway over them, his actions and omissions alike setting the country's political course. Within the lifetime of Francis, Metternich recognized that a state bound by such formal rigorism was doomed to failure; yet he was unable to rouse himself to make a decisive stand against tradition, to throw off his role of passive onlooker—he lacked the moral conviction.[6]

One might quibble with the observation that the state was "doomed," but the essence of his critique points to one of the central themes we have explored in this work. The Habsburg dynasty had another century to go, but the mystery of this man and his place in history is made difficult due to what appears to have been a deliberate policy of staying out of the limelight except on rare occasions. Francis never entered Paris in triumph 1814 with Alexander and Frederick William of Prussia, sending Schwarzenberg in his stead while he went to visit his daughter. He refrained from personal intervention in the Congress of Vienna, remaining a shadow in the background. Francis had developed a personal style of rule that made him the final authority, without question, but out of the public eye. This had the convenient consequences of his avoiding personal blame when things went wrong, as they often did, but also for creating a historical void, where he is concerned, within the most powerful Empire in continental Europe during his reign.

Desmond Seward makes the same point in his biography of Metternich in this way:

> Yet for all his kindness, Francis was a harder man than his chancellor. In 1848 Metternich would tell Count von Hübner that if the Emperor had taken his advice on foreign affairs, he had not done so on internal matters. 'As chancellor, I had the right to speak but I did so very moderately, and only during real crises when vital principles were at stake.' Surveillance of writers, artists and musicians was encouraged by Francis, not by Metternich. Nor would he take any notice when the chancellor spoke of the need to reorganize the Monarchy.[7]

It is all the more ironic, when the truth is known, that the system of repression in Germany and Italy, both internally and internationally, came to be known as the "Metternich System," forever linking the more liberal minister to an increasingly despised method of government. Staying out of the public eye or the records of posterity, however, was not the same as relinquishing power. The image of a genial, Biedermeier ruler was one cultivated by Francis and not atypical of hereditary monarchies, certainly of this era. It perpetuated the myth, in the popular imagination, of the infallible near-deity. When mistakes were made, when things went wrong, conventional wisdom was that the Emperor had been ill-advised or poorly served. A change of ministry or sacking of a general would put things right.

Nonetheless, it is not clear why Francis and Austria are given especial censure for what in later times would be called "human rights." The existence of a free and unfettered press was by far the exception to the rule in the world of 1815–35 in just about every country. Francis' regime was hardly unusual in this respect and may even have been more tolerant than some. Francis was resolved not to fight a revolution within his empire with bloody suppression of organized resistance to the law and institutions of his government. He had seen that in France, during his lifetime and knew where it led. The Carlsbad decrees and other measures taken to detect and suppress sources of internal dissent and potential revolution, as he would have seen it, were intended to pre-empt and forestall mob violence and rebellion before they ever reached that point.

Furthermore, the conservative suppression of open and organized dissent in his day and age resembled nothing like the fascist or communist police states that would arise a century later. There were no concentration camps, nor enforced ideological conformity, nor mass executions or terrors. In fact, as Pieter Judson points out, the coffers of the *Geheime Staatspolizei* of the Austrian state were so under-funded that it could not begin to run anything like a wide-ranging spy network while also carrying out all the other roles the regime demanded of it or for which it was given such credit later, particularly in English- language books and periodicals.[8]

One must also remind oneself of other more odious suppressions of liberty in the day and age of Francis. It would not be until 1833 that slavery was abolished in the British Empire. The United States was becoming embroiled in an ever-deepening national debate over slavery. In 1808 Congress forbade the further importation of slaves into the country. In 1820, the Missouri Compromise was reached, in which Congress admitted two new states to the Union; one slave and one free after fierce debate. The United States would continue to enslave over ten percent of its population until 1865. Twenty percent of the population of Kentucky were slaves; forty-seven percent of the population of Louisiana were enslaved. Brazil only abolished slavery in 1888.

Austria had no slaves, had never had slavery, and had abolished serfdom at about the time of the American Revolution.

Interestingly, after the early 1820s, neither Francis nor his ministers seriously believed that there was any significant danger of revolution or threats to the Monarchy. Instead, the focus of the police evolved. Initially, the regime imposed upon the police the duty to monitor foreign travelers to Austria and to carefully watch their contacts in Austria.[9] Anyone arriving in Vienna immediately became involved with the authorities and possibly with the censor as well. Books had to be presented on arrival and if they failed to comply with Austrian censorship, had to be surrendered and deposited.[10] It is easy to understand why, as the years went on, Austria received rather dismal reviews by English speaking travelers, for example, who found such restrictions tiresome, to say the least.

Over time, however, the focus evolved to rooting out civil servants unfit to govern. Its inquiries tended to delve into the moral character or failings of servants of the state, reflecting the Emperor's own, increasingly puritanical viewpoint and his fear that scandal could arouse contempt or hostility to the government. To Francis, the presence of moral failings, such as drunkenness, womanizing priests, homosexuality, extra-marital relationships, or failing to regularly attend Mass became disqualifiers for civil service, imposing a conservative orthodoxy upon the Empire.[11]

Secondly, the secret police often sympathized with the disaffection of Francis' most neglected, impoverished subjects and their complaints about the inadequacy or failings of the imperial or, most often, local government. The secret police pushed up to the top a steady stream of feedback and criticism of governance that Francis and his ministers read with interest.[12] It is perhaps for this reason that, deep into the 19th century, Austrian civil servants, governors and bureaucrats were generally, scrupulously incorruptible compared to former Turkish, Italian or Polish overlords that preceded them.

There can be no doubt, however, that as the Austrian Empire became more and more urbanized with the dawn of industrialization in areas clustered around Vienna, Trieste, Milan, western Bohemia and Lower Austria, the strict, conservative censorship became increasingly intolerable to intelligent, educated society. This resentment would eventually boil over into the riot and revolt that Francis dreaded in 1848–49. In some respects, this may have been due to the relatively educated society over which Francis ruled, as compared to much of the rest of Europe and particularly Eastern Europe and the Balkans. In Vienna, particularly, the Biedermeier period would see a blossoming and wide popularity of theatre and plays, stimulating the works of Franz Grillparzer, Nikolaus Lenau, Friedrich Halm, Johann Nestroy and Ferdinand Raimund. Grillparzer complained of the censor in his autobiography, but all of them could have their work banned.

Nonetheless, Austrians found ways to mitigate the censor. In the first place, the hobbled funding meant that those individuals working for the censor, reviewing books, literature, plays and so forth, did so at very low wages and, consequently, often had little understanding of the material they were supposed to curate. The authors became adept at the ingenious *bon mot*, the clever double entendre, the disguised metaphor that floated past the police, but delighted audiences. As one historian has remarked, the censorship was a nuisance rather than a tyranny.[13]

Of course, as with the spy network, there were censors who sympathized with the authors and some cities were known to be friendlier than others and were chosen as sites for publications that would have been banned elsewhere.[14] Particularly in Vienna, private libraries and "reading club rooms" sprang up where the censor and the police rarely interfered. Much of high society, including high ranking members of the government and bureaucracy, could and did discretely partake of foreign journals and books in these salons and clubs. Despite occasional raids, the exclusive membership of such associations and societies kept the authorities largely at bay.[15]

This is not to excuse the Biedermeier era's restrictive, conservative structure, the secret police, censorship or surveillance; merely to explain the reality of its function and its comparative impact with other contemporaneous societies in Europe and America. Open and free public expression is essential to any civilization that is forced to compete with others over time. The raucous, unruly and sometimes misguided opinions that populate freer societies are necessary to stimulate recognition of deficiencies and self-correction once errors have been discovered. When, like Austria, your country existed in a hyper-competitive neighborhood, cheek-by-jowl with other states whose receptivity to innovation eventually transformed into socio-economic or military power, the closure of channels of free expression produced short-term security at the price of long-term competitiveness. In this regard, Francis' short-sighted insistence on passive socio-political orthodoxy, while understandable and not even particularly unique among European leaders of his day, planted the seeds of his fledgling empire's decline and eventual dissolution.

SEEDS OF DESTRUCTION: ECONOMIC STAGNATION

Perhaps nowhere was the conservative suspicion of innovation and change more telling than in the road not taken during the post-war period with respect to the Austrian Empire's economic development. The other two Eastern monarchies were in the same relative position as Austria in 1815, but one of them, the Prussian state, made a virtue of necessity and the hard choices that would transform it over the succeeding decades into the most dynamic and powerful state in continental Europe. The seeds of Prussian ascendency were planted in this era.

In the development of the Austrian economy during the Biedermeier period, the inherent conservatism and suspicion of innovation, especially from abroad, would eventually result in Austria falling far behind its potential and then actual continental rivals, Prussia and France. All European economies had been stricken by the wars, except Great Britain whose "take off" into the industrial age had begun earlier in the late 18th century and exploded during and after the Napoleonic period. Like the United States after the Second World War, Britain's economy had grown and strengthened during and because of the war.

Continental Europe, on the other hand, experienced economic constriction and deprivation. While the economies of the various European states gradually improved with the resumption of agriculture and commerce in the years following the war, progress would be uneven. The industrial revolution that had essentially begun and taken off in Britain would spread to France, Belgium, the Netherlands and western and northern Germany as the years went on, but the Eastern empires would lag.

Austria would remain a first-class political power during Francis' lifetime but its geopolitical position masked an increasingly, comparatively weak economic base that would eventually prove to be its undoing. The hammer blows to Austrian predominance in continental Europe would come from France in 1859 and even more so from Prussia in 1866. Those debacles are outside the scope of our story but the seeds of Austrian destruction were sown within it and must be considered to give a full and fair account of the undoubted influence that Francis and his ministers had on the eventual fate of his country.

In the first place, industrialization was viewed with suspicion by Francis and his ministers because it was believed to encourage migration of masses of workers into urban centers, such as the capital, that provided tinder for the spark of revolution, such as the mobs in Paris. Francis' Minister of Police, Johann Anton von Pergen, was of equal mind and warned the Emperor against the "mob" arising from an urban proletariat as a potential source of social upheaval.[16] A simple but stark example to illustrate Austrian mistakes in the all-important economic sphere during the Biedermeier era is to contrast them with the choices made by its arch-rival during the same period.

Prussia's award of the Rhineland areas and Westphalia at the Congress of Vienna had not been the kingdom's first choice. Prussia had wanted Saxony, an eastern kingdom like itself and which would have been contiguous with the homeland of Brandenburg-Prussia and the Polish territories it had absorbed decades earlier. Instead, it received a large swath of territories along the Rhine, far more influenced by the Enlightenment and later revolutionary, liberal, French ideas. These newly annexed lands were, or soon would be, in the "take off" phase of industrialization. Indeed, the Rhine/Ruhr area would become in time the heartland of German industrial might for centuries to come.

This disparity between the largely agricultural, traditional, conservative society of peasants and feudal lords in "old" Prussia contrasted with a more urban, intellectual, western society of the Rhineland that was in the beginning stages of industrialization forced the monarchy in Berlin to make some choices that would have fateful consequences. Politically, the western half of the kingdom would have to accept a much stricter, conservative governance from Berlin than the former duchies and kingdoms that had existed previously had exercised. In the economic sphere, however, the reverse became true. The new, expanded Prussia whose territories now spanned the width of Germany would become an industrialized, modern state while Austria increasingly fell behind in relative terms.

The impetus for all this was the fact that Prussia's two halves were not continuous. And this anomalous situation posed a problem for Prussian commerce and trade. Like Austria, much government revenue was generated by "internal" tolls and tariffs that inhibited domestic, let alone international trade and commerce. One Prussian writer bemoaned no less than ten internal tolls when goods passed from one end of the kingdom to another. Like Austria, the royal government was reluctant to deprive itself of the revenue produced by internal tariffs. Further, Prussia's problem included tolls and tariffs that were charged by the 38 other German states that surrounded and, in some cases, were interposed between Prussia's non-contiguous parts. The solution, almost forced upon Prussia's conservative elite, was the Zollverein.

Prussia's first, tentative moves were cautious but nevertheless difficult. In 1818, the Prussian government eliminated internal tolls and external tolls for the importation of raw materials. A uniform ten percent tax was imposed on manufactured goods imported into Prussia, usually but not always from Britain. On the other hand, a heavy tax was placed on goods transported through Prussia which had the tendency to pressure other German states to join. In 1819, Schwarzburg-Sondershausen did so. In 1822, Weimar Gotha, Merchlenburg-Schwerin, Schaumburg-Lippe, Rudolstadt and Hamburg also joined.

Significantly, during this period, Austria was not excluded but declined to show any interest in joining any customs union at all, nor to create one of its own. The reason was essentially the reluctance to give up revenues desperately needed by the crown to pay off debt and balance the books, but also resistance by merchants and agricultural interests—the landed gentry and aristocracy—to competition from abroad. Finally, as we have seen, Francis was advised by his Minister of Police that industrialization necessarily meant urban "mobs" who were prone to revolution. Austrian economic policy was, therefore, steeped in a kind of mercantile rigidity that isolated it from the rest of the world.

However painful it may have been to wean government revenues from internal and external duties and taxation, the benefits of freer trade and competition would eventually compensate and then surpass the loss in time. The example provided by Prussia was evidently not lost on other German states.

In 1828 Bavaria and Württemberg saw the light and created their own South German customs union, seeking the benefit of free trade between themselves but reluctant to join the Zollverein, dominated by Prussia. They were soon joined that same year by Saxony, Hesse-Cassel, Hanover, Brunswick Hamburg, Bremen and Frankfurt. Austria still abstained from joining and inevitably leading a rival customs union to the Zollverein. The golden opportunity did not last long.

In 1831, Hesse-Cassel defected to the Zollverein followed in 1834 by Bavaria and Saxony. By 1837 most of the German States had joined the Zollverein, creating a free trade zone and uniform tariff program on all frontiers of the German Confederation, excluding Austria. Proceeds from tariffs would be divided among the members in proportion to population. Austria would not attempt to join the Zollverein until it was too late; after the 1848 revolutions. By then, the government in Berlin had experienced thirty years of growing economic power and leadership in Germany and was not about to cede any of it to Austria. By then, Austria was left with the hollow political leadership of the Confederation. Austria was not admitted to the Zollverein in 1849 and had to settle for some limited tariff concessions from the Zollverein members.

The costs and benefits of free trade and international competition on national economies is controversial in many respects, even to this day, but the arguments tend to revolve around their distribution within a given society rather than the overall impact on participating states. There is no reason to think, for example, that the Austrian Empire would not have developed an industrial economic base equal to any of the other German states, even if its benefits were unevenly distributed across the vast Empire. As it was, there were green shoots of industrial growth in Lombardy, Austria and Bohemia despite its economic isolation, although the supremacy of agriculture in Hungary, Galicia, and Transylvania, for example, maintained those societies in the same condition they had been in the 18th century.

What Francis and particularly his finance minister, Franz Anton von Kolowrat, failed to grasp was a fundamental fact about largely agrarian empires. "The elemental truth must be stressed that the characteristic of any country before its industrial revolution and modernization is poverty . . . with low productivity, low output per head, in traditional agriculture . . . any economy which has agriculture as the main constituent of its national income does not produce much of a surplus above the immediate requirements of consumption."[17]

Adam Smith's *Wealth of Nations* had been published for forty years by the conclusion of the Napoleonic Wars; a half century by the mid-1820s when Austria should have joined one or the other German customs unions or, perhaps, created one of its own that might have included northern Italy. Nor was Smith's book obscure. The fundamental philosophy of capitalist resource allocation and the "invisible hand" had been debated in the British Parliament by North, Fox and Pitt in the 1780s. James Madison in the United States would rely on the arguments put forth in Smith's book in 1791 to oppose a national bank in Congress. Thomas Jefferson thought it the "best book to be read. . . ."[18] Metternich himself warned Francis of the potential economic domination of Prussia and urged him to permit Austria to join the Zollverein, if only to balance Prussian influence, but Kolowrat supported by parochial Austrian business interests prevailed in the argument.[19]

The conservative fog that shrouded Francis' government did not influence only the monarch himself, but permeated the aristocracy in Biedermeier society that was dominated by the usual desire to maintain its own privileges and income without change. And not all changes from rapidly accelerating industrialization were pleasant and appealing. Austrians with sufficient means and interest to travel abroad, particularly to London, could not have been entirely impressed with what they saw.

Dickensian Britain was to the toiling masses a brutal and soul-destroying process of wage enslavement, urban slums, child labor, horrific working conditions and exploitation by a rising class of bourgeois capitalists. The relatively mild, agrarian economy of the Austrian Empire of the Biedermeier period, punctuated here and there by limited industrialization in and around Milan, Linz, Prague, or Vienna seemed much less fearful and dystopian, by contrast. The magnates and great families whose income as landlords maintained them in their magnificent country *schlossen* and urban residences, sitting at the peak of a quiescent agrarian peasantry, understandably had little incentive to change much at all, and in this, they were in accord with the Kaiser in Vienna.

The Austrian government in Vienna did little to directly subsidize the growth of industry within the Empire, but then again, neither did most European governments. Austria was not unique in this respect. This was the infancy of *laissez-faire* capitalism in which investment in some infrastructure—roads and bridges, canals, sewerage, primary school education—was all that anyone expected or desired, but here the Austrians also lagged. Infrastructure investment in parts of Austria and Bohemia were made, but the cash-strapped treasury did little for Hungary, Galicia, Dalmatia, and other more peripheral areas.

Chapter Sixteen

LATE REFORMS AMID REPRESSION

One positive contribution made was the founding of the Imperial-Royal Polytechnic Institute in Vienna in 1815. This institution, which survives to this day as the Vienna Institute of Technology, was meant to compliment the University of Vienna, which had been in existence since 1365. The purpose of the new institution was to educate and promote the study of practical and utilitarian skills and knowledge for modernization, as contrasted with the emphasis on humanistic, legal and philosophic studies of the ancient University.[20]

Another was the founding of the Austrian National Bank ("Österreichische *Nationalbank*") in 1816. In 1815, Francis had appointed Johann Philip Stadion as Finance Minister, a post he would hold until 1824, resurrecting his career that had temporarily ended in 1809 with his resignation as Foreign Minister after Wagram. The bank would improve the rampant inflation that had arisen in the last stage of the war to underwrite Austrian military expenditures, embarking on a policy of devaluation of the Austrian currency. The bank would also provide a new source of public and private credit for the government and entrepreneurs. The Austrian National Bank survives to this day.

On the one hand, in the immediate post-war period, Francis might be forgiven for failing to foresee that the economic isolation of his realm would lead to its faltering 50 years hence and crumbling a century later. Few national leaders then or now can be credited with that sort of prescience and vision. On the other hand, it cannot be denied that Frederick Wilhelm III of Prussia and most of the other German kings and leaders grasped, to some extent at least, the short-term benefits if not the ultimate result of their decisions. Austria would have internal tariffs until 1918 with Hungary and suffered accordingly.

In the economic sphere, then, Francis presided over the beginning of a slow and this time final decline of Habsburg power that would gather speed over time. It was not seen at the time and indeed, it would have taken a very extraordinary ruler to have wrenched a conservative society out of its entrenched and comfortable existence. It would become far more apparent during the reign of his son and grandson. The suspicion of foreign ideas, economic or otherwise, that might germinate and propagate revolution engendered censorship and stifled healthy debate, self-criticism, self-correction and reform within the Empire.

Metternich, so often blamed for this blinkered policy, cannot be given the ultimate blame for it any more than he should be given ultimate credit for Austrian geopolitical maneuvering during the war. He served a monarch and not the other way around. If his undoubted intelligence, insight and brilliance had been successful, over time, in persuading Francis of the need for economic reform, including free trade and interaction among and with the other

German and Italian states, he would deserve far more credit than is due him. Instead, he largely contented himself with being the "coachman" of Europe, cultivating the support of the equally conservative, fearful courts of Prussia and Russia, and dominating those of the lesser German states by facilitating the suppression of liberal dissent wherever and whenever it was found or even suspected.

The occasions for suppression were not lacking. Austrian soldiers intervened regularly in Italy, for example, propping up the traditional monarchies and the Catholic church. Austria intervened with military force in the kingdom of Naples in 1821 and Piedmont in 1823.[21] It supported the Bourbon French monarchy in its intervention in Spain to save the throne of King Ferdinand in 1826.

Many of these exertions required Austrian military intervention, or the threat of it, especially in Italy. As liberal uprisings against often corrupt, backward Italian puppet kingdoms were put down, public opinion in Britain and, in due course, the British parliament began to look at Francis' Austria as the "jailer" of Italy and Europe. The unfortunate consequence of cooling British opinion coincided with the rapidly rising expansion of Britain's overseas empire, especially in India. Britain began drifting away from the Quadruple Alliance and quietly, one of the supports of the "five-sided checkmate" gradually but largely withdrew from continental affairs.

In fact, it was Austrian intervention in Italy that drew the most international notoriety, probably due to the advanced culture and international standing the land of the Renaissance had, as compared to Austria's own eastern possessions or Germany, where native monarchies were equally reactionary and asked for no Austrian help to stifle dissent. By contrast, revolts and popular agitation against local rulers and "foreign" Austrian dominance in northern Italy were far more frequent and violent than anywhere else Francis held sway and engendered more sympathy accordingly. The seeds of aggressive Italian animosity toward Austria that would result in wars in 1848, 1859, 1866 and 1915–18 were planted and fertilized during this time. Austria would have no more implacable enemy for the rest of its existence than among the Italians and violent Austrian repression using military force would incur more popular, international censure of Austria and Francis than almost anything else done during his reign.

In addition, the perceived need to maintain a substantial, standing army at the ready to garrison, occupy or put down riot and rebellion burdened the Austrian Empire's treasury. The cost was a constant, annual drain, impairing investment in other necessary or desirable improvements, including military/technological innovations, without raising taxes. This Francis was wont to do because it would inevitably arouse hostility from the merchant and aristocratic classes and that could lead to pressure on the monarchy itself.

In fact, the cost slowly exhausted Austria's military potential, as against another great power in a war, should it become necessary. This was disguised, however, by its active interventionism and the relatively large population from which a very large army could be recruited. But mere numbers in the age of the industrial revolution would prove to be a deceptive indicia of real military power. Subsisting on an increasingly meagre economic base with limited access to capital, the high expense of a military establishment served to accelerate the erosion of relative Austrian military power over time. It would not be put to the test against another great power in Francis' lifetime, but that would change in the middle of the century.

NOTES

1. Kennedy 163.
2. Taylor, *The Habsburg Monarchy* 39,40.
3. Richter, Ludwig, *Lebenserinnerungen eines Deutschen Malers* (German Edition), (Charleston: Createspace Independent Publishing Platform, 2014) 211.
4. Judson 100, 101.
5. Taylor 40.
6. Waissenberger, Robert. *Vienna in the Biedermeier Era, 1815–1848*, (Lombard: Mallard Press, 1986).
7. Seward 289.
8. Judson 131.
9. Ibid.
10. Waissenberger 82.
11. Ibid.
12. Waissenberger 132.
13. Taylor, *The Habsburg Monarchy* 39.
14. Judson 132.
15. Ibid.
16. Häusler, Wolfgang. "Von der Manufaktur zum Maschinensturm, Industrielle Dynamik und soziale Wandel in Raum von Wien." *Wien in Vormärz*, (Vienna: Verein für Geschichte der Stadt Wien: Kommissionsverlag Jugend und Volk, 1980) 49.
17. Mathias, P., *The First Industrial Nation: An Economic History of Britain 1700-1914*, (London: Routledge, 1969) 5.
18. Smith, Adam, An *Inquiry into the Nature and Causes of the Wealth of Nations: A Selected Edition*, (Oxford: Oxford Paperbacks, 2008).
19. Seward 313.
20. Rampley, Matthew. *The Vienna School of Art History*. State College: The Pennsylvania State University Press, 2013.
21. Romani, George. *The Neapolitan Revolution of 1820–1821*, (Santa Barbara: Greenwood Press; New Edition, 1978).

Chapter Seventeen

Family

After an eight-year marriage, Francis' third wife, the Empress Maria Ludovica, died shortly after the Congress of Vienna at the age of 28. Her vivacious personality had proved an asset to her husband. Johann Wolfgang von Goethe, whom she met in 1812, was swept off his feet by her intellect, describing her to be well read, cheerful and a "wonderful creature" in a contemporaneous letter to a friend. She had been quite active in planning entertainments and hosting banquets for her husband and proved to be immensely popular while interacting with many of the famous personalities at the Congress. No less a personality than Talleyrand expressed admiration for her grace and charm, despite her failing health.

In retrospect, it appears the Empress had already contracted tuberculosis which had an increasingly deleterious impact on her health. In 1816, after the Congress adjourned, Maria Ludovica and Francis embarked on a trip to Italy, the childhood home for them both. The sunshine and warmth of Italy failed to revive her from a disease that took an ever-increasing number of lives each year as the 19th century wore on and urban centers grew. In fact, the Empress' disease progressed rapidly during the trip. She became too weak to return to Vienna and died on April 7, 1816 in Verona. As had been the case with his uncle, Francis did not catch the disease notwithstanding what must have been close contact with his wife. He returned with her body to Vienna thereafter where she was buried in the Habsburg Imperial Crypt.

Once again, Francis did not wait long to remarry; this time to Karoline Charlotte Auguste, the daughter of his old rival, the king of Bavaria. Princess Karoline was 24 years old and had previously been married to the crown prince of Württemberg. This was an arranged "political" marriage between the two royal houses to avoid either of their children having to marry a Bonaparte. The two of them had lived apart and asserted their marriage had never been consummated to Pope Pius VII, who obligingly annulled the marriage in August 1814, after the defeat of Napoleon.

The new Empress would become popular in Vienna and long outlive her husband, dying in 1873 in Salzburg, just one day after her 81st birthday. She and Francis would have no children. She was popular in Vienna during her nearly twenty-year reign as Empress, becoming involved in social work, founding several hospitals and residences for the poor. She was quite close to her Wittelsbach family in nearby Bavaria. Her half-sister, Sophie, married Francis' son Franz Karl, and it was through that marriage that the Habsburg-Lorraine dynasty would flow to its last two emperors, Franz Joseph and Karl. Her half-niece, Elisabeth, would eventually marry Franz Joseph continuing the unfortunate Habsburg tradition of close familial intermarriage to the end.

The Emperor's daughter, Marie Louise, took up residence in Parma with Adam von Neipperg, but her son remained in Vienna with Francis. The boy's father, Napoleon, died of stomach cancer on May 5, 1821 at the age of 51 on the island of St. Helena. Napoleon's son was just ten years old and had never consciously known his famous father. It was his misfortune that he would also not know his mother well either, as an adolescent or adult. As far as he was concerned, she had essentially abandoned him at the age of five, although that was not actually the case.

Marie Louise gave birth out-of-wedlock to her first child with von Neipperg, Albertine, in 1817 and a second, William Albert, in 1819. With the death of Napoleon, she married von Neipperg on August 8, 1821. She had a third child with him, Mathilde, after her marriage, but the child died in the first year after her birth in 1823. William Albert was eventually made Prince of Montenuovo by Francis. His son, the second Prince Montenuovo, became the chamberlain to Kaiser Franz Joseph in 1909. Both were descended from Francis.

FERDINAND

Francis' son Ferdinand reached the age of 21 on April 19, 1814. While not as grotesque as the last Habsburg king of Spain, Ferdinand was not a normal appearing or acting boy or young man. He had a huge head, due to hydrocephaly. He stammered. He was subject to frequent, violent epileptic attacks since epilepsy could not be controlled by any medication in these times. In the early years of his life, "Nandle," as he was called by his family, was attended by women servants and kept by his parents from public view.

At the age of six, he received his first male tutor. Learning was difficult for him, but it appears that the boy was not burdened with low intelligence, as some later incorrectly assumed without understanding the nature of his physical or mental afflictions. More has become known today thanks to modern medicine and science. Histories and biographies that have mentioned Ferdinand as a man or as Emperor routinely described him as "retarded," "feeble minded" and similar labels that were routinely used in those times that would, today, be regarded with dismay but, more importantly in the case of this man, as inaccurate.

It is not clear exactly what the nature of his learning disability was, but he showed great interest and enthusiasm for diverse subjects such as heraldry, farming, and modern technology. Nonetheless, the tragic figure of the little boy with the huge head, shuffling around the halls of the palace, minded by servants and courtiers, was a sight that his mother and father frequently witnessed.

Ferdinand's mother, Maria Therese, died when he was 14 years old. Francis' new wife, Maria Ludovica, was probably the greatest influence in his life. There is no doubt she brought a breath of fresh air and had a profound impact on the boy. She took a strong interest in Ferdinand right away as his step-mother. She felt that Ferdinand should be brought out of seclusion and exposed to a more normal environment and better instruction. For example, he still could not read and write. Maria Ludovica dismissed Ferdinand's tutors and appointed Josef von Erberg to instruct the boy. Von Erberg was a botanist and historian and managed to develop a deep rapport with his pupil. He completed Ferdinand's education to the age of 21.[1]

It seems that the aggressive insistence of the Empress on treating the child as normally as possible and Von Erberg's diligent, gentle instruction had a great and positive impact on the crown prince. Slowly Ferdinand learned to read and write, to dance, to ride horses, fence, play the piano and to draw. He started keeping a diary, which he did to the end of his life and which often contained very perceptive and witty observations of people and situations. In all, Ferdinand appears to have been rescued by his step-mother and escaped the dreadful treatment of "imbeciles" that was common in that day and for centuries to come.

Francis apparently loved his son unreservedly, despite his disabilities, and almost to a fault. He acquiesced in Maria Ludovica's experimental methods, hopeful of some improvement in the shadow life Ferdinand had led to that point, known only to himself and the most trusted servants and advisors. Yet Francis' presence as a father who enjoyed nothing more than spending time secluded with his family at Laxenburg must have been a factor in the willingness of the young Ferdinand to struggle against his infirmities. There are contemporaneous accounts of Francis wheeling the young boy around the parks at Laxenburg in a wheel barrow, for example.

Francis seems never to have seriously considered the possibility that Ferdinand should not succeed him, although in adolescence, he was advised by the court physicians that they doubted he could consummate any marriage. Francis began including his son in briefings and conferences with his ministers by 1829 when he reached the age of 34. In 1830, he insisted his son be crowned king of Hungary, clearly signaling his intent that the succession would devolve to Ferdinand.

In 1832, Ferdinand was married to Maria Anna, daughter of the king of Piedmont. Reportedly, his attempt to consummate the marriage triggered a succession of five epileptic seizures on the night of his wedding. His attempt to do his duty by his father and the dynasty had to be considered nothing less than remarkable under the circumstances. In December 1832, Ferdinand is reported to have suffered no less than twenty violent seizures. Francis' doctors thought he might die.

Despite the young man's difficult and often heroic progress in overcoming his disabilities, Ferdinand's condition was kept secret from all but the most trusted court functionaries and servants. His public appearances were care-

Figure 17.1. Ferdinand, Archduke of Austria by Caspar Jele, circa 1834. Monastery of Stift Wilten, Innsbruck

fully stage managed. Ferdinand and his father dreaded the possibility that he might have an epileptic seizure during one of these events. Paintings of the imperial family invariably depicted him as a normal, handsome young man disguising his unusual appearance and disabilities from the public.

The curious intransigence of Francis regarding the succession of his son defies logical understanding in historical hind-sight. In part, it appears to arise from the blind love of a parent for a child with special needs. Ferdinand's remarkable progress may well have exaggerated his father's estimation of his capabilities to some extent that only those with such children of their own can understand. In part, it may be attributed to an excessive value placed by Francis on the principle of legitimacy and, in particular, the now hereditary monarchy he had instituted after the collapse of the elective monarchy of the Holy Roman Empire. And yet, even Francis recognized at some level that Ferdinand could not be entrusted with the fate of his new Empire, exercising the power of a supreme autocrat in a complex European geopolitical environment which would inevitably pose new challenges after Francis' death.

In due course, the conflict led to a compromise in the mind of the monarch. Ferdinand would succeed him but he would be guided and directed by a secret state council, the *Geheime Staatskonferenz*, who would actually rule the empire after Francis' death. Three councilors would rule in Ferdinand's name. Francis' brother Ludwig, twenty years younger and only eight years older than Ferdinand, would chair the council. The other two councilors would be Metternich and Count Francis Anton von Kolowrat. This arrangement lasted until 1848 when revolution would shatter Francis' best-laid plan and result in the abdication of his son in favor of Francis' grandson, the eighteen-year-old Franz Joseph who was born in 1830 at Schönbrunn.

BEETHOVEN IN VIENNA

Ludwig van Beethoven had risen to new heights of popularity and fame after receiving his annual pension from Prince Archbishop Rudolph in 1809. During the later war years, he had composed the Seventh Symphony in the Bohemian town of Teplitz in 1811–1812 and Wellington's Victory, both of which were premiered in Vienna on December 8, 1813 at a charity concert for wounded soldiers. Beethoven conducted the concert himself and addressed the audience before the presentation, saying "We are moved by nothing but pure patriotism and the joyful sacrifice of our powers for those who have sacrificed so much for us."[2] By 1813, Beethoven's attitude toward Napoleon had become like that of most Germans who had, in Napoleon's earliest days, seemed the embodiment of the French revolution but was now seen as an oppressive tyrant.

With the death of his brother, Beethoven became involved in a bitter custody battle in the courts with his sister-in-law over his nephew, Karl. This battle would rage for five years, between 1815-20 until finally, he succeeded. The relationship between him and his nephew would eventually lead to Karl attempting to commit suicide.

In 1822, Beethoven met Gioachino Rossini who had recently come to Vienna after the success of his opera *The Barber of Seville*. Reportedly, Beethoven congratulated Rossini saying that the opera would be "played as long as Italian opera exists" and that he should continue to write comic opera because "any other style would do violence to your nature."[3] In 1823, Beethoven met the eleven-year-old Franz Liszt at his residence, having been importuned to do so by Liszt's teacher, Carl Czerny. After hearing the boy play, Liszt recalls Beethoven saying to him "You are one of the lucky ones. . . . It will be your destiny to bring joy and delight to many people and that is the greatest happiness one can achieve." Liszt claimed that this was "the proudest moment of my life."[4]

On May 7, 1824, the *Theater am Kärntnertor* in Vienna was sold out for the premiere performance of Beethoven's Ninth Symphony. The evening would include an appearance by the composer himself; his first public concert since 1813. Beethoven was completely deaf at this point in his life. Nonetheless, he had actively recruited some of the most famous, celebrity singers to perform the vocal solos and duets and ensembles including the eighteen-year-old prodigy, Henriette Sontag, and 21-year-old Vienna native, Caroline Unger. Michael Umlauf would conduct the largest orchestra ever assembled which included the Kärntnertor house orchestra and the Vienna Music Society. Beethoven himself would share the stage with Umlauf.

The Ninth Symphony some would argue was Beethoven's most stupendous work. It combined three movements of strictly orchestral music with a fourth movement in which a chorus and soloists joined the orchestra; the first "choral symphony" ever composed. In any event, the performance was unique in every respect. A thunderous applause cascaded from the packed and excited audience after the choral finale. Beethoven himself was facing the orchestra when the piece concluded, momentarily unaware of the reaction it had caused. At that point, Caroline Unger approached him and gently turned him around to face five standing ovations. The audience waved handkerchiefs, threw hats in the air and waved their hands so that their greatest composer could see their ovation gestures.

Ludwig van Beethoven was unquestionably the greatest composer of his age and, perhaps, of any age. Beethoven's Vienna was likewise the epicenter of European classical music and attracted musicians and composers from all over Europe, not just in Beethoven's lifetime, but into the next century. He died less than less than three years later, on March 26, 1827. Eyewitnesses in his room at the time of his death reported that at the last, a thunderstorm was underway when a loud thunderbolt crashed. The composer lifted his arm with his hand in a fist at the sound and then expired. Some 20,000 mourners lined the streets near what was then the Church of the Holy Trinity at 17 Alser Strasse. Franz Schubert was one of the pallbearers. The funeral prayer for him was written by Franz Grillparzer, one of the most famous Austrian playwrights of his day.

NOTES

1. Grafenauer, Bogo. *Erberg, Joseph Kalasanz*. Ljubljana: 1991
2. Goldschmidt, Harry, *Beethoven Werkeinführungen,* (Leipzig: Reclam, 1975) 49
3. Fisher, Burton D. *The Barber of Seville (Opera Classics Library Series)*. Grand Rapids: Opera Journeys, 2005
4. Keiler, Allan. "Liszt and Beethoven: The Creation of a Personal Myth." *19th-Century Music. 12. no. 2.* (1988) 116–131.

Chapter Eighteen

Francis and the Post War Era

On February 11, 1818, Francis reached the age of 50. His life and his reign was already longer than both his father's and his uncle's. Only his grandmother, in living memory, had lived and reigned longer. Contemporary accounts suggest that, even at the Congress of Vienna, Francis appeared older than his actual age. Always of slight build, he appeared increasingly thin and frail. He still had a full head of hair, but it was now white and with a receding hairline. His face in other portraits was often made to appear fuller and rounder than it was but in still others, the premature aging, the bony cheeks and large watery blue eyes are less disguised. A portrait of Francis in 1820 by Joseph Kreutzinger is undoubtedly embellished but still shows a thin, wary man of 52 years gazing out of the canvas.

Another, painted by the foremost English portrait painter of his day, Sir Thomas Lawrence, depicts Francis in a far more flattering, softer pose. It hangs in the Waterloo Chamber of Windsor Castle. The painting depicts a man in his early 50s with snow white hair and the fading after-glow of middle age. It is the face of a man who sought peace and repose and what enjoyment of life might still be there to salvage before he died. Having seen quick and sudden deaths of three wives and four children by then, not to mention the early deaths of his father and uncle, Francis must have contemplated the possibility that his own life could end suddenly, at any time and sought to enjoy it while he could.

In January 1820, King George III died at Windsor Castle. In Europe, Francis became overnight the longest reigning monarch living of a Great Power. Charles IV of Spain had died the year before. Frederick William III of Prussia and Alexander I of Russia had both come to their thrones while Francis was Emperor and Louis XVIII of France had been placed on the French throne only in 1815. The new King of the United Kingdom, George IV, had been

figure 18.1. Joseph Kreutzinger's portrait of Francis at 52 years of age. Heeresgeschichtliches Museum, Vienna.

regent for his father for some ten years due to the mental incapacity of George III in his later years and now became the newest sovereign among the Great Powers of Europe.

In many ways, the personalities and interests of George III and Francis were quite alike, although the two men never met. Both had rather puritanical, socially conservative views and abhorred scandal. George III had once snubbed Lord Nelson at a levee after having gotten wind of his affair with the wife of his ambassador to Naples. Both enjoyed nature. George III was an avid lover of farms and agriculture, as was well known to his subjects. Francis loved botany, landscape gardening and puttering around his greenhouses. And of course, Britain had been Austria's ally in every single war against Napoleon, supported Austria's opposition to Russian and Prussian expansion at the Congress of Vienna and generally supported Austrian primacy on the continent of Europe as the great fulcrum of the balance of power. Had they met and come to know each other, Francis would probably have gotten more pleasure out of the relationship with George III than he did with any other monarch in Europe.

Francis' private interests and pleasures can best be seen at the park and palace at Laxenburg, which remains a significant tourist destination to this day. It was here that Francis made his own mark. The estate today actually comprises three palaces located on approximately 700 acres of woodland, ponds and fields in the village that bears the name, almost due south of Vienna. Francis had inherited the property upon the death of his father. It had been a treasured retreat for his grandmother and his uncle where they could escape the etiquette and formalities of the Hofburg in a much smaller palace, the "Blue Court" or *Blauerhof*, largely free of servants, courtiers, chamberlains and ministers.

As mentioned earlier, Francis and his second wife, Maria Therese, spent an enormous amount of time with their children at Laxenburg for this very reason. A famous painting shows the Emperor rowing an un-named man in a boat on one of the ponds on the estate, giving an idea of the atmosphere of informality and normalcy that Francis preferred.

By 1801, Francis began to employ his talents in botany and landscape gardening to the grounds and structures. Formerly, the gardens near the *Blauerhof* had been created in the formal French style that was popular in the late 18th century. Francis changed all that to the more informal English garden style replete with *faux* grottos and temples, a knight's tomb, and the wide, sweeping open lawns and fields characteristic of this style. A canal runs

figure 18.2. Francis rowing a man on the pond at Laxenburg by Johann Krafft. The Belvedere, Vienna. The castle he built—Franzensburg—can be seen in the background. A typical Biedermeier scene that Francis seemed content for his subjects to see.

through the estate with stone bridges built over them. The park and gardens have remained in the style Francis brought to it to the present time.

Francis also had constructed a repository for his collections and a museum to honor the Habsburg dynasty which became known as Franzensburg. It was a collection of towers, gates and a castle that was never intended to be inhabited inspired by the ancient Habsburg castle in Switzerland from which the family derived their name; the Habichtsburg. The buildings were constructed on an artificial island in the middle of a large pond on the grounds. In it, he placed many of his art treasures, furnishings, furniture and other collectibles that remain.

This domestic and artistic side of Emperor Francis is rarely mentioned. His love for natural beauty and bucolic rural or wooded settings fit into the Biedermeier period, whose artists and painters reveled in the beauty of nature and simple, rural pleasures. The Laxenburg estate and the Franzensburg stand witness to this part of the Emperor's personality. By contrast, he would not spend much time during his life at Schönbrunn, the stunning palace built by his grandmother as a grand showcase of Baroque splendor. That palace was preferred by the Emperor's grandson who was born there in 1830 and died there in 1916.

REVOLUTION RETURNS

The early 1820s witnessed the collapse of the Spanish empire because of protracted revolution and civil war in the Americas. While this event hardly affected Francis in a geopolitical sense, even watching from afar, the news of the demise of Spanish rule because of popular uprisings could only confirm in his mind the dangerous consequences of failing to "nip in the bud" any sign of disloyalty or defiance. The end of the War of Mexican Independence by September 27, 1821 when the rebel army entered and occupied Mexico City marked the end of Spain as a Great Power. Mexico, or "New Spain" as it had been known, was by far the crown jewel of the Empire which had been crumbling piece by piece since Napoleon had crippled the Spanish monarchy by his coup and invasion in 1808.

The fall of the Spanish empire was followed on December 2, 1823 by a declaration by the United States that further efforts by European nations to take control of any independent state in North or South America would be viewed as "the manifestation of an unfriendly disposition toward the United States."[1] The doctrine was duly noted in Vienna. The "Holy Alliance" to which Austria was a party included the right to intervene to maintain Bourbon rule in Spain and its colonies.[2] Metternich noted in his private papers that the doctrine was a "new act of revolt" by the United States that would grant "new strength to the apostles of sedition and reanimate the courage of every conspirator."[3] There is little doubt Francis shared this view, but British support for the doctrine and the formidable obstacle of the Royal Navy made the establishment of republics in South and Central America an irreversible fact in the changing world of post-Napoleonic Europe. The example these fledgling republics and the United States posed was not lost on European intellectuals and would contribute in time to popular resentment at exclusion from participation in government.

In Europe, however, the trend was still toward absolutism and reaction. On September 16, 1824, Louis XVIII died and was succeeded by his brother, the Count d'Artois who became Charles X. Charles had been the leading light of the émigré forces that had opposed the French Revolution and importuned Francis' father to sponsor the Pillnitz Declaration that triggered the French Revolutionary Wars in 1792. Louis had ruled France with a soft and deft hand in the nine years since the restoration of the Bourbon monarchy. Charles X would be much more aggressive in promoting the principles of absolutism that would lead to his overthrow just six years later.

Figure 18.3. Sir Thomas Lawrence's portrait, circa 1818. Waterloo Chamber, Windsor Castle.

In the meantime, however, Francis could look to Charles as a strong friend and supporter of Austrian policy. He knew Charles well personally and there was a cordial personal relationship between the French king, Francis and his ministers with whom Charles had collaborated in the dark years of Napoleonic rule. In 1832, after his overthrow, Francis gave Charles sanctuary in Prague and he died in Gorizia in 1836 where he was buried. He is the only king of France not to have been buried in France.

Shortly after December 1, 1825, Francis received news of the death of Tsar Alexander I. He was 47 years old. The Tsar had contracted typhus on a trip to southern Russia with his wife and suddenly, he was gone. A complex but mercurial ally, the relationship between Francis and Alexander had always been tinged with a certain amount of distance and coolness. Alexander had been an immensely important figure who had to be handled, to Francis. As for the Tsar, Francis and Metternich had won him over to the practical virtues of conservatism and were two of the very few people on earth to whom he would usually, although not always defer, the Greek independence movement being an example of the latter. His successor would be his brother Nicholas.

Whatever history might make of the conservatism of Francis and the Austrian Empire, the new Tsar of Russia would place them and his late brother, Alexander, in the shade. Considered by many historians the most reactionary ruler in Europe in the first half of the 19th century, Nicholas I would second the interventionist policy of Austria to snuff out the first signs of revolutionary stirrings. His policy was simple and self-proclaimed: autocracy. Francis would have no fears of conflict with this leader in the East. Relations between Austria and Russia would remain warm, friendly and cooperative until the Crimean War, long after Francis' death, in 1854.

Even in Britain, nervousness about liberal reforms fueled conservative reaction. On January 22, 1828, the Duke of Wellington succeeded Lord Goderich as prime minister. The "Iron Duke" was adamantly opposed to reform or any expansion of the miniscule electoral franchise. In fact, the "Iron Duke" moniker had nothing to do with his military legacy, but was acquired when riots broke out against his stubborn resistance to the Reform Bill for franchise expansion. When mobs outside his house broke the windows of his London home, Apsley House, he installed iron shutters over the windows.

The 1820s therefore saw the screws of conservatism and reaction turned tighter and tighter with rulers of the various Great Powers becoming more conservative, not less, as the decade wore on. Occasional and sporadic revolts in Europe encouraged the belief among the European monarchies that revolution was a constant threat and engendered hyper-vigilance against the slightest claims by their subjects for political participation and rights against arbitrary rule. Preemptive measures, such as the Carlsbad decrees, censorship and surveillance were backed by armed force if need be. All this stirred growing resentment, especially among the educated classes, who remembered the French and American revolutions and predicted that, eventually, it would happen in their own country. The sputtering fuse flickered and flared in the 1820s, but would never go out. It would ignite the powder keg by 1830.

HUNGARY

The kingdom of Hungary would in time become one of the major fault lines in Francis' empire that would lead to the end of the unitary empire he created in 1804. Hungary, as noted previously, had been the bane or the salvation of the Habsburg monarchy since the dynasty had become its rulers in 1526. In the time of Francis' grandmother, the Hungarian aristocracy had risen in support of her call to arms against Prussia, but in response to the aggressive reforms of his uncle, the Hungarians came to the brink of revolution. During the Napoleonic Wars, a time of supreme danger, the Hungarian Diet and nobles had largely been compliant with the needs of the monarchy for soldiers and money, but by the end of the wars, as we have seen, Francis had imposed taxes without the consent of the Diet out of perceived necessity.

Now that the wars were over, the high aristocracy expected a return to the status quo which preserved to them more rights and power than in any other part of the Austrian Empire. The basis for this distinction is complex, but involved concessions made to the Hungarian nobility when the Habsburgs were initially elected king, in the Pragmatic Sanction that Charles VI had conceded to ensure the succession of his daughter and in further concessions made by Leopold II after the near uprising caused by his brother's reforms and Prussian agitation. The last concession, known as Law X or *Regnum Independens* enacted by the Diet in 1791, had confirmed Hungary's unique status as an independent kingdom ruled by the Habsburg king who was subject to Hungary's laws. No imperial institutions could be involved in the kingdom's internal government.

The conspiracy in Hungary by Ignac Martinovics in 1795, together with the continuous danger of intermittent warfare with France, made the danger of another internal revolt intolerable. This, in turn, fostered a close alliance between the crown and the aristocracy. Francis and the *Geheime Staatspolizei* enforced internal surveillance and compliance with the needs of a monarchy frequently at war with the active collaboration of the high nobility who feared French-style jacqueries by their peasants and the unthinkable consequences that might bring to their elite status and power.

The problem was that the high nobility, the landowning "magnates" in Hungary who jealously guarded their economic, political and legal rights shackled the population in poverty and low productivity. This population included a much larger, lower aristocracy or gentry and a largely rural peasantry. Hungary was a vast, impoverished and comparatively backward kingdom and was going nowhere. Compared to Upper and Lower Austria, Bohemia, Moravia and Lombardy, conditions in Hungary were primitive. The kingdom had suffered depopulation due to poverty, disease and war and an influx of non-Magyars from abroad, including Germans, Romanians, Jews, and Slavs. Many of these non-Magyars were encouraged to settle and farm there by the dynasty essentially to colonize it.

So long as their rights were not challenged, the Hungarian nobility showed loyalty to the Habsburg dynasty, but the price was high. Controlling much of the wealth of the kingdom, such as it was, they were exempt from taxation. They were the law on their vast estates and subject towns and villages, dispensing justice as they saw fit without recourse to the courts of the state. Economic reform was anathema because it threatened the privileged, agrarian society of the land-owning magnates.

Yet economic reform was needed even more desperately in Hungary than in the rest of the Empire. While all of Europe's economies were agrarian-based until the very end of the 18th century, the contrast between Hungary's society and that of the rest of the Habsburg Empire, or Europe for that matter, was not so pronounced. As the early 19th century unfolded, Hungary increasingly became an economic backwater, contributing little to the development of the Empire's economic strength beyond agriculture and serving to enrich a tiny elite. More than that, however, the Faustian bargain between the monarchy and the nobility would also result in the estrangement of the Hungarian gentry and peasantry—in time the Hungarian nation—from the rest of the Empire. In its societal paranoia to preserve its Magyar identity, the nobility and gentry would oppress all other non-Magyar minorities such as the Croatians, Romanians and Serbs in ways that would have driven them to revolution had the Austrians pressed it on them. The seeds of future discord would be planted in this era and ripen to deadly levels in the next.

In Francis' time, the resentment of the gentry and peasantry smoldered, unrelieved by any attempt by the crown to reform or revive the country that would mean breaking the power of the nobles. In the case of the gentry, it gradually built into a paranoid, nationalistic resentment against foreigners living in the kingdom and Austrian predominance in the affairs of the kingdom as a whole. They perceived that Hungary was being ruled as a province from Vienna, rather than as a co-equal partner.

István Széchenyi would be the first and most moderate of a series of Hungarian political leaders to raise the challenge, both to the monarchy and the nobles. He first came to prominence in 1825 when, after fourteen years, Francis summoned the Hungarian Diet. Széchenyi shocked his fellow delegates by delivering his speech in the Magyar tongue, instead of Latin or German, supporting higher education. He published a critique of the magnates in a book called Credit, in which he argued that the privileges of the nobility were immoral and indefensible. Further, the economic consequences in some ways hurt their income. For example, since banks could not foreclose on the lands of the magnates, they could not raise loans for investment for raising the productivity of their lands.

Széchenyi was loyal to the dynasty, however, favoring strong ties with the Empire. He proposed taxation of landowners, establishment of a national bank, and wages for the peasants who worked the lands. Opposition by the conservative upper house of the Diet, however, composed exclusively of the landowning, high nobility, doomed these measures.

The next challenge would come from the gentry who organized around Lajos Kossuth who was born and raised in this era. By 1830, he was twenty-eight years old, a lawyer and one of the most spellbinding orators of his day, whether he was speaking his native Magyar or in English. He had become an accomplished writer and publicist as deputy to a member of the Diet and was publishing a gazette that circulated widely in political circles, spreading news of speeches and debates of the Diet and animating popular discussion of national issues. Eventually, the censor stopped their publication as they were causing what was perceived to be dangerous levels of public discourse. Kossuth became an active advocate for freedom of speech and the press while Francis was king and that would only be the beginning for him. He listened to the speeches and policies advocated by Széchenyi which formed the core of his later ideas.

These years of benign collaboration between Francis and the Hungarian nobility succeeded in his lifetime in maintaining peace and quiet, but set the stage for a long, painful and ultimately ruinous relationship between the monarchy and the kingdom that would play out until the end of the Empire in 1918.

NOTES

1. United States Department of State. "The Monroe Doctrine (1823)." *Basic Readings in U.S. Democracy.*

2. Herring, George C. *From Colony to Superpower: U.S. Foreign Relations Since 1776.* New York: Oxford University Press, 2008.

3. Ibid.

Chapter Nineteen

Luxury and Austrian Biedermeier Culture

While the Austrian Empire was slow to industrialize, the Biedermeier era saw the growth and fame of several crafts, most famously, furniture making and Bohemian glass. The Biedermeier style of design was an evolution from roots in the French Empire and Directoire style as well as 18th century English styles, but simplified and more utilitarian. Austrian Biedermeier furniture was designed for its functionality, elegance and high quality. Cabinetmaking shops and factories boomed in post-war Vienna. Some transformed themselves into furniture factories, such as the one by Josef Danhauser, employing 100 workers in 1808. Danhauser sold not only furniture in his factory, but also home furnishings such as drapes, carpets, clocks and even glassware.

Bohemian crystal had achieved early fame in the Renaissance era and remains world famous to this day. The term "crystal" normally denotes the presence of lead oxide in glass that gives it clarity and distinct physical characteristics as opposed to mere "glass" which does not contain lead. Bohemian crystal is a generic term meaning a unique kind of glass produced without lead, but with the same or even superior qualities in some respects. In the centuries of production and experimentation, Bohemian glass also became famous for its exceptional cut and engraving. Bohemian glass chandeliers, vases, pitchers and cut glass services were commonly purchased and installed in palaces, opera houses, and in the homes of the rising bourgeois classes.

Porcelain, whose secrets were not revealed to Europe until 1708 in Dresden, was the subject of exquisite manufacture in Vienna in the Biedermeier era. Founded in 1718, the Vienna Porcelain Manufactory was the second to be established in Europe. The Congress of Vienna, with its influx of foreign monarchs, aristocracy, diplomats and other luxury-loving visitors immediately vaulted its products into unprecedented popularity throughout Europe.

Augarten porcelain, established in 1923 is the successor to the Manufactory and produces fine porcelain products to this day.

Painting changed too. Typical Biedermeier paintings were far more realistic and detailed than the classical painters of the 18th century. Scenes of typical, daily life were popular among the bourgeois consuming class rather than religious or historical events. Landscapes were also popular, often depicting spectacular scenes from the varied landscape of the Empire with emphasis on nature. Finally, with new affluence, portrait painting became immensely popular with single or group portraits of families of the bourgeoisie.

Ignaz Bösendorfer, the son of a carpenter, had studied at the Vienna Academy of Fine Arts and then accepted an apprenticeship with the piano manufactory of Joseph Brodmann. In 1828 he succeeded Brodmann as owner of the business, receiving his license from the authorities in Vienna on July 28, 1823. Bösendorfer's eye for beauty and craftsmanship led to a refinement of piano making as furniture of the highest art form, but it did not stop there. Bösendorfer's friendship with and advice from Franz Liszt, whose aggressive, flamboyant playing style demanded the maximum in technical endurance and sound quality, raised the quality of the Bösendorfer piano to the highest in the world. In 1830, Francis appointed Bösendorfer the official piano maker to the imperial court. The reputation and popularity of the "Bösendorfer" remains to this day at the pinnacle of pianos in the world; the "Rolls Royce" of pianos.

The Biedermeier period saw Vienna rise to compete with Paris for luxury commodities. The Biedermeier spirit of bourgeois comfort and utility married to style and fashion spread out over the continent particularly, but by no means exclusively, in central Europe.

But the Biedermeier term comprises more than art and culture. It embraces a lifestyle and frame of mind during the last two decades of Francis' rule. It permeated society, as time went on but its foundation was a rising and expanding bourgeois class in the urban areas of the Empire, particularly Vienna. Below the surface, the wealthiest bourgeois families often obtained prominence in Biedermeier society by becoming financial patrons of the arts including writers, composers, painters, singers and contributing to the cultural blossoming of the times. They also were the hosts to literary and other cultural societies and salons that were often the entrée of rising talents into celebrity. No longer was music the province of the nobility and the crown. In 1812, the Association of Friends of Music—*Gesellschaft der Musikfreunde*— was founded by bourgeois patrons and grew in popularity as the years went by, hosting concerts and promoting musical art and talents.

In this, Francis contributed in two ways. The first was negative; the nearly complete exclusion of the bourgeoisie from participation in political decision-making in the Empire which was confined to trusted members of the nobility, except for the military. With no means of entry to high political position in the state, except by ennoblement by the crown, the bourgeoisie looked to enriching their personal lives in other ways that created a cultural infrastructure independent of the crown and the nobility. Acquisition of art and furnishings, enjoyment of music, dancing, fine arts, literature and theatre, and generally seeking to live a comfortable, pleasant life with their families. It was a time when ordinary citizens enjoyed coffeehouses, amusement parks such as the Prater in Vienna, spending hours eating and drinking new wine at a Heurigen tavern and, of course, waltzing.

The second was that the emperor himself embraced the Biedermeier mentality and lived his own life much like his bourgeois subjects. His example encouraged more of the same. Francis sought more and more the bucolic pleasures of the country life, gardening, art and literature. His abhorrence of imperial pomp and ostentatious displays of his own wealth and power, except as a device of statecraft, fostered his image among his subjects as one of them. He is one of the very few monarchs of his time to be painted in ordinary, bourgeois clothing, appearing as a country gentleman.

It is doubtful that this was by accident. The Emperor's love of peace and quiet in the conduct of all foreign and domestic affairs was consistent with his own personal life and what he believed to be the desire of his people, to enjoy the good life while you can. There is every reason to suppose that the Emperor consciously cultivated the aura of a modest, frugal and simple Biedermeier man, which in fact he was, and understood well that his personal popularity, and that of the monarchy, was reinforced by this perception by his people.

Chapter Twenty

Revolution and Reaction

By 1830, Francis had reached the age of 62. The policies of preemptive repression and prompt suppression of revolutionary activity certainly would have appeared as a success that could and should be sustained for as long as Francis could foresee. None of the cracks and fissures that would emerge that would ultimately bring down the Empire would have been obvious to any but the most critical and discerning observer. There was no obvious challenge to the political or military power of the Austrian Empire on the continent of Europe. The wisdom of the "balance of power" system conceived and implemented at the Congress of Vienna seemed vindicated. Europe was not being wracked by near constant warfare, as had been the case in the preceding century and a half and many an observer of that time would have attributed this to the collective political unanimity of Europe's conservative monarchies.

Alan Palmer, in his book on Metternich, describes Francis at this point in his life as a perfect, Biedermeier gentleman:

> Francis was unimaginative, unpretentious and commonsensical, with a sardonic sense of humor. He had simple tastes and preferred a quiet life. He rode in an old-fashioned green calèche. He dressed in a shabby brown coat and hat. He had a conservatory full of plants, where he liked to garden. His idiosyncrasies included cooking toffee on the royal stove and greeting his subjects affably in the Prater in a broad Viennese dialect.[1]

Yet just as some measure of self-satisfaction must have been entertained as the Austrian Kaiser tended his gardens in the summer of that year, the whole system attributed to his Staatskanzler was about to face its most severe challenge. As usual, the conflagration began in Paris.

On July 25, 1830, Charles X signed the "July Ordinances" to face down popular dissent against the government which suspended freedom of the press, dissolved the just elected Chamber of Deputies and abrogated all rights of the bourgeoisie to participate in any future elections. The prevailing trend toward greater conservatism, not less, would stop here. The uprising in Paris erupted within two days with massive crowds in the streets agitating for revolution and the king's head. In three more, Charles X and his family fled Paris for their lives to London. The provisional government, rather than declaring a republic, perhaps with memories of the Terror, invited Louis Philippe d'Orleans, a distant cousin of the king, to succeed Charles and a liberal, constitutional monarchy was established that would last almost two decades, known as the "July Monarchy."

While France was transformed in an almost bloodless manner in a matter of days, things did not end there. It was as if a signal had been given. The news flashed across Europe. In a month, the Belgians rose against the Dutch monarchy. This revolution also succeeded and established another constitutional monarchy in Brussels to rule the new and independent kingdom of Belgium.

The next to rise were the Italians. In an apparent excess of enthusiasm for the liberal cause, Louis Philippe encouraged the Carbonari leader, Ciro Menotti, that should he attempt the overthrow of Austrian rule in northern Italy and Austria intervened, he would support him with French military

Figure 20.1. Louis Philippe d'Orleans—the wily king of the French. Artist Unknown. Musée Condé, Chantilly, France.

force. On February 3, 1831, the Carbonari revolted in Modena triggering the expected reaction from Vienna. While temporarily successful, the Duke of Modena put down the revolt backed by Austrian troops. Menotti was hanged.

Nonetheless, the flames of revolution fanned out and down the Italian peninsula. The Papal States experienced revolts against the Pope who, in that time, ruled Rome and vast territories around it as a virtual king. Revolutions in Bologna, Forli, Ravenna, Imola, Ferrara, Pesaro and Urbino overthrew the Papal authorities and declared a united Italy. The Emperor's daughter, Marie Louise, fled Parma due to upheavals there. Pope Gregory XVI appealed to Austria for help and Francis answered.

The first response was a blunt warning issued by Metternich to Louis Philippe that French support for the rebels would be met with Austrian bayonets. It was enough to deter the French king. No French military support would be forthcoming after all. Then came the army. A slow moving but methodical campaign crushed resistance in each and every province. Arrests of revolutionary leaders followed until monarchical rule was restored everywhere.

On November 29, 1830, the cadets of Congress Poland's military academy in Warsaw led by Piotr Wysocki revolted against Russian occupation, arming themselves with weapons from their garrison and attacking the palace of the Russian Grand Duke Constantine, the Tsar's brother. There had been rumors that Tsar Nicholas, who by the terms of the Congress of Vienna was also king of Poland, intended to use the Polish army to suppress the revolutions in France and Belgium that provoked the revolt. The Grand Duke escaped capture, but the cadets next raided the city arsenal and were joined by civilians who sought constitutional restraints on royal power. The masses of armed citizens and the cadets forced the withdrawal of the Russian army from Warsaw. Risings then followed in cities in the Ukraine, Estonia and Belarus. On December 13, the Polish Sejm essentially declared independence from Russia.

Shocked by the suddenness and virulence of the revolt, Tsar Nicholas nevertheless issued a decree that there would be no concessions. Further, on January 7, 1831, he demanded the complete and unconditional surrender of Poland "to the grace of their Emperor." On January 25, 1831, the Sejm declared that Nicholas was no longer king of Poland, ending the "personal union" of Russia and Poland imposed by the Congress of Vienna. The Polish nation would offer the crown to whomever it felt worthy.

The heavy hand of Nicholas now fell on Poland. On February 4, 1831, over 100,000 Russian troops crossed into Poland. By February 25, the Polish army repulsed the Russians outside of Warsaw, forcing it to retreat and saving Warsaw from occupation.

Europe was stunned. Elation at the revolution and the triumph of Polish arms reverberated in Paris, London and even New York where American committees collected money to help the rebels. Lafayette held meetings in Paris. Yet no real help was forthcoming. The reaction in Vienna was to close the border to Poland to prevent any arms or assistance from reaching the rebels. Prussia did the same.[2] Lord Palmerston in Britain declined to allow assistance on the theory that an independent Poland would automatically be allied with France, disturbing the balance of power.

Nonetheless, the national resistance stubbornly fended off successive Russian attacks. A new army under Grand Duke Michael Pavlovich suffered several successive defeats, but the casualties sustained by the Poles mounted in these bloody battles. Slowly but surely the Russian army encircled Warsaw and by October, it was all over. Remnants of the Polish army and its leaders crossed into Prussia and Austrian Galicia where they laid down their arms and surrendered rather than capitulate to the Russians. The fate of Poland was harsh. Nicholas abolished Congress Poland and annexed it to Russia as a mere province where it would remain until 1918. From then on, Poland would be subject to the same unbending and oppressive autocracy as the rest of Russia.

While much British and American historiography of the 19th and 20th century uniformly condemned the conservative or reactionary policies and actions of the Eastern monarchies of the Holy Alliance, particularly Nicholas and Francis, one must ever remember the context of the times and weigh leaders of an era in relative terms. As conservative as Francis might appear in the light of succeeding centuries, and from the viewpoint of liberal, democratic societies, those same societies tend to forget their own nation's reactions to popular uprisings against repression even more egregious.

For example, in 1831 in Southampton County, Virginia, in the United States, the largest slave uprising in American history occurred on August 22, known as Nate Turner's Slave Rebellion. Approximately sixty white men, women and children were killed by rampaging black slaves. The rebellion was crushed in two days and fifty-six of the rebels were killed or executed. A hysterical and paranoid white population in the American South, excited by false rumors of more slave rebellions, then executed hundreds more blacks in the ensuing weeks by mobs and militias as far away as Alabama. In a letter to the *New York Evening Post*, Reverend G. W. Powell wrote that "many negroes are killed every day. The exact number will never be known."[3] The Richmond *Whig*, writing "with pain," described the scene as "the slaughter of many blacks without trial and under circumstances of great barbarity."[4]

On Christmas Day, 1831, another slave revolt in Jamaica that began as a strike against British colonial plantation owners there for wages quickly degenerated into violence and violent repression. Jamaica had some 300,000

Figure 20.2. Lord Palmerston—British Foreign Secretary. Francis Cruikshank circa 1855.

enslaved African workers of which an estimated 60,000 participated under the leadership of a black Baptist preacher, Samuel Sharpe. Fourteen whites were killed as against over 200 blacks, killed or executed by the British colonial militia garrisoned there. As in Virginia, a bloodbath of reprisal followed by white mobs resulting in the deaths of over three hundred more.[5] In one account, a witness described how the courts commonly executed three or four persons simultaneously with bodies piled up until workhouse African slaves carted the bodies away at night and buried them in mass graves outside town.[6]

The events of 1830-31 undoubtedly confirmed again, for Francis, the ever-present, lurking danger of popular revolution which could spring up at any time. The wisdom of Austria's own policies of domestic tranquilization and preemptive censorship appeared vindicated, since there were no serious risings or revolutions within the Austrian Empire or, indeed, the German Confederation. Yet tensions were simmering in Francis' realms too.

In January 1832, journalists banded together to seek freedom of the press and free speech against the Bavarian government and the Carlsbad Decrees of 1819. The Bavarian monarchy immediately banned the group who then called and organized a "fair" located at the ruins of the Hambach Castle, near Heidelberg. Some 20,000-people appeared, many of whom were radicalized students who took an oath to seek freedom from the repressive laws of Bavaria and the German Confederation, of which Francis was head. The fair was over in three days, before the authorities could act. One of the organizers, Johann Wirth, was arrested and imprisoned for two years. The other three main organizers fled the country.

Furthermore, there was now a crack in the formerly unanimous European monarchical order: France. The July Monarchy of Louis Philippe had considered taking up arms and opposing continued Austrian dominance in Italy in 1830. The king's nerve had faltered; however, it was the first time that one of the Great Powers had parted ways with the post-Napoleonic order. To the other continental monarchies, Louis Philippe was playing with fire, seeking popular approval for liberal ideas that had been anathema to Charles X and his brother.

In Belgium, Louis Philippe responded to a call for assistance by the fledgling Belgians when a Dutch army sent by the arch-conservative king of the Netherlands, Willem I, crossed the border to re-capture the region. The French Armée du Nord was dispatched into the new kingdom to support the Belgians, which caused the Dutch to withdraw, except from Antwerp. The French laid siege to the city and eventually forced the Dutch to capitulate and withdraw, ending the Dutch attempt to restore the king's territorial claims granted at the Congress of Vienna.

Moreover, the new French king had dangerous pretentions. Upon his accession to the throne on August 9, 1830, he had chosen the title "King of the French" instead of "King of France" to emphasize his connection with the people, rather than the land. He reveled in his popular acclaim as the "Citizen King" or "Bourgeois King." These were not qualities that recommended him to Francis, Frederick William of Prussia or Tsar Nicholas. He would have to be watched.

NOTES

1. Alan Palmer, *Metternich* (London, 1972), 81, 86.
2. Tucker, S.C., *A Global Chronology of Conflict, Volume Three:1775–1860*, (Santa Barbara: ABC-CLIO, LLC, 2009) 1156.
3. *New York Evening Post*, September 5, 1831, quoted in Aptheker, *American Negro Slave Revolts*, p. 301.
4. Richmond *Whig*, September 3, 1831, quoted in Aptheker, *American Negro Slave Revolts*, p. 301.
5. Mary Reckord. "The Jamaican Slave Rebellion of 1831," *Past & Present* (July 1968), 40(3): pp. 122, 124–125.
6. Révauger, Cécile, *The Abolition of Slavery—The British Debate 1787–1840*, (Paris: Presse Universitaire de France, 2008)107–108.

Chapter Twenty-One

Franciscan Twilight

In 1832, the internationally famous, Austrian portrait artist Friedrich von Amerling painted Francis in formal, imperial regalia in perhaps the most famous portrait of him of all the hundreds painted in his lifetime. Seated on a throne, he is wearing the crown of Rudolf II that Francis himself selected and adopted as the official Imperial Crown of the Austrian Empire. It was created in 1602 for the mad Emperor Rudolf II in Prague by his court jeweler, Jan Vermeyen. In his gloved, right hand, he holds the Imperial scepter made by Andreas Osenbruck in Prague between 1612–15 for the Emperor Matthias. He is cloaked in the Mantle of the Austrian Empire, made of red velvet, ermine and white silk, created by Philipp von Stubenrauch for the coronation of his son, Ferdinand, in 1830 as king of Hungary. Spread over the throne beneath him are the coronation robes of the Kingdom of Lombardy-Venetia. It is an immensely impressive showpiece portrait that symbolized the wealth and power, tradition and style of the longest reigning monarch in Europe.

Yet a closer look at the portrait and especially the face of the Emperor conveys a different story. Amerling's "realistic" style of painting subtly captured the glassy, blue eyes that gaze downward, rather than outward at the viewer, as if distracted or lost in thought. The long, narrow nose casts a slight shadow, beyond which is seen thinning facial skin, reddish puffiness under his left eye and pronounced hallowing of his cheeks. The mouth is firmly set with the trademark, protruding Habsburg lower lip. Overall, the impression, although unquestionably regal, is a portrait of a troubled, older man attired in the pompous finery he personally detested, brooding and perhaps distracted. Von Amerling's portrait viewed as a whole is striking, but in its detail of the Emperor captured a personality that no photograph likely could have done.

Figure 21.1. Francis in formal regalia by Friedrich von Amerling, 1832. The Hofburg Schatzkammer, Vienna.

Figure 21.2. Close up of Amerling's portrait.

    The portrait was painted at around the same time as the death of the Kaiser's grandson, Franz, on July 22, 1832 at the age of 21. Francis was in Linz on that day when he received a note from Metternich in Vienna informing him of the death: "It is fortunate for your Majesty that the Duke, who could not have been saved, passed away before your return. Your Majesty has been spared a heartrending spectacle. I have recently visited him, and I do not remember ever to have seen a more terrible wreck." The Emperor, on hearing the news, broke down and wept, and then replied to Metternich: "With his complaint [illness], my grandson's death was a blessing for himself, and perhaps also for my children and the world in general; he will be a loss to me."[1] The young man's doctor, Johann Malfatti, had suspected he had contracted tuberculosis as early as 1830 and treated him for it as aggressively as he could, but the disease continued to debilitate him in the last two years of his life.

    As with all his children and grandchildren, Francis had developed a deep affection for Napoleon François since he had come to Vienna with his mother in 1814 at the age of three. His fourth wife, Karoline Augusta, came to love him as if he were her own son. The child's French nurses were soon dis-

Figure 21.3. Napoleon François, grandson of Francis and Duke of Reichstadt. Leopold Bucher, 1832.

Figure 21.4. Napoleon Franz in family portrait, third from left, by Leopold Fertbauer, 1828.

missed and replaced with Austrians to ensure that he grew to manhood as a German prince. Instead of his first name, his family and the Austrian court always called him by his second; Franz in German.

In 1818, at the age of seven, Francis made him the Duke of Reichstadt. The boy delighted him, sat next to him when dining and often visited his grandfather in his study at the Hofburg or the Blauerhof. He was uncommonly handsome, even as a young child, taking after his mother, with blonde, curly hair. As a young man, he grew to six feet in height. Much as he loved his grandson, however, Francis understood that due to his birth, the only legitimate child and heir of Napoleon, he would have to be carefully watched and managed. He was the object of Bonapartist intrigue in Paris as the rightful heir to the imperial throne. For the same reason, he was regarded by the ultra-Royalists as a menacing pretender to the Bourbon dynasty. Rumors of bribes being paid for his assassination or abduction were taken very seriously.

Francis saw to it that he got an excellent education. He assigned Maurice Dietrichstein, a former military officer and aide-de-camp to General Mack in the Ulm campaign, as the boy's governor in 1815 and they remained lifelong friends. Dietrichstein was an intellectual and very active in Vienna's musical scene. He was joined in educating the young duke by Jean-Baptiste Foresti, a former military officer, and Mathias de Collin, a professor of history and philosophy. By the age of 12, in 1823, he was made a cadet in the Austrian army. Not surprisingly, given his paternity, the boy took a passionate interest in military life. By 1831, he had risen to the rank of colonel and was given the command of a battalion, but by then, his health made it impossible for him to pursue his military career further.

In January 1831, Franz came down with a serious fever and was brought to the Hofburg to recover. His health continued to decline, however, and he was brought to Schönbrunn palace in May where it was thought he could recover by walks in the fresh air and gardens. In June, his mother, Marie Louise arrived to be with her son and was appalled at his debilitated condition. Metternich visited him on June 7 and wrote in his papers: "The Prince's condition is in keeping with his malady. His weakness increases in proportion as his illness progresses, and I see no possibility of saving him." By July, the end was near. On July 19, he refused all nourishment and by July 21, his breathing had become so difficult that he gasped to his mother and his doctors that all he wanted was to die.

The entire court and family were grief-stricken when he passed away in the early morning hours of the following day. It is perhaps this latest tragedy that Von Amerling captured in his most famous portrait of Francis.

DIPLOMATIC TURBULENCE IN EUROPE AFTER 1830

With the passing of the Revolutions of 1830–32, the attention of the Emperor and Metternich turned to the Mediterranean and the travails of the ever-weakening Turkish Empire of the Ottoman dynasty, currently headed by Mahmud II. Beginning in 1831, the Sultan's government had faced a rebellion by the governor of Egypt, Pasha Mehmet Ali when his army invaded Ottoman Syria. Mehmet Ali had long planned to detach Egypt and Sudan from the Turkish Empire and create his own hereditary dynasty. Syria was quickly overrun and at the Battle of Konya on December 21, 1832, Ali's army routed a Turkish army in Anatolia, clearing the way for an assault on Constantinople itself.

The Sultan appealed to Nicholas I to save the situation and the Russians quickly landed an army outside of Constantinople to defend the city and the government. The Russian landing alarmed the British and the French who now joined the fray in support of Ali. The dangerously escalating situation was a prelude to the Crimean War twenty years later and placed Francis and Austria in a delicate situation. In May 1833, the crisis was temporarily averted when the Great Powers brokered a peace agreement between the Sultan and Pasha Ali in which Syria and other territories were ceded to Ali, but independence was withheld.

The agreement was not going to last very long, but temporarily averted war among the European powers and Russia. The ominous presence of growing Russian power over the declining, disintegrating Turkish Empire was confirmed months later. In return for a Russian alliance, the Sultan signed the Treaty of Hünkâr İskelesi on July 8, 1833. The alliance between the two powers was directed against further Egyptian aggression but also, among other things, obligated the Sultan to close the Straights of the Dardanelles to foreign warships at Russia's bidding.

In September 1833, Francis and Metternich went to the Bohemian town of Münchengrätz to meet Tsar Nicholas and his foreign minister, Karl Robert von Nesselrode. They were joined by the Crown Prince of Prussia, representing King Frederick William III. Nicholas was anxious to re-affirm support from his partners in the Holy Alliance in the face of rising and increasingly aggressive Franco-British opposition, led by Lord Palmerston. Austria was anxious to restrain, but not break with Russian power, and forestall a general European war. The result was a Convention with public and secret parts that bound Austria and Russia to work "in union" with one another with respect to the Ottoman Empire. In general, they would oppose Mehmet Ali's campaign but provided for contingencies, in the secret articles, in case the Ottoman dynasty should collapse.

Lord Palmerston was convinced that Austria and Russia had secretly agreed to partition the Turkish Empire, but the truth was the opposite. Both

Figure 21.5. Count Franz von Kolowrat by Johann Ender

signatories sought to preserve a weak but intact Ottoman state. Austria gained the assurance from Tsar Nicholas that Russia would not act unilaterally in case the worst should happen and there would be a sudden breakdown of Ottoman control, especially in the Balkans. The fate of that corner of Europe had been a concern and interest of the Habsburg dynasty since the Ottoman invasions of the 15th century and would continue to concern Austrian emperors and ministers until 1918. On the one hand, the region was so poor and primitive that it no longer had much appeal for Habsburg expansion. On the other hand, it was against Austria's interest for a new and vigorous power, such as Russia, to replace a weak, compliant Ottoman presence and threaten its southern flank which had been quiet since the end of Joseph II's war. The delicate balancing act would be tested again in 1839, after Francis' death.

In these latter days of Francis' reign, a new political figure had emerged, Franz Anton von Kolowrat-Liesteinsky. A Bohemian noble of the very highest social standing, he had been in the Austrian civil service since 1799, rising to become governor of Bohemia in 1810. He professed to be an admirer of Czech culture and political pretensions and was a founder of the Prague National Museum in 1818. In 1826, he was summoned by Francis to become a member of the State Council ("*Staatsrat*") and was placed in charge of the Empire's finances. Described as a "bad tempered, aggressive nobleman, a curious combination of great landowner and bureaucrat who became what in effect was minister of the Interior" he was the antithesis of the suave, wily Metternich and the two developed an increasingly deep distaste for one another.[2]

Kolowrat's obsession with the imperial finances drove him to oppose the continuing, heavy expenditures on Austria's military establishment. Over Metternich's objections, he recommended and obtained Francis' approval for deep cuts in military expenditures, describing them as "a shield which weighed down the rider." By 1829, Kolowrat had succeeded in balancing Austria's state budget for the first time in many decades, which further ingratiated him with Francis. As far as the preemptive, military interventions favored by Metternich, Kolowrat reportedly criticized them as nothing more than "a forest of bayonets" and by "leaving this as they were, he was playing into the revolutionaries' hands."[3]

By 1834, Metternich was still the most influential advisor to Francis, but his power, as ever, rested on the Emperor's special favor. Kolowrat was also a seasoned, tough political advisor and had been in office long enough to gain Francis' trust, particularly in internal, domestic affairs and finances.

DEATH

The end began where it had begun, in Vienna's *Burgtheater* where Francis' grandmother had breathlessly interrupted a performance to announce his birth to his family on February 19, 1768. Francis and his family had attended a performance at the same theatre on a cold, snowy evening in February 1835 and sat in the same loge where Joseph II had heard the news from Maria Theresa. Shortly after the performance, Francis "caught a chill." By February 23, Melanie von Metternich wrote that she had heard from her father that the Emperor was "dangerously ill." The chill progressed to pneumonia. By February 28, she recorded that "we see death approaching."[4]

Francis was conscious until almost the last moments before his death. On the night of February 27–28, he met with Metternich at the Hofburg Palace for the last time. Metternich described the meeting in a dispatch to Tsar Nicholas shortly after Francis' death:

> The Emperor Francis died as he had lived. His last thoughts bore the impress of rectitude and simplicity, and were concerned far more with the interests of the country than his own. It was thus that, in the night of February 27-28, in the midst of an aggravated attack of his malady, he worked for four hours, some-

times writing down with his own hand, sometimes dictating his last wishes. He has drawn up a will, regulating every private affair of importance. . . . The dying monarch who bequeaths his love to his people, his gratitude to his army and the servants who served him so well in the State, has listened to the voice of his heart, the voice which, throughout the course of his long life, has been so powerful, and which, now that he is dead, will ensure him the pious gratitude of those whom it has been his lot, under Providence, to govern for so long a period-and what a period! In a letter addressed to his son, the Emperor has laid down, under the form of counsels, the principles which have served as the basis and guide of his own government.[5]

The "political testament" Francis left for Ferdinand included the following instructions:

Do not disturb the foundations of the edifice of state; rule and change nothing. Stand fast upon fundamental principles by constant observation, of which I have steered the Monarchy, not only through the storms of difficult times. . . . Honor acquired rights. . . . Vest in Prince Metternich, my truest servant and friend, the trust that I have devoted to him over such a long succession of years. Do not come to any decisions about public affairs or people without having listened to his opinion on them. . . .[6]

In the early morning hours of March 2, 1835, after having been given the Catholic sacrament of extreme unction and surrounded by his family, Francis died. His death happened to fall 43 years and one day after the death of his father. He was the same age as George Washington—sixty-seven–on the day he had died at Mount Vernon of the same disease. He left his wife a widow at the age of 43. Melanie von Metternich wrote of a visit with the Dowager Empress on April 7, 1835:

She was pale and haggard. She spoke to me in touching terms of our adored Emperor. . . . She told me that she almost died the night he was carried to his room in the chapel where he was to be exposed. She talked much about the Emperor's last moments. . . . The courage she displayed gives strength.[7]

Shortly after the Emperor's death, his heart was severed and removed from his body for separate interment in the *Herzgruft*, a burial chamber containing the hearts of members of the Habsburg dynasty located behind the Loreto Chapel in the Augustinian Church within the Hofburg. Today, there are 54 such urns; the Emperor Francis' heart is in urn 43.

The Emperor's body was then prepared and dressed for his funeral. For three days, his body lay in the Chapel of the Hofburg as an immense throng of his subjects filed past, paying their respects. The body was then transported by an immense, black hearse to the Imperial Crypt beneath the Church of the

Capuchins where his body was entombed and lies to this day surrounded by the tombs of his four wives.

NOTES

1. De Wertheimer, Edward, *The Duke of Reichstadt*, (London: John Lane The Bodley Head, 1906).
2. Seward 311–312.
3. Ibid, p. 312.
4. Seward 314.
5. Metternich, Richard, *Memoirs of Prince Metternich, 1830–1835, Volume V*, (New York: Charles Scribner's Sons, 1882) 472.
6. Wheatcroft 254.
7. Richard Metternich 11.

Epilogue

Francis had fallen ill and died suddenly, a fate that was all too common in this era when a contagious disease could take life with little warning. As news reached the far corners of his Empire, no doubt many of his subjects paused to think about what the late Emperor meant to them. He had been suddenly called to rule at the age of twenty-four on a day and in an age most Austrians could hardly remember in the Spring of 1835. They would recall his stubborn resistance to Napoleon despite innumerable military set-backs and defeats. They would remember his eventual triumph and the celebrations on his return to his homeland from Paris in 1814.

There was genuine heartsickness and sorrow at the death of this man who had endured so much, both in his personal life and as their sovereign. The English writer, Frances Trollope, traveled widely in her lifetime in Europe and America and, among her other works, wrote travel books. In 1838, she published one entitled *Vienna and the Austrians*. In this book, she recounted a scene she witnessed nearly two years after the death of the Emperor, on All Souls Day, when Catholic Vienna tended to its dead in its cemeteries and attended mass to pray for their souls:

> . . . The great point of general interest, however, is the crypt of the church belonging to the convent of the Capuchins, for there lie interred the imperial family of Austria. The vaults on this day open to the public . . . the crowd of pilgrims who came, upon this day, to gaze upon the coffin that contains their idol the late Emperor, Francis the First of Austria, was too numerous to permit any very accurate examination of them. Were I simply and fully to describe to you the strong emotion manifested by the throng, still passing on, but still renewed when at length they had won their way across the imperial sepulcher to the grating which gave them a sight of the Emperor Francis' coffin, you would hardly give credence to the truth of my tale. You would not think it false, but you would

Figure E.1. Sarcophagus of Francis, last Holy Roman Emperor and First Austrian Emperor, Imperial Crypt, Vienna.

suspect that it was exaggerated.... And yet, perhaps, of all the spectacles I have ever witnessed it was the most striking! ... The old and the young, the rich and the poor, pressed on together to the tomb of their common father; neither sex, age, nor condition were observed in this unparalleled melee of general emotion. ... We watched tears stealing down many a manly cheek from eyes that seemed little used to weeping, and listened to sobs that spoke of hearts bursting with sorrow and remembered love, beside the tomb of one who had already lain there above two years–and that one an Emperor! ... Between him and the people that thus freshly weep for him, there must have been a tie more closely drawn than we, in our land of freedom, can easily understand. ...[1]

The dynasty would see three more emperors before 1918 and the fall of the six-hundred-year dynasty at the conclusion of the First World War. That cataclysm erupted a century after the defeat and abdication of Napoleon in 1814 in which Francis and his new Empire had played such a pivotal role. The Congress of Vienna that Francis had hosted, after centuries of repetitive and destructive European wars, had succeeded in preventing another general European war for a century; an accomplishment which may never be repeated. In that century, European ascendency and predominance over nearly the entire globe was achieved.

Francis lived a relatively long life for the era in which he lived. What can be said about him, in the end, as a man and as a ruler?

He lived an extraordinary life, that cannot be denied. To some extent this would be expected of one born into royalty and destined to inherit a throne, a monarchy, a dynasty. Clearly, though, the times in which he lived and ruled and the impact he made on the history of his country, of Europe and of the world contributed to the extraordinary life recounted here.

He was born and raised as a child of the Enlightenment in a loving family in Florence, one of the foremost cultural and historical cities in Europe, then as it is today. As an adolescent, at sixteen years of age, he entered a completely different world, far different than anything he had known, and was exposed to a difficult, exacting mentor that shaped and matured him into a worthy heir of a dynasty he had not chosen, but into which he had been born and fate had determined for him. He saw much and learned much that would guide him for the rest of his life, for better or worse.

As a young man, in his twenties, he experienced tragedy at a young age, with the death of his wife, his uncle and then his father and found himself at twenty-four years of age, the ruler of a vast Empire, in a matter of a little more than two years' time. He was immediately faced with war by a revolutionary power such as the world had never seen that had to be fought by an empire whose treasury had already been drained and would never be balanced for most of his reign of forty-three years. He would suffer defeat after defeat

Figure E.2. Bust of Francis I of Austria by Camillo Pacetti, Kunsthistoriches Museum, Vienna

against an extraordinary opponent bent on the complete reorganization of the European continent to the detriment of his own inheritance and his country.

Further personal tragedies, including the deaths of several children and three wives were intertwined with the geopolitical and domestic challenges he faced, time and again. He adapted to them, perhaps not perfectly and certainly not with the benefit of hindsight, and overcame them one by one in his own way.

The Franciscan era in Austrian history is, due to Francis' personality and as an absolute monarch, a mixed legacy to be sure. The phoenix-like triumph of 1814 must rank in modern European history as one of the greatest and would not have happened without the patient, stoic and determined ruler Francis had evolved to be over the years. In the second half of his reign, the obtrusive and persistent censorship and surveillance of domestic and foreign citizens alike that so often has defined him, must be fairly balanced against the context in which it was imposed, its comparative weight as against other regimes in Europe, and the lessons Francis and his contemporary rulers felt they had learned from the French Revolution and its aftermath.

The Franciscan era saw great opportunities gained and missed. In law, education and culture, there were advances for which he is rarely, if ever, given credit. The transformation of his capital into one of the greatest cities in Europe, blossomed in his time. In economic development, for his failure to comprehend and grasp the nettle of industrialization, as compared to some of the other states of Europe, Francis can be fairly blamed. And yet, it would have taken an even more gifted leader to have foreseen the eventual consequences of this failure decades later.

As a human being, he was by every account, a loving father, grandfather and husband. His immediate family meant more to him than it did to other royal sovereigns of many of the other ruling houses of Europe. He had no mistresses. He was accessible to his subjects, reserving two half-days per week to grant personal audiences to essentially anyone who made an appointment to see him. His self-effacing, bluff personality endeared him to his people and his intimates and was consistent with his disdain for pomp, ceremony and ostentation of any kind where he was concerned, unless it served the purposes of the state. His example personified the Biedermeier era. His love of nature, botany, making candy and playing the fiddle with his wife and children, landscaping the gardens and parks at Laxenburg, are also part of this man who has been written off as cold, dour and forbidding.

Francis was not a hard man, although he was forced to make some hard decisions throughout his life and reign. He did not choose the life he lived, but accepted it without complaint and did the best he could for his country and his dynasty, learning from his mistakes and often placing others in the position to take credit for his successes, which did not seem to concern him. And they did.

As a man, it is interesting to note that nearly all the people who knew him—his ministers, generals, diplomats, civil servants, fellow sovereigns–appear to have liked him personally and were loyal to him to a fault, through thick and thin. His family adored him. And while his people may have chaffed under his conservative persona, they respected and obeyed him and when he had died and left them, felt a great and personal loss at his passing. And, after all, that is not such a bad legacy for any man who ever lived.

NOTES

1. Trollope, Frances. *Vienna and the Austrians*. London: Forgotten Books, 2016.

Bibliography

Abbott, J.S.C. *The Monarchies of Continental Europe.* New York: Mason Brothers, 1861. Print.

Aksan, Virginia. *Ottoman Wars 1700-1870: An Empire Besieged.* London: Longman/Pearson, 2007.

Andress, David. *The Terror: The Merciless War for Freedom in Revolutionary France.* New York. Farrar, Straus and Giroux, 2005.

Arneth, Alfred. *Marie Antoinette; Joseph II, und Leopold II.* Vienna: Wilhelm Braumüller, 1866. Print.

Austrian State Archive. "Points d'education pour les enfants." *Haus-, Hof- und Staatsarchiv, Faszikel 56, Erziehungsplane betr. Die Erziehung der Kinder Leopolds II.* 1775–1784, Konvolut 7, folios 1–4.

Beales, Derek. *Joseph II, In the Shadow of Maria Theresa.* New York: Cambridge University Press, 2008. Print.

Bernstein, Leonard. *The Infinite Variety of Music.* New York: Simon & Schuster, 1966. Print.

Blanning, T.C.W. *Joseph II.* London: Routledge, 2013.

Brezis, Elise and Crouzet, François. "Seven Centuries of European Economic Growth and Decline." *Journal of European Economic History, 24:1.,* London: 1995.

Castelli, I.F. *Memoiren meines Lebens.* Milltown: Hansebooks, 2017.

Castle, Ian. "The Battle of Wagram." *The Campaign of 1809 Symposium.* Vienna: 2009.

Cochrane, Eric. *Florence in the Forgotten Centuries 1527–1800.* Chicago: University of Chicago Press, 2013. Print.

Connelly, Owen. *Blundering to Glory: Napoleon's Military Campaigns*; 3 ed. Lanham: Rowman & Littlefield Publishers, 2006.

Coxe, William. *History of the House of Austria.* London: Bell & Dalby, 1873. Print.

Crankshaw, Edward. *The Fall of the House of Habsburg.* London: Penguin Books; Reissue edition, 1983.

Dallas, Gregor. "Metternich: The Autobiography, 1773–1815." *The Napoleon Series.* April 2005.

Davies, Norman. *Europe: A History.* New York: Harper Perennial, 1998. Print.

De Marbot, Jean Baptiste. *Memoires Du General Baron de Marbot, Vol. 2.* Charleston: Nabu Press, 2010.

De Saint-Amand, Imbert. *The Happy Days of the Empress Marie Louise.* Miami: HardPress Publishing, 2010.

De Wertheimer, Edward. *The Duke of Reichstadt.* London: John Lane The Bodley Head, 1906.

Esmein, A. *A History of Continental Criminal Procedure With Special Reference to France.* London: Forgotten Books, 2012.

Feil, Joseph. "*Kaiser Joseph II. Als Erzieher*" in Sylvester-Spenden eines Kreises von Freunden vaterländischer Geschichtsforschung. Vienna: 1852.

Fiebeger, G.J. *The Campaigns of Napoleon Bonaparte of 1796–1797.* West Point: 1911. Print.

Fisher, Burton D. *The Barber of Seville (Opera Classics Library Series).* Grand Rapids: Opera Journeys, 2005.

Fisher, Henry. *Remember to Tell the Children: A Trilogy Book One; The Pioneers.* Bloomington: Authorhouse, 2006.

Fournier, August. *Napoleon I, Eine Biographie.* Vienna: Verlag von F. Tempsky, 1904. Print.

Frasier, Antonia. *Marie Antoinette: The Journey.* London: Phoenix, 2002. Print.

Goldschmidt, Harry. *Beethoven Werkeinführungen.* Leipzig: Reclam, 1975.

Grafenauer, Bogo. *Erberg, Joseph Kalasanz.* Ljubljana: 1991.

Häusler, Wolfgang. "Von der Manufaktur zum Maschinensturm, Industrielle Dynamik und soziale Wandel in Raum von Wien." *Wien in Vormärz.* Vienna: Verein für Geschichte der Stadt Wien: Kommissionsverlag Jugend und Volk, 1980.

Herring, George C. *From Colony to Superpower: U.S. Foreign Relations Since 1776.* New York: Oxford University Press, 2008.

Holland, Arthur William. "The French Revolution." *Encyclopedia Britannica, 11th ed.* Cambridge University Press. Cambridge: 1911.

Holmberg, Tom. "Metternich: The Autobiography, 1773–1815." *The Napoleon Series.* April 2005.

Ingrao, Charles. *The Habsburg Monarchy, 1618–1815.* New York: Cambridge University Press, (2nd edition), 2000.

Isaacson, Walter. *Kissinger, A Biography.* New York: Simon & Schuster, 2013.

Jefferies, F. *The Gentlemen's Magazine, Vol. 79, part 2.* London: 1809.

Judson, Pieter M. *The Habsburg Empire, A New History.* Boston: Belknap Press of Harvard University Press, 2016.

Kagan, Frederick W., *The End of the Old Order, Napoleon and Europe, 1801-1805.* Boston: Da Capo Press, 2006.

Kann, Robert. *History of the Habsburg Empire.* Berkley: University of California Press, 1974. Print.

Keiler, Allan. "Liszt and Beethoven: The Creation of a Personal Myth." *19th-Century Music. 12. no. 2.* 1988.

King, David; *Vienna, 1814*; New York: Broadway Paperbacks, 2008.
Kelly, Michael. *Reminiscences of Michael Kelly, of the King's Theatre, and Theatre Royal Drury Lane.* London: H. Colburn, 1826. Print.
Kennedy, Paul. *The Rise and Fall of the Great Powers.* London: Vintage Books, 1989. Print.
King, David. *Vienna 1814.* New York: Random House, 2008.
Khan, Razib. "Inbreeding & the downfall of the Spanish Hapsburgs." *Discover,* April 14, 2009.
Langsam, Walter. *Francis the Good.* New York: The Macmillan Company, 1949. Print.
Leggiere, Michael V. *The Fall of Napoleon: Volume 1, The Allied Invasion of France, 1813–1814*; New York: Cambridge University Press, 2007.
Madelin, Louis. La *Jeunesse de Bonaparte.* Paris: Hachette, 1937. Print.
Mahan, Alexander. *Maria Theresa of Austria.* Whitefish: Kessinger Publishing, LLC, 2010. Print.
Malleson, George. *Life of Prince Metternich.* Philadelphia: J.B. Lippincott, 1888.
Mathias, P. *The First Industrial Nation: An Economic History of Britain 1700–1914;* London: Routeledge, 1969.
Metternich, Clemens. *Metternich, The Autobiography, 1773–1815.* Welwyn Garden City: Ravenhall Books, 2004.
Metternich, Richard. *Memoirs of Prince Metternich, 1830–1835. Volume V.* New York: Charles Scribner's Sons, 1882.
Mitchell, B.R. *British Historical Statistics.* Cambridge: Cambridge University Press; Reissue edition, 2011.
Nester, William R. *Titan: The Art of British Power in the Age of Revolution and Napoleon.* Norman: University of Oklahoma Press, 2016.
Palmer, Alan. Metternich. London: Faber & Faber, 2010.
Palmer, Robert. *The World of the French Revolution.* London: Routledge, 1971. Print.
Perlin, David and Cohen, Ann. *The Complete Idiot's Guide to Dangerous Diseases and Epidemics.* Royersford: Alpha, 2002. Print.
Rampley, Matthew. *The Vienna School of Art History.* State College: The Pennsylvania State University Press, 2013.
Révauger, Cécile. *The Abolition of Slavery—The British Debate 1787–1840.* Paris: Presse Universitaire de France, 2008.
Richter, Ludwig. *Lebenserinnerungen eines Deutschen Malers* (German Edition). Charleston: Createspace Independent Publishing Platform, 2014.
Roberts, Andrew. *Napoleon—A Life.* London: Penguin Books, 2014.
Roider, Karl: *Baron Thugut and Austria's Response to the French Revolution.* Princeton: Princeton University Press, 2014.
Romani, George. *The Neapolitan Revolution of 1820–1821*, (Santa Barbara: Greenwood Press; New Edition, 1978).
Rossi, Joseph. *Denkbuch für Fürst und Vaterland, Herausgegeben von Joseph Rossi, 2 vols.* Vienna: J.B. Wallishausser, 1814–1815.
Rothenberg, Gunther E. *Napoleon's Great Adversary.* New York: Sarpedon Publishers, 1982.

Sandholtz, Wayne. "Prohibiting Plunder: How Norms Change." *European Journal of International Law*. Oxford: Oxford University Press, 2007.

Seigworth, Gilbert R. "Bloodletting Over the Centuries." *New York State Journal of Medicine*. New York: December 1980.

Seward, Desmond. *Metternich, The First European*. London: Viking Penguin, 1991.

Silagi, Denis. *Jakobiner in der Habsburger-Monarchie*. Vienna: Verlag Herold, 1962. Print.

Smith, Adam. *An Inquiry into the Nature and Causes of the Wealth of Nations: A Selected Edition*. Oxford: Oxford Paperbacks, 2008.

Stewart, John Hall. *A Documentary Survey of the French Revolution*. New York. Macmillan, 1951.

Szabo, Franz A. J. *Kaunitz and Enlightened Absolutism, 1753–1780;* Cambridge: Cambridge University Press, 1994.

Taylor, A.J.P. *The Italian Problem in European Diplomacy, 1847–49*. Manchester: Manchester University Press, 1970; *The Habsburg Monarchy 1809–1918*, (Chicago: University of Chicago Press, 1976).

Trollope, Frances. *Vienna and the Austrians*. London: Forgotten Books, 2016

Tucker, S.C. *A Global Chronology of Conflict, Volume Three:1775-1860*. Santa Barbara: ABC-CLIO, LLC, 2009.

United States Department of State. "The Monroe Doctrine (1823)." *Basic Readings in U.S. Democracy*.

Vovk, Justin. *In Destiny's Hands, Five Tragic Rulers, Children of Maria Theresa*. New York: iUniverse, Inc., 2010. Print.

Waissenberger, Robert. *Vienna in the Biedermeier Era, 1815–1848*; Lombard: Mallard Press, 1986.

Wheatcroft, Andrew. *The Habsburgs: Embodying Empire*. London: Penguin Books, 1997.

Winslow, Robert and Melissa Francescut. "Crime and Society: A comparative criminology tour of the world." *San Diego State University*. www-roan.sdsu.edu/faculty/rwinslow.

Wolfsgruber, Cölestin. *Franz I. Kaiser von Österreich, und Sein Zeitalter*. Vienna: Wilhelm Braumüller, 1899; "Diocese of Tarnow." *Catholic Encyclopedia, Volume 14*. New York: 1913. Print.

Zamoyski, Adam. *Moscow 1812; Napoleon's Fatal March*. New York: Harper Perennial, 2004.

Index

Absolutism, 11, 229
Adams, John, 87
AGBG [Allgemeines Burgerliche Gesetzbuch], 119
Alexander I, Tsar of Russia, 73, 112, 127, 132, 146, 153, 156, 157–159, 164, 171, 180, 184, 206, 225, 230; Congress of Vienna, 188–191, 193; Sixth Coalition, 174–175, 177–178, 181–182; Third Coalition, 96, 98, 105–108
Alvinczi, Joseph Baron von Borberek, 25, 135, 157
Amerling, Friedrich von, 245, 246–247, 249
Aspern Essling, Battle of, 64, 133, 135, 143
Austerlitz, Battle of, 104, 106–109, 112, 115, 12, 1310–121, 125, 156–157, 178,
Austrian Empire, 38, 49, 52, 74, 231, 85–86, 99, 104, 109, 137, 151, 154, 230, 239, 243, 245; economic issues, 74, 208–209, 204, 212–213, 215, 235; kaiserlied, 86; National Bank, 214; reforms, 115–121; Salzburg, Bishopric of, 67, 88, 137, 158, 218; Sixth Coalition, 163, 187, 194; Tyrolea, 108, 113, 128, 131, 158, 205; Vorarlberg, 108, 113, 128
Austrian Netherlands, 26, 38, 41, 44, 46, 59, 64, 66, 70, 77–78, 99, 111, 116,
Austrian Succession, War of, 10, 89
Austro–Hungarian Empire, 115, 204
Austro–Prussian War, 193–194

Balkans, 24–26, 37–39, 41, 109, 153, 200, 208, 251,
Batavian Republic, 77, 83
Bavaria, kingdom of, 20, 40, 50, 67, 70, 72, 83, 98–99, 106, 108–109, 113, 129, 131, 137, 158, 167–169, 212, 217–218, 243–244
Bavarian Succession, War of, 9, 32, 40; Charles Theodore, Elector of Bavaria, 99; Maximilian, king of Bavaria, 99, 113, 168; Sophie, von Wittelsbach, 218; Wittelsbach, dynasty, 99, 218
Beethoven, Ludwig van, 4, 20–21, 33–34, 101–103, 221–222; Unger, Caroline, 222
Belgium. *See* Austrian Netherlands
Bellegarde, Marshal, 143, 151, 153,
Biedermeier, 52, 104, 187, 199–201, 206–211, 213, 227– 228, 235–237, 239, 259

266 *Index*

Blois, Chateau de, 184, 187107
Bohemia, 8, 26, 37–38, 42, 44, 67, 70–73, 99, 111, 116, 133, 138, 192, 205, 208, 212–213, 221, 232, 250–251
Bonaparte, Jerome, 103, 114, 183
Bonaparte, Napoleon, 4, 13, 25, 61–62, 64–66, 73, 77, 94, 117–122, 141–142, 144–145, 148–149, 151, 157, 190, 192, 194–195, 218, 221; Marie Louise, marriage to, 146–147, 184–186; Metternich, relationship with, 112, 126, 158, 160–162; Russian campaign, 153–156; Third Coalition, 95–96, 98–99, 103–104, 106–109, 113–115; Second Coalition, 78–80, 86–88; Sixth Coalition, 163–165, 167,169–172, 182–184; Toulon, Siege of, 61; Wagram, 125,127, 129–137
Bourbon, dynasty, 3–4, 39, 117, 171, 183–184, 190, 193, 215, 228–229, 249; Charles X, king of France and Count d'Artois, 41, 46, 184, 229–230, 240, 244; Louis XV, king of France, 4, 73–74, 89, 115, 145; Louis XVI, king of France, 4, 39, 41, 46, 50, 52–53, 73, 147, 184; Louis XVIII, king of France, 184, 225, 229; Louis Philippe d'Orleans, king of France, 240–241, 244
Bukovina, 74, 76
Bundestag, 202–203
Burschenschaften, 202–203

Campo Formio, Treaty of, 66–67, 71, 74, 83, 86, 88
Carlsbad Decrees, 117, 201–203, 207, 230, 243
Castelli, Ignatz Franz, 131
Castlereagh, Robert Stewart, Viscount, 115, 171, 189–193
Catherine II, Tsarina of Russia, 23, 42, 52, 83–84, 178, 180

Catholicism, 11, 185, 205, 215, 253, 255
censorship, 32, 52, 116–118, 203, 205–206, 208–209, 214, 230, 233, 243, 258
Charles, Archduke of Austria, Duke of Teschen, 37, 44, 59, 63–65, 87, 92–96, 98–99, 104–107, 109–110, 129–130, 132–136, 143, 149, 157
Chaumont, Treaty of, 183
Cobenzl, Johann Ludwig, Graf von, 88, 95–96, 105, 141
Cobenzl, Johann Philipp, Graf von, 66, 75, 112–113
Colloredo–Waldsee, Graf von, 11–12, 15, 17, 88, 95–96, 135, 141
Congress of Vienna, 103, 165, 184–187, 189–195, 206, 210, 217, 225–226, 235, 239, 241, 244, 257; Quadruple Alliance, 194, 215; Quintuple Alliance, 194
Continental System, 125–126, 145; Berlin Decree, 125; Orders in Council, 125

D'Enghien, Duke of, 96
Danhauser, Joseph, 235
Danton, Georges, 52–53, 61
Davout, Louis–Nicholas, Marshal of France, 113
Duka, Peter Baron von Kadar, 94, 143
Dresden, Interview at, 158, 161, 163, 167
Duke of Wellington see Wellsley, Arthur, 4, 129, 157, 170–171, 230
Dumouriez, Charles Francois, 59

Eichrodet, Ludwig, 199
Erberg, Joseph von, 219
Erblande, hereditary lands of Habsburg dynasty, 38, 70–71, 109, 119–120
espionage, 51, 120, 192
estates, 26, 38, 70–71, 93–94, 117, 121
Eylau, Battle of, 157, 180

Index

Florence, 3–7, 10–13, 18, 27, 29, 31–32, 64, 88–89, 257
Ferdinand I, Emperor of Austria, 35, 91, 199, 218–221, 245, 253
Ferdinand, Charles Wilhelm, Duke of Brunswick, 44, 59
finanzpatent of 1810, 150–151
Fisher, Henry, 75
First Coalition, 44, 47, 52, 57–58, 62, 66, 77, 80, 85, 184
Florin. *See* Gulden
Fontainebleau, Treaty of, 184
Fouché, Joseph, 118, 127, 172
Frankfurt Proposals, 174, 183
Franz Joseph, Emperor of Austria, 22, 25, 44, 69, 165, 201, 218, 221
Friedland, Battle of, 114, 125–126, 1, 46, 56
French Revolution, 29, 40–41, 43, 63

Geheime Staatskonferenz, 221
Geheime Staatspolizei, 118, 119, 158, 205, 207, 231
Gentlemen's Magazine, The, 137
Gentz, Frederick, 95, 111, 128
George III, 39, 47, 52, 74, 83, 85, 109–110, 117, 125, 180, 225–226
Germany, 24, 26, 57, 62–66, 77–78, 86, 92, 96, 99, 104, 108–109, 113–114, 127–129, 131, 146, 158, 160–161, 169–170, 177, 181–183, 187, 194, 199, 201–205, 207, 210–212, 215; Bonn, 21, 33–34; Frederick Augustus, king of Saxony, 41; Hanover, kingdom of, 70, 108, 113, 212; Hesse-Kassel, 62, 169; Westphalia, Kingdom of, 103, 114, 183, 210; Zollverein, 211–213
Goethe, Johann Wolfgang von, 217
Great Britain, 4, 39, 83, 86, 126, 155, 191–192, 200, 210
Gregory XVI, Pope, 241
Grillparzer, Franz, 208, 223
Gulden, 57

Habsburg, Habsburg–Lorraine, 7–12, 20, 22, 31, 34, 36, 38–44, 53, 61, 89–90, 99, 103, 105, 109, 130, 146–147, 162, 165, 193, 228, 231–232, 245, 251; Amalie Theresa, 92, 121; Caroline Ludovika, Archduchess, 92; constraints on power, 49, 52, 57–58, 69–73, 120; Elisabeth, von Wittelsbach, 218; Elisabeth Wilhelmina, von Wurttemberg, 22, 28, 42; epilepsy, as hereditary disease of Habsburgs, 35, 64, 91, 218; Ferdinand, Archduke of Austria–Este, 34, 93, 105–107; Franz Karl, Archduke of Austria, 218; intermarriage, genetic deficits, 35, 64, 91, 218; Johann Nepomuk, Archduke, 34, 92, 121; Joseph Franz, Archduke, 89, 91, 92, 121; John, Archduke, 87, 93; Marie Christine, Archduchess, 17; Rudolph, Archduke, 103, 221
Hager, Franz Baron von, 189, 192
Haugwitz, Friedrich, Wilhelm, 25
Haydn, Joseph, 4, 34, 86, 101
Hofer, Andreas, 131
Hofkriegsrat, 95, 99, 105, 143, 150–151
Hofmannsthal, Hugo von, 204
Hohenlinden, Battle of, 87–88, 93, 109, 115
Hohenlohe, Frederick William, 59
Hohenwart, Sigismund von, 12, 204
Holy Alliance, 194, 228, 242, 250
Holy Roman Empire, 26, 33, 44, 66–67, 69–72, 74, 98–99, 109, 113, 194, 221; Charles VI, Holy Roman Emperor, 231; Imperial Diet, 67, 70; Pragmatic Sanction, 231
Hungary, kingdom of, 26, 35, 37–38, 41, 70–72, 93, 116, 119, 129, 203, 205, 212–214, 220, 231–232; Anne, of Hungary, Jagiellon, 72; Budapest, 50, 52, 93, 116, 119, 136,

205; Kossuth, Lajos, 233; Regnum Independens, 231; Széchenyi, István, 232–233
Hunter, William, 22

Imperial Royal Polytechnic Institute, 214
infectious disease, 9, 25; tuberculosis, 21, 25, 27, 53, 217, 247
Italy, 39, 63, 65–66, 76, 78, 80, 88, 96, 98–99, 104, 108, 113, 181, 183, 185, 193–194, 200–201, 207, 213, 215, 217, 240–241, 244

Jacobins, 40, 47, 51–52, 59, 61, 75
Jamaica, 242
Jefferson, Thomas, 87, 213
Jemappes, Battle of, 59, 64, 157
Jena Auerstedt, Battle of, 113, 125, 178
Joseph II, Benedikt August, Holy Roman Emperor, 4, 8–11, 15–17, 19–21, 23–25, 27–29, 38–40, 50, 53, 57, 66, 72, 74, 99, 116, 118, 121, 201, 204, 251–252
Judson, Pieter, 116, 119–120, 187, 203–204, 207

Kann, Robert, 12–13
Kaunitz, Eleonore von, 111
Kaunitz-Reitberg, Wenzel Anton, 8, 11, 27–28, 31–32, 39, 43, 47, 66, 74, 76, 111, 113, 137, 144, 189
Keinmayer, General, 106–107
Kellerman, Francois, 59, 61
Kelley, Michael, 21
Kennedy, Paul, 73
Kolowrat, Franz Anton von, 212–213, 221, 251–252
Kotzebue, August von, 202
Kreutzinger, Joseph, 90–92, 225–226
Kutuzov, Mikhail, 106–107, 156, 178

Landwehr, 128–129
Langsam, Walter Consuelo, 12

Lawrence, Sir Thomas, 65, 142, 174, 225, 229
Leipzig, Battle of, 116, 158, 167–171, 175, 177, 182, 188, 192, 194
Leopold II, Holy Roman Emperor, 3–4, 6–7, 10–13, 17, 19, 21, 27, 31–43, 46–47, 53, 58, 64, 73, 93, 103, 116, 118, 120, 144–145, 231
Lichtenstein, Johann Prince von, 136, 148–150
Liszt, Franz, 222, 236, 103
Loeben, Armistice of, 65
Lombardy, kingdom of, 65, 96, 193, 200, 212, 232, 245
London, 34, 213, 230, 240, 242
Lunéville, Treaty of, 87–89, 93, 98, 113

Mack, Karl von Lieberich, 95, 99, 104–107, 249
Manfredi, Frederick Ferdinand, 12
Mantua, Siege of, 65, 77, 96
Marengo, Battle of, 87, 115
Maria Anna, Empress of Austria (wife of Ferdinand), 220
Maria Ludovica, Empress of Austria (third wife), 122–123, 217, 219
Maria Luisa, Grand Duchess of Tuscany, 3, 7
Maria Theresa, Dowager Empress, Archduchess of Austria and Queen of Hungary, 4, 8–11, 14, 32–33, 37–39, 42, 50, 71–72, 74, 115–116, 120–121, 144–145, 147, 162, 201, 252
Maria Therese, Holy Roman Empress (second wife Francis), 34, 36, 89, 91, 121, 219, 227
Maria Carolina, Queen of Naples (aunt), 34, 91
Marie Antoinette, Queen of France, Archduchess of Austria, 4, 40, 52–53, 66
Marie Louise, Archduchess, Empress of France, 42, 89, 122–123, 144–147, 184–186, 218, 241, 249

Index

Martinovic, Ignac, 51, 231
Maximilian, Count von Merveldt, 65
Maximilian Franz, Archduke, 33–34
Mendel, Gregor, 35
Menotti, Ciro, 240–241
Metternich, Klemens von, 4, 11, 44, 49, 51, 59, 67, 75, 105, 122–123, 185, 213–214, 221, 228, 230, 239, 241, 247, 249, 250, 252–253; appointed foreign minister, 135–138, 141–147; Carlsbad Decrees, 200–202, 204–207; collaboration with Napoleon, 153–154, 156–158, 160–164; Congress of Vienna, 189–193, 195; early diplomatic career, 110–112, 126–127, 129; Sixth Coalition, 167, 169, 172–175, 177, 180–183
Metternich, Melanie von, 252–253
Mexico, 228
Monroe Doctrine, 228–229
Moore, Sir John, 130, 138
Mozart, Wolfgang Amadeus, 4, 20–21, 34, 37, 86, 101

Naples, Kingdom of, 80, 105, 193, 215,
Napoleon, Francois Charles, Duke of Reichstadt, 147, 247–249
Nate Turner Slave Rebellion, 242
Neefe, Christian, 33
Neipperg, Adam Albert von, 185–186, 218
Nelson, Horatio Lord, 87, 226
Nesselrode, Karl Robert, 250
Nicholas I, Tsar of Russia, 230, 250

Ottoman Empire, 86, 109, 250; Hünkâr Iskelesi, Treaty of, 250; Konya, Battle of, 250; Mahmud II, Sultan of Turkey, 250; Mehmet, Ali Pasha, 250; Münchengrätz, Convention of, 250

Palacký, Frantisek, 115
Palmer, Adam, 239
Palmerston, Lord, 242–243, 250

Papal States, 80, 96, 241
Paris, Treaty of, 184
Parma, Duchy of, 78, 80, 184–186, 193, 218, 241
Peninsular War, 126
Pergen, Johann Anton von, 119, 210
Piedmont, Kingdom of, 64, 77–78, 80, 83, 193, 200, 215, 220
Pillnitz, Declaration of, 41, 43–44, 62, 229
Pitt, William, 39, 58, 74, 85, 96, 110, 213
Pitti Palace, 3, 7, 21, 64
Pius VII, Pope, 218
Poland, Kingdom of, 42, 44, 62–63, 66, 74, 76, 113–114, 119, 145, 168–169, 190–192, 241–242; Warsaw, City of, 241–242; Wysocki, Piotr, 241; Zamoyski, Adam, 144
Portugal, 58, 126
Potato War, 32
Pressburg, Peace of, 108, 112, 115, 126, 129, 137
Prussia, Kingdom of, 52, 57–58, 83, 95–98, 107–112, 130, 157, 178, 195, 200–201, 206, 215, 225–226, 231, 242, 244, 250; Basle, Peace of, 62; Congress of Vienna, 188–190, 192–194; Frederick II, king of Prussia, 9, 40; Frederick Wilhelm II, king of Prussia, 26; Frederick Wilhelm III, king of Prussia, 214; Hardenberg, Karl August von, 193; Jena, aftermath and Tilsit, 113–114, 125–126, 130, 137, 145; rapprochement, 42–47, 61–63; rivalry in Germany, 10, 12, 26, 32, 37–41, 70, 72–73, 75–76, 168–170; Sixth Coalition, 156, 160–167, 174; Stein, Heinrich Baron von, 169–170; Valmy and Partitions of Poland, 59, 62, 66; Zollverein, 209–214

Radetzky–Radetz, Joseph Graf von, 130, 144–145, 148–151, 153, 157, 163, 167, 171, 177, 181–182

Rastatt, Congress of, 66–67
Reichenbach: proposals, 160, 162;
  Treaty of, 40–41
Rivoli, Battle of, 65, 76–77, 115
Robespierre, Maximilian, 52, 61
Rossi, Joseph, 187, 203
Rossini, Gioachino, 222
Rothschild, Salmon Mayer, 119,
Rousseau, Jean Jacques, 4, 12
Russia, Russian Empire, 50, 52, 58,
  83–84, 95, 109, 112, 116, 119, 125,
  144–148, 153, 188, 200, 226, 230;
  Catherine II, the Great, 23–26, 32,
  37–47; Congress of Vienna, 189;
  Friedland, Aftermath and Tilsit, 114,
  126–127, 129, 137; invasion and
  Sixth Coalition, 154–161, 163–164,
  167–171, 174, 178, 180, 182;
  Nicholas I, 230, 241–242, 250–251;
  Paul I, Tsar of Russia, 52, 63, 180;
  Poland, 62–63, 75
Romanov Dynasty, 23, 42, 180; Third
  Coalition, 96–98, 105–107
Russell, John Lord, 117

Salieri, Antonio, 34, 103
Sand, Karl Ludwig, 202
Schwarzenberg, Karl Phillip, Prince
  von, 106, 109–110, 112, 130, 146,
  155–157, 163, 171, 177, 181–182,
  184, 206
Second Coalition, 83, 86, 88, 93, 110,
  193; Amiens, Peace of, 95
Serbia, 24–25, 38, 153
Seven Year's War, 10
Seward, Desmond, 206
Schönbrunn, Treaty of, 134, 137, 146,
  151
Sharpe, Samuel, 243
Sixth Coalition, 156, 158, 163, 184
Smith, Adam, 213
Sorel, Albert, 141
South German Customs Union, 212
Spain, Spanish Empire, 3–4, 50, 62–63,
  87, 125–137, 129–130, 137–138,
  160, 169, 183, 215, 218, 228; Bailen,
  Surrender at, 129; Charles II, king of
  Spain, 35; Charles III, king of Spain,
  3, 4; Charles IV, king of Spain, 126,
  225; Ferdinand VII, king of Spain,
  126
Stadion, Johann Phillip Graf von,
  111–113, 125–129, 135–136, 141,
  143, 214
Suvarov, Alexander, 25–26
Swieten, Gerard van, 11

Talleyrand, Maurice de, 108, 112, 115,
  127, 172, 184, 189–190, 192, 217
Teplitz Accords, Treaty of Töplitz, 168,
  173, 177, 182
The Hague, Treaty of, 77
Third Coalition, 95–96, 98–99, 101,
  104, 112–113, 178
Thugut, Johann Amadeus Francis
  Baron de Paula, 74–76, 83, 88,
  111–112
Tilsit, Treaty of, 114, 125–126, 178
Trafalgar, Battle of, 125–126
Transylvania, 37–38, 41, 70, 72, 116,
  205, 212
Turkish Empire. See Ottoman Empire
Turkish War (also Austro–Turkish and
  Russo–Turkish War), 22, 24–27, 32,
  37–38, 57–58, 105, 148, 150; Lacy,
  Franz Moritz von, 24–25, 148;
  Laudon, Ernst von, 25–26, 105, 148;
  Sistova, Treaty of, 38, 41
Turner, Francis, 57
Tuscany, Grand Duchy of, 3–4, 6, 13,
  31–32, 38, 70, 78, 80, 88, 93, 117, 193

Ulm, Battle of, 95, 104, 106–107, 109,
  112, 115, 131, 249

Valmy, Battle of, 59, 62, 66, 75–76
Venice, Republic of, 65, 80, 88, 96,
  104, 205
Victor Amadeus III, king of Piedmont,
  78, 80

Vienna, 37–38, 50, 65, 73, 78, 87, 96, 98–99, 103–104, 106, 115, 119, 123, 131–134, 137, 148, 185–186, 188–190, 205, 217–218, 249, 252, 256; and *The Austrians* (book), 255; Biedermeier Period, 206–210, 213–214, 235–237; Blauerhof, Schloss von, 227, 249; Bösendorfer, Ignaz, 236; Burgtheater, 4, 20, 86, 102, 252; Congress. *See* Congress of Vienna; Hofburg, Palace of, 4, 18, 20, 29, 42, 160, 189, 200, 227, 249, 252–253; Josephin Vienna, 20–27, 29; Laxenburg, Palace of, 89, 93, 219, 226–228, 259; musical legacy, 34, 101, 221–222; Schönbrunn, Palace of, 9, 20, 188, 221, 228, 249

waltz, waltzing, 20, 237
Waissenberger, Robert, 206
Wallachia, 25, 38
Wallis, Joseph Graf von, 150, 153
Warsaw, Duchy of, 114, 137, 145, 147, 161, 193
Washington, George, 4, 39, 87, 253
Wellsley, Arthur, Duke of Wellington, 4, 129, 157, 170–171, 230
Willem I, King of the Netherlands, 244
William Albert, Prince of Montenuovo, 218
Wolfsgruber, Cölestin, 75

Znaim, Battle of, 136, 143

About the Author

Chip Wagar is a life-long history explorer in his travels and writing. A lawyer in New Orleans by day, Chip enjoys writing about history, particularly Central European history and the Balkans. His interest in this region began with his attending the Austro-American Institute in Vienna during his college years, abetted since then by extensive travel and exploration of the areas covered in his award-winning books. This is his third book and first non-fiction work.